MW01045972

ARTFUL PRACTICES

ARTFUL PRACTICES
The Political Economy of Everyday Life

Volume 5
Critical Perspectives on Historic Issues

edited by
Henri Lustiger-Thaler and Daniel Salée

**BLACK
ROSE
BOOKS**

Montréal\New York
London

Copyright © 1994 BLACK ROSE BOOKS LTD.

No part of this book may be reproduced or transmitted in any form, by any means — electronic or mechanical, including photocopying and recording, or by any information storage or retrieval system — without written permission from the publisher, or, in the case of photocopying or other reprographic copying, a license from the Canadian Reprography Collective, with the exception of brief passages quoted by a reviewer in a newspaper or magazine.

BLACK ROSE BOOKS No. X222
Hardcover ISBN 1-895431-93-X
Paperback ISBN 1-895431-92-1
ISSN 1195-1869
Library of Congress No. 93-73927

Canadian Cataloguing in Publication Data

Main entry under title:

Artful practices: the political economy of everyday life

(Critical perspectives on historic issues; 5)
Includes bibliographical references.
ISBN: 1-895431-93-X (bound) —
ISBB: 1-895431-92-1 (pbk.)

1. Economic history — 1990 – . I. Lustiger-Thaler, Henri, 1951 – . II. Salée, Daniel
III. Series.

HC59.15.A78 1993   330.9′049   C93-090624-1

Photo on front cover: *Cain and Abel*, Barbara Rose Haum,1993.

Mailing Address

BLACK ROSE BOOKS
C.P. 1258
Succ. Place du Parc
Montréal, Québec
H2W 2R3 Canada

BLACK ROSE BOOKS
340 Nagel Drive
Cheektowaga, New York
14225 USA

Printed in Canada
A publication of the Institute of Policy Alternatives of Montréal
(IPAM)

Contents

Part I: Lives, Livelihood and Strategies of Survival

Part II: The Community Versus the Market: The Ups and Downs of Practices of Resistance

Part III: Mapping New Citizenship Practices

Notes on the Contributors

Henri Lustiger-Thaler is a professor of Sociology at the School of Social Sciences and Human Services, Ramapo College of New Jersey, New Jersey, USA.

Daniel Salée is a professor of Political Science and the Vice-Principal of the School of Community and Public Affairs, Concordia University, Montreal, Quebec, Canada.

Gavin Smith is a professor of Anthropology at the University College, University of Toronto, Toronto, Ontario, Canada.

Jane Wheelock is a professor of Sociology in the Department of Social Policy at the University of Newcastle upon Tyne, Newcastle, United Kingdom.

Enzo Mingione is a professor of Urban and Rural Sociology at the University of Messina, Italy.

Ivan Laughlin is a private consultant with Human Settlements Consultants, Ste. Augustine, Trinidad.

Larissa Lomnitz is a professor of Anthropology at the Instituto de Investigaciones en Matemáticas Aplicadas y en Sistémas, at the Universidad Nacional Autónoma de México, Mexico.

Ana Melnick is a researcher at the Instituto de Investigaciones en Matemáticas Aplicadas y en Sistémas, at the Universidad Nacional Autónoma de México, Mexico.

Menachem Rosner is a professor of Sociology at the Institute for Research of the Kibbutz and the Cooperative Idea, University of Haifa, Israel.

Maurice Roche is a professor in the Department of Sociological Studies at Sheffield University, Sheffield, United Kingdom.

S. Michael Miller is a professor emeritus of Sociology and Economics at Boston University, Massachusetts and a Senior Fellow at the Commonwealth Institute, Boston, USA.

Warren Magnusson is professor of Political Science at the University of Victoria, Vancouver, British Columbia, Canada.

Preface

The origins of this book are several. First and foremost, it reflects our concerns about the relationship between political theory and social and cultural practices. There is a tendency among social scientists to ignore the reality, meaning and consequences of everyday strategies of economic survival. But it seems that these constitute more and more the ongoing informal activities of a growing sector of the population. We need to know more about how people construct their everyday lives from a policy and sociopolitical perspective. We hope that this book can repair this neglect.

These concerns are eloquently expressed by the international collection of academics and community activists who contributed to this book.

Most of the chapters gathered here have been selected from papers presented at the fourth international conference of the Karl Polanyi Institute of Political Economy held in Montreal in 1992. They are now part of a series entitled "Critical Perspectives on Historic Issues" jointly sponsored by Black Rose Books and the Karl Polanyi Institute of Political Economy.

We wish to thank the Social Sciences and Humanities Research Council of Canada and Québec's Fonds FCAR for their generous support of the conference from which these papers emanate. We would also like to acknowledge the logistic and moral support of the Karl Polanyi Institute, its Director, Dr. Marguerite Mendell, and Black Rose publisher, Dimitri Roussopoulos.

The editing of this volume has been greatly facilitated by the technical expertise of Ana Gomez and Robert J. Collins. Their always cordial cooperation under duress of deadlines made this book an easier task. At Black Rose Books we would like also like to thank Nathalie Klym and Tom Holzinger for their diligent and expert work.

Introduction

The Quest for a Politically Effective Language of Everyday Life

Henri Lustiger-Thaler and Daniel Salée

Tactical prudence ensures that subordinate groups rarely blurt out their hidden transcripts directly. But, taking advantage of the anonymity of a crowd or of an ambiguous accident, they manage in a thousand artful ways to imply that they are grudging conscripts to the performance.

James C. Scott, *Domination and the Arts of Resistance*

The modern world is experiencing unprecedented levels of change and flux. The social, economic, and political institutions we have lived with since the postwar settlement are undergoing radical transformations that deeply challenge received notions of universality, the nature of the market, and, most importantly, the role of citizenship. These transformations beg pressing questions: What are the social and political consequences of changing patterns of power relations? What life strategies and new institutional practices are emerging to deal with these changes? The answers offered in response to such questions in contemporary political, economic, and social analyses are usually unsatisfactory, as they tend to neglect the subtle role of human agency embedded in the process of change.

Indeed, behind the current reality of transformation, a larger life drama is unfolding as broad segments of the population are increasingly marginalized, left alone to fend for themselves and face the tyranny of ever triumphant market forces. This is creating new patterns of social interactions and forms of solidarity in the face of a welfare State that no longer holds sway. As social agents are forced to enter into fierce competition over scarce resources, the terms of the social contract are being incrementally renegotiated. Exactly what this new contract holds is still difficult to determine, but clearly its redefinition involves an inordinate remodelling of once dominant patterns of social relations and power.

The practices of social agents coping with these massive changes through the informalization of labour power, the "upgrading" of the local in a global environment, the shifting relationship of the family to subsystems of social order and containment, etc., all point to novel ways of grasping the complexity of everyday life. This book is about the range and extent of human possibilities, the artful practices, of which people avail themselves in the political economy of everyday life. These are practices that ensure presence and agency in a hostile world where economic exploitation and social domination are all too common features. But, as the debilitating effects of global restructuring lay waste to national and local economies, we notice everywhere a resurgence of collective sentiments. These sentiments may not always succeed in staving off existing patterns of domination, but they foreground a sense of purpose that refuses to be silenced. Whether this manifests itself in social movements (through issues of difference and identity), or in transformations within the formal organizations and institutions of civil society and the State, the search by individuals for a *sensus communis* is not easily suppressed. Indeed, the "sense" and meaning of community is the end result of many of the social practices documented in this book.

The notion of community is a complex and contested term, one that is best grasped as a process of reconstituting social relations, endeavouring to create something *in common* (Nancy, 1991). In the modern world condition, the task of finding something *in common* is alone an act of resistance against the fragmenting power of capital and its "creative destruction." The practices of the many groups surveyed in this book contain resonances and echoes which go beyond the political banality of contemporary meta-discourses, or particularistic identity-based versions of community. The former too often absorb differences into a false unity; the latter collapse them within the helical spins of postmodernism.

The chapters in this reader ask different questions. They point to the importance of cultural practices in the social, political and economic realms. These practices become quests for community but are not figured in terms of membership; they underscore, rather, a project of discursive and practical possibilities. These are best grasped in the everyday web of social struggles and collective redefinitions of self, of others, and not least, of the State.

Indeed, everyday life is a critical public space for mutual and collective reconstitution, a wellspring for a new, politically effective language around human needs. From this viewpoint, the contours of everyday life contain unbounded ideological fields, border crossings which individuals traverse as they respond to crisis in a host of innovative ways. Their responses may or may not work, may or may not improve their condition, but they always reflect an unremitting search for an alternative to the restricting, institutionalized fetters of market forces.

The poles of crisis and innovation, and how people deal with them, rest at the core of this book. Most of the case studies, or theoretical analyses, in some shape or form address this relationship as a phenomenon embedded in practice. Whether under the rubric of issues such as family strategies in England, the informal economy, community mobilization in Trinidad and Tobago, reanimating a socialist ethic on the Israeli kibbutz, or the project of radical municipal politics, individuals respond and reconstitute their world through a variety of practices which engage the relationship between knowledge and authority. These practices are inherently dialectical in nature, producing a motor-like force which propels collectivities forward as they negotiate formal and informal economic and social arrangements.

The relationship between crisis and innovation is, in fact, a tightly knit one, where innovative reshaping already takes place as the economic and communal crisis deepens. As crisis reshapes the economy and everyday life, individuals emerge with multiple cultural "definitions of the situation" and their possible solutions. And, it is often at the height of crisis that the most innovative survival practices reveal themselves. In this Goffmanesque world of rules, counter-rules, front-stages (crisis), and back-stages (innovations), society is remade in its most intricate narratives and ethnographies.

Such are the practices to which the contributions gathered in this book refer. They bring us to consider the following questions: How do individuals respond to the everyday order of social relations which affect their lives, particularly their relations to economic, social and cultural institutions? Do they contest these institutions with counter-hegemonic ideologies? Or are their practices of a more culturally appropriative sort, blurring the lines between ideologies, appealing both to older cultural traditions and new ethical interpretations of memory and traditions?

In compiling the chapters for this book we were struck not only by the relationship of crisis and innovation, and its resemblance to

Polanyi's double movement of society, but also by the types of agencies individuals are engaged in. These are not always self-evident to the naked eye. The works of Scott (1985, 1990) and of Jordan, Redley, and James (1993) have been helpful in fathoming this deeper understanding of social practices, as people build on discourses of dissatisfaction while strengthening and emboldening their social networks. Jordan, Redley, and James, for example, argue that individuals do this by "pursuing their own purposes and interests within the roles and rights accorded to them" (1993:205).

The importance of this insight is that it points to the necessity of understanding practices *in their own right,* as containing clues to how people act in their social relations. Clearly, people relate to forces of exploitation and domination through complex practices of social and mutual recognition, rather than solely through a sense of abstract justice. These forces of recognition bridge institutional and noninstitutional moments, and their accompanying ideologies, from the level of practice. This is a theme that runs through this volume.

The nine essays collected here examine case studies from Italy, the United Kingdom, Chile, Trinidad and Tobago, the United States, Canada, and Israel. They offer us substantively different views about how societies respond to dramatic internal and external changes. Perhaps more striking are the family resemblances these countries emit in terms of an ethical and moral master-framing of their claims.

Citizenship on the Frontiers of Experience

Certain terms seem to be very appropriate for capturing the experience of people, regardless of their national and cultural contexts. Concepts such as autonomy, authenticity, and dignity fulfil that mandate well; they can be visualized here as the three points of a triangle outlining a new "politically effective language of everyday life," the title of this introductory essay. These points can be seen as conceptual markers which express certain types of social relations, their practices of subjection and resistance (Scott, 1990; see also Maheu, 1995). They can also be seen as bridging concepts between the informal realm and the formal institutionalization process. One of our contributors speaks, in very similar terms, about the political economy of respect and disrespect within social relations as powerful concepts about how we encounter otherness. We can use the notion of autonomy to speak of how one is positioned in a world of rights and obligations, figured through the grid of a statist "moral mode of regulation." Through their practices, individuals insert and locate discourses into a universe that is not only political and social, but deeply ethical and intercalated with discretionary power: the power of the State to draw moral borders around scarcity and well-being. The ongoing struggle for (relative) autonomy suggests that the State/civil society relationship is contingent and highly ambivalent, lest it escape politics.

Autonomy, as an artful practice, is about multiple agencies, both formal and informal, that are expressed in how one frames claims about livelihood, community, and well-being. Autonomy is about how one deals with institutions. Authenticity refers to the way individuals form their identities through experiencing Self and Others. This is perhaps the concept that is nearest the notion of community we are employing, through finding something *in common*. Authenticity refers to the way one sustains a contesting practice, embedding it in everyday understandings of difference and experiential knowledge, what Stuart Hall has called "the voicing of the margins" (Hall, 1988). Dignity is the last point of our didactic triangle of a "politically effective language of everyday life." Here, the emphasis is relational, and it concerns the effects of power. Dignity refers to the way one endures, confronts, and experiences the exercise of asymmetrical power relations. From this viewpoint, we have the long and bitter history of class relations as a struggle for many things, not the least of which is dignity. In a condition of persistent structural inequality, dignity becomes an ethical baseline, a moral challenge, for constructing relations with known, unknown, and distant Others (Wolfe, 1989).

Autonomy, authenticity, and dignity, as the three corners of the triangle of a politically effective language of everyday life, are ways to broach a very different basis for citizenship claims than that founded on rights and new areas of entitlements. Though these three concepts certainly point to problems of social membership, and to the complex interplay of identity which they raise, they bring the discussion of citizenship to a more fundamental level of social practice and social experience.

Citizenship, as several writers have insisted, is a crossroads for the moral agent in a condition of mounting diversity. It is also a place to construct alternative notions of politics (Bottomore, 1992; Fraser and Gordon, 1992; Cohen and Arato, 1992; Turner, 1986; Jenson, 1993). It is a place where ethical interpretations around liberal rights are contested on the terrain of the State or in the environment of State largesse. In his classic discussion of *Citizenship and Social Class* (1950), T. H. Marshall was perhaps the first to shed light on the structural context within which citizens find themselves. Marshall's early analysis presupposed an ethical justification for the postwar welfare regime; his insights have served as a platform for mounting new theoretical investigations. These range from analyses of citizenship practices within supra-national contexts (Held, 1991; Beitz, 1991), to questions of the moral complexity that contemporary citizenship practices raise in terms of the conflicts between our experiences and our acquired rights; these are discussed in chapter 7 of this book.

Part of the problem, certainly in the way that Marshall spoke of citizenship, was that he left little space for individuals to participate in the creation of their own political, social, and cultural well-being; he offered no link between practice, agency, and justice. Perhaps most critically, Marshall did not examine closely enough the effects of market-led ideologies and their relationship to rights embedded in civil and political citizenship; these have found their way into the discourse of social citizenship. Social citizenship, in this regard, while a creation of the State and civil society (and part of the class compromise), became a key moment in the moral mode of regulation about the nature of entitlement.

It is important to examine the collapsed moments that are subsumed under this process, through the stirring-together of social entitlement within the discourse of rights and market-led formulas. This has brought writers, such as Nancy Fraser and Linda Gordon (1992), to argue that the modern welfare State's commitment to civil and political citizenship is a dubious measure for envisioning new foundations for more caring and substantive forms of social citizenship. What, then, might this measure be, in terms of building a practice of social citizenship for modern times, a social citizenship beyond the market? Our sense is that the basis for this is contained in everyday practices of people and their reconstitutive agencies which inevitably inform present and future politics.

This book is clearly not about the discourse of rights: its emphasis is elsewhere. Family, community, and small entrepreneurial survival strategies, new emancipatory possibilities of citizens and their cities, and even laments for what once were progressive visions now lost in the melee of market relations form a litany which points to a recognition of the need for a profound moral recoding of social relations.

There is a lesson to be grasped here by Left theory and practice. New emancipatory sources will most likely appear in hybrid and institutionally camouflaged forms, bending the divisions between the formal and informal spheres. These will articulate increasingly oppressive modes of regulation with reconstitutive practices using State largesse and market conditions in subversive and reconstructive ways. This emphasizes the cultural side of politics, as people struggle to regain dignity and control over their communities and lives.

In so doing, it is the practices of individuals which contain the possibility for creating a new basis for deliberating citizenship, but not as a linchpin in the inclusion/exclusion debate around liberal rights (the "underclass" debate is an example of this). Rather, the reconstitutive practices of individuals and communities underscore new ethical standards for communality beyond the market, as an expression of the new citizenship, imploding the very boundaries of the concept. As these chapters demonstrate, the critical components at work here are not the commodified relations of exchange, but the artfulness of human relations, negotiating the borders of experience.

Lives, Livelihood, and Strategies of Survival

This book is organized into three sections, each one probing a particular dimension of the political economy of everyday life. The first section is mainly concerned with strategies of survival and livelihood in the face of adverse and transformative economic circumstances. Three chapters bring together views from different national contexts (Spain, England, and Italy). They shed light on the deftness with which individuals recreate their everyday lives and maintain their dignity in difficult times. But, from a more general standpoint, they also convincingly illustrate the eminently social nature of economic activity, and indicate ways to rethink the material conditions of growing informal economies as well as the identity consciousness of individuals taking part in that process.

The primary goal of Gavin Smith's *Western European Informal Economies in Historical Perspective* is to offer a fresh methodological position from which to view the informal. Essentially, he proposes to look at the informal as *idiosyncratic forms of livelihood*. Drawing from both an historical interpretation of the European experience with the informal, as well as recent field work conducted in Alicante,

Spain, Smith makes us realize that the informal is more complex than a mere social space from which to contest the formal sector. It is also an emerging field of regulation which hinges on dominant forms of Fordist and post-Fordist modes of regulation. To drive his point home, Smith examines the nature of idiosyncratic forms of livelihood within nineteenth century European civil society; he argues that this was both an arena beyond the State, as well as one incorporated by the State. The informal is characterized by a similar process of exclusion and incorporation.

Smith purposely relates idiosyncratic forms of livelihood to the nineteenth century understanding of civil society. He does this in an effort to prompt us to move away from the narrow focus that utilitarian reason has imposed on economics. In so doing, he forcefully restates Polanyi's theoretical intuition regarding the social embeddedness of the economy: he calls for a sociological form of inquiry that would go beyond understanding strategies of livelihood simply as a function of the production process. New inquiries must be simultaneously sensitive to structural conditions, instrumental practices, and the interpretive understanding of cultural production. The process of labour is more than a mere economic affair to be grasped in narrow, profit-maximizing terms. People seek livelihood through a complex of activities that are culturally loaded. To neglect this reality amounts to an undue dismissal of shadow economies as unimportant and peripheral. It leads to a misunderstanding of the very process of livelihood.

Smith's concerns are shared in Jane Wheelock's *Survival Strategies for Small Business Families in a Peripheral Local Economy* and Enzo Mingione's *Family Strategies and Social Development in Northern and Southern Italy*. Through more pointed observations of actual case studies, they show that strategies of livelihood and survival are intimately linked to cultural patterns which mould the economic process. In such patterns, traditions of solidarity, reciprocity, compassion, kinship, and loyalties loom large.

Wheelock looks at strategies of survival among small family businesses in Wearside, a town in the rapidly de-industrializing northeastern region of England. She points out how in times of market instability family businesses exhibit forms of rationality that have little to do with the usual formal objectives of profit maximization and accumulation. In fact, her empirical material confirms that forms of rationality based on family and affective relations, as well as on traditional loyalties, are quite significant during downward-spiralling economic periods. Wheelock's study authoritatively demonstrates that sheer economic interest is not what drives individuals in society.

As Wearside's small-scale entrepreneurs attest, there is a will to reciprocity and social solidarity that accounts for a large part of an individual's so-called economic decisions. They are prepared to be exploited so as to play their part in a two-pronged social enterprise; they want to be a part of a co-operative family based on reciprocal values as well as to respond to the natural need of people to pursue work and means of livelihood. Although self-employment locates the individual outside the larger, more formal networks of market activity, it provides for personal dignity. Wheelock gives the lie to those who believe in the self-interested motivations of individuals and points ultimately to the need for replacing the dehumanizing Fordist and Taylorist frameworks with flexible forms of labour organization.

Enzo Mingione writes from a more macrosociological point of view. He emphasizes the importance of adaptation capacities and changes in reciprocity networks around family or kinship strategies. These are juxtaposed against the particular orientations of economic or industrial development. He argues that individual economic strategies are conditioned by complex mixes of reciprocity and loyalty. These are formulated in such a manner as to allow people to cope, at the personal level, with the exigencies of utilitarian modernity over which they initially had little control. Drawing from the Italian case, Mingione offers a broad analytical perspective that allows us to understand the individual strategies at play in post-Fordist transformative and adaptive societal conditions.

Mingione convincingly illustrates how the individualization and competitive utilitarian behaviour which supposedly characterize modern societies are, in fact, highly inadequate views of things. Complex social realities encompass ascriptive and optional loyalties, non-monetary and non-utilitarian goals, and relationships. Much like Smith and Wheelock, Mingione also confirms Polanyi's thesis about the embeddedness of economics in social relations.

The Community Versus the Market: The Ups and Downs of Practices of Resistance

Community practices at the local level offer new patterns of intervention which challenge the policy orientations of a State increasingly bent on accommodating market imperatives. The second section of this book examines social and institutional practices of resistance and containment, aimed at countering the negative effects imposed by markets on the socioeconomically disadvantaged. The three chapters in this section evaluate strategies which, while directed at the State, actually try to reconstitute civil society and hence promote a more autonomous constituency of citizens.

In this process, however, all is not as encouraging as one might hope. The outcome of the tug-of-war between the atomizing tendencies of market forces and the forces of community resistance sometimes provides a humbling reality check. The grouping of community forces is not, in itself, a sufficient guarantee of the defeat or appeasement of market exigencies. This section relates three stories of critical, community-based struggles in different national contexts (Trinidad and Tobago, Chile, and Israel) and the efforts in each to counteract the consequences of an uncompromising market logic.

The first story is told by Trinidad community activist and consultant, Ivan Laughlin. In *The Sou Sou Land Possibility: Survival and Community Mobilization in Trinidad and Tobago,* he recounts the process of mobilization which led to the struggle for survival by landless squatters outside Port-of-Spain. This resulted in the establishment of a tremendously successful, non-governmental, non-profit land reform initiative, the *Sou Sou Land,* rooted in and born out of the local community.

Laughlin shows the critical importance of people's direct involvement in both the development process and the implementation of desired changes in living conditions. The worth of the Sou Sou Land experience rests in the possibilities it raises in terms of adapting development goals and instruments of livelihood to match the needs of people, rather than the other way around. Here, as in the cases discussed in the preceding section, solidarity and a strong will to regain a lost dignity in the face of structural adversity emerged as important parts of the social portrait of the affected population.

The narrative of Larissa Lomnitz and Ana Melnick, which animates *Middle Class, Social Networks, and the "Neo-Liberal" Model: The Case of the Chilean School Teachers 1973-1988,* is not as happy. It is the story of the destruction of existing social networks of solidarity as a result of the brutal enforcement of market principles; it is also a recounting of the difficult reconstruction of alternative networks, which barely succeed in maintaining a modicum of dignity.

While the plight of the Chilean school teachers may not seem objectively comparable to that of Trinidad's landless squatters —

because of the obvious differentials in living conditions — the socioeconomic downgrading they have experienced under Pinochet's policy of privatization of educational and social programmes has the makings of a human tragedy.

Lomnitz and Melnick illustrate all too well the dramatic consequences of market-driven policies and their effect on individuals. Before the coup, like most members of the middle class, Chilean school teachers enjoyed reasonably good standards of living, job security, and access to social networks, based on their connections to State apparati. These guaranteed relative material comfort, an enviable symbolic status, and some socioeconomic privileges. The privatization of education led to the virtual annihilation of the social networks, and it introduced a criterion of competitiveness which dealt a severe blow to pre-existing patterns of solidarity. In a way not unlike Wearside's small entrepreneurs, Alicante's jobbers, or southern Italy's farmers, Chilean school teachers have come to depend increasingly on kinship and family loyalties to pull through. Yet, as Lomnitz and Melnick argue, in spite of the realigning of family solidarities as a means of coping with radical policy changes, the experience of Chilean school teachers was a negative one. Their study serves as a reminder that the political economy of everyday life can spell dire consequences in situations where the market forces operate in unchecked and unfettered ways.

In *Beyond the Market in a Market Economy: The Kibbutz Experience,* Menachem Rosner tells a story that is almost as disconcerting as that of Lomnitz and Melnick. Rosner relates the current attempt within Israel's kibbutz communities to move away from their original communal principles in order to introduce free market mechanisms into their mode of functioning. Since these structures are known for their eminently community-based approach to livelihood as well as for their autonomy from national market networks, this abandonment of traditional practices represents a significant rupture.

The severe crisis of the Israeli economy since 1985 has led to the accumulation of a large debt, accompanied by high interest and capital payments which have negatively affected ongoing economic activities. As Rosner explains, after fifteen years of unprecedented growth and expansion of the kibbutz economy, this crisis prompted many to believe that it could be overcome by allowing market forces and profit considerations priority over social and value-related considerations. The new guiding ideas were to promote greater individual autonomy in all spheres of kibbutz life and enhance consumer sovereignty. For all intents and purposes, the New Kibbutz Concept seeks nothing less than the "de-embedding" of the economy from its social framework. Indeed, its explicit goals are to separate business from community, and to "liberate" the economic units from the limitations and principles of the kibbutz.

Rosner takes firm issue with the New Kibbutz Concept, and he painstakingly points to its inherent weaknesses. Of more significance is his empirical analysis of the reaction of kibbutz communities to the concept. While a relatively low percentage seem to have bought into it — generally those marked by social instability or low standards of living — most are resisting the intrusion of market-led hierarchical mechanisms. Rosner's findings do not indicate that a process of decommunalization is sweeping kibbutz communities. Yet he admits that normative changes are occurring, and that more often than in the past these take utilitarian expressions. In some communities, confidence in the future of the kibbutz is dwindling. The battle against market forces is not lost in the land of the kibbutz, but it is clear that the market is posing extreme challenges to community practices. Rosner's essay articulates the predicament that even a deeply grounded community logic has to constantly face and overcome.

Mapping New Citizenship Practices

The final section of the book examines new spaces for collective action by considering the institutional and affective contexts for emerging social and political practices. These transformative spaces are linked to significant changes in politics "writ large"; as importantly, they are also linked to perceptions about politics that have emerged in Western societies in the last decades.

The following issues signpost the concerns of authors in this section: the breakdown of enduring myths about citizenship and its patterns of entitlements; the transformation of the nation-State through inter-local and global-local networks linking municipalities; and the centrality of "social sentiments" which individuals carry about themselves and their relationship to others through the medium of respect and self-respect. The tone of this section differs somewhat from the preceding ones; its more general and politically speculative nature is intended as a reflection on the social realities mapped out in the other sections. Maurice Roche, Warren Magnusson, and S. M. Miller all cast their net fairly wide so as to contextualize and offer explanations about the phenomena observed by the other contributors; in the process they point to new paths of critical thinking.

In *Citizenship and Social Change: Beyond the Dominant Paradigm,* Maurice Roche argues that the critical standards and contexts of social citizenship are rapidly breaking down; the dominant paradigm of citizenship as an integrating ethos of the liberal-democratic State is in irreversible crisis. Roche argues that the basis for this crisis is not only ideological but is also tied to structural transformations in political economy within late twentieth century capitalism. Given tumultuous changes in the nature of class, work, and labour markets, the social citizenship that accompanied us from the Keynesian postwar compromise into the *fin de siecle* has become irrevocably outdated. So, too, are the political strategies that hope to resuscitate it. Post-industrial capitalism has newly called into existence the foundations for its "creative destruction" by making categories of non-citizenship for a self-reproducing underclass, a proportion of which now must be said to incorporate the working poor.

These sea-changes, affecting the employment, income, and welfare of growing sectors of the population, are further complicated by powerful forces of globalization. Roche looks to the European Community (EC) and debates surrounding the Social Charter as prefigurative of a post-industrial and post-national world where the problem of citizenship becomes one of intense moral complexity. This, he argues, must be understood from a variety of viewpoints if the transmission of poverty and its institutionalization in non-citizenship statuses is to be grasped.

Maurice Roche's structural concerns with moral complexity are taken up with a different nuance, and in a different language, in *A New/Old Frontier of Inequalities,* where S. M. Miller makes the argument that respect and self-respect are key to contemporary policy issues. He states in uncategorical terms: "How a society regards particular groups affects how it treats them." Miller's insight underscores the importance of moral perception as a political condition that mediates between self and others. Respect, in this regard, acts as a scarce resource that is carefully distributed; as a result, it functions as an ethical starting point for a host of social interactions. The notion of respect, or what Miller ingenuously refers to as *a political economy of respect,* opens the door to a series of interrogations.

Primarily, the shift from structural to perceptual categories permits a focused view into the density of class relations and everyday life that is redolent of Richard Sennett's *The Hidden Injuries of Class.*

Miller, however, moves beyond Sennett by drawing examples which are more attuned to the cultural and social diversity that mark us as moderns. Looking at popular culture, Miller demonstrates the ubiquitous manner in which the oppressiveness of daily media and its commodified images reproduce circuits of disrespect through stereotyping and discriminating institutional practices.

Building respect as a policy concern must, as Miller insists, be integral to the future design of citizenship. How marginal groups are treated — respect as a resource — and the manner in which they help themselves — self-respect as a resource — are critical to the struggles for social, cultural, gender, and economic equality now so current on the political agenda. Miller's policy position maintains, then, that intercalating self-respect and mutual aid within public programmes would have an effect on untangling the tightly wrapped roots of disrespect. It would also engender responsibility for one's actions towards others, away from an outside party — the welfare State — and towards more localized expressions of solidarity.

In *Dissidence and Insurgency: Municipal Foreign Policy in the 1980s*, Warren Magnusson tackles similar issues, but from the institutional perspective of the municipality as an empowered agent which makes moral, ethical, and ultimately political choices. Magnusson examines the ambivalent political spaces that municipalities occupy between the State, the market, and everyday life. Municipalities are privileged sites that can be socially and politically mobilized against the expanding vortex of relations of domination. Municipalities, though this is never guaranteed, have the power to disrupt the global system of exploitation.

Magnusson offers examples of various local initiatives that have networked with national or international unions of local authorities, United Nations agencies, and wider social movements that are not contained within any given national or spatial context. Examples of dissident municipalities declaring themselves to be "free zones," appealing to international law and the need for new standards of morality, position the city in a unique counter-hegemonic stance. Municipalities have the potential to thread the local and the global in intricate patterns of social relations, recreating the groundwork for the emergence of new practices and their social effects.

The last three chapters of this collection poignantly underscore the following and concluding assertions. To map the shifting frontiers of citizenship statuses in late modernity requires continuous and mutually involved enterprises, pursued from a variety of perspectives. No single discipline contains sufficient scope in and of itself, as societies become increasingly intertwined both on the level of politics and everyday life.

Conclusion

The changing structural contexts of the national and international welfare State, how we perceive "distant and unknown others," and the place from which we build our perceptions in a bewildering context of globalization, harbour critical questions for contemporary social and political analysis. As we attempt to come to firmer grips with new patterns of global and local inequalities and the practices that arise to meet and challenge them, it becomes abundantly clear that the questions posed by the contributors to this book are critical. These questions are now ours to debate and critique. They will not go away.

The importance of this book is contained in the very nature of the social practices that it raises for contemporary theory and political analysis. These chapters comprise an ethnographic composite of practices which can no longer be ignored by social scientists and policy makers. Indeed, these forms of collective actions raise significant issues for the future of markets and the welfare State.

Practices of survival, born out of the inherent limitations of a failing socioeconomic logic, are exceedingly real, not only in their appearances in everyday life but in their human consequences as well. They must be known, named, and acknowledged, not as mere sociological or anthropological curiosities but as concrete challenges to the social, economic, and political institutions of modern societies. They are clarion calls signalling the increasing illegitimacy of the dominant socioeconomic system and its societal mode of regulation.

We organized this reader with the express purpose of addressing both practice and theory. The first two sections offer vivid empirical evidence of the astounding ability of communities to reconstruct themselves in the face of adversity. The last section offers, through the grid of rigorous theoretical analysis, conceptual redefinitions of the dominant frameworks of social interaction. Those of us concerned with the search for an alternative to the present state of our political economy, and its distribution of mass unemployment and immiserization, should find in the following contributions abundant food for thought and helpful guidelines for action.

References

Beitz, Charles R., (1991), "Sovereignty and Morality in International Affairs," in *Political Theory Today*, edited by David Held (Cambridge: Polity Press).

Bottomore, Tom, (1992), *Citizenship and Social Class* (London: Pluto Press).

Cohen, Jean, and Andrew Arato, (1992), *Civil Society and Political Theory* (Boston: MIT Press).

Fraser, Nancy, and Linda Gordon, (1992), "Contract Versus Charity," *Socialist Review*, 22, 3, pp.45-49.

Hall, Stuart, (1988), *The Hard Road to Renewal: Thatcherism and the Crisis of the Left* (London: Verso).

Held, David, (1991), "Democracy, the Nation State, and the Global System," in *Political Theory Today*, edited by David Held (Cambridge: Polity Press).

Jenson, Jane, (1993), "Deconstructing Dualisms: Citizenship Claims in Canada," in *New Approaches to Social Welfare Theory: Making and Sorting Claims*, edited by G. Drover and P. Kierans (Cheltenham, U.K.: Edward Elgar).

Maheu, Louis (ed.), (1995, forthcoming), "Introduction," *Social Movements and Social Classes: New Actors and New Agendas* (London: Sage Publications).

Jordan, Bill, Marcus Redley, and Simon James, (1993), "Putting the Family First," (mimeo).

Marshall, T.H., (1950), *Citizenship and Social Class and Other Essays* (Cambridge: Cambridge University Press).

Nancy, Jean-Claude, (1991), *The Inoperative Community* (Minneapolis: University of Minnesota Press).

Scott, James C., (1985), *Weapons of the Weak: Everyday Forms of Peasant Resistance* (New Haven: Yale University Press).

Scott, James C., (1990), *Domination and the Arts of Resistance* (New Haven: Yale University Press).

Sennett, Richard, (1972), *The Hidden Injuries of Class* (New York: Knopf).

Turner, Bryan S., (1986), *Citizenship and Capitalism* (London: Unwin and Hyman).

Wolfe, Alan, (1989), *Whose Keeper? Social Science and Moral Obligation* (Berkeley: University of California Press).

Part I

Lives, Livelihood and Strategies of Survival

Chapter One

Western European Informal Economies in Historical Perspective

Gavin Smith

[I was] the slave of circumstances . . . like a feather on the stream . . . continually whirled along from one eddy to another. Amid the universal transformation of things in the moral and physical world, my own condition has been like a dissolving view and I have been so tossed in the rough blanket of fate, that my identity, if at any time a reality, must have been one which few could venture to swear to.

James Dawson Burn, artisan, 1885
(Vincent, 1981:70)

You think we are like cunning old spiders weaving a wide web but you are wrong. We are like the flies caught in the web. And you know what happens to the fly. Each twist and turn to be free just strangles it a little more.

Lima Shantytown dweller, 1973
(Smith, 1989:96)

Everybody's fiddling somewhere. It's impossible to pay the taxes the Socialists have brought in if you work all up front. And what are the increased taxes for? They take money from me so I can't support my mother in her old age, to give it to the mother of someone who wouldn't support his anyway. So now, on Fridays when I need extra cash to pay my women I go and get it from my mother's pension cheque.

Valencian small work-distributor (July 1993)

S tudies of informal economic activities, be they in the West, the post-socialist regimes of eastern Europe, or the third world, variously stress the features brought out by these quotes: the sense workers have of being helplessly tossed around, the victims of an uncontrollable world; the perpetual focus on strategizing and then the acknowledgement of its severe limitations; and the bizarrely nightmarish way of dealing with State actions in order to turn them back upon themselves. Macro studies that generate statistics on the "extent of informal economies" in country X or Y, for example, have the effect of stressing the passivity of actors. Ethnographic work among "informal economies" tends often toward an overemphasis on the role of strategy as a pre-eminent feature of people's lives; something picked up here by the Lima informant, above. And "cultural" studies can frequently give us a sense of the Byzantine worldview so often necessary for actors, yet somehow lose sight of the material conditions so strongly felt in the first of these quotations.

The purpose of this chapter is to begin the task of trying to bring these separate perspectives together. It seems to me that insofar as the informal economy is "informal," we study it as a kind of civil society, as opposed to the more formal society firmly under the panoptic gaze of the State; and insofar as we see it as an "economy," we study people's activities therein in terms of "labour." What I do here, then, is to shift away from any one contemporary "informal economy" towards the past, when our understanding of civil society and social labour were far less taken for granted than they are among social enquirers today. By doing so, I hope to open the door to possible new formulations and hence, ultimately, new methodologies in dealing with informal economic activity.[1]

To begin with, I should dispense with that term. Not, I'm afraid, for anything better (yet). The way people are gaining a livelihood in contemporary western Europe, and also of course in the East, is indeed undergoing change, if only in terms of the degree of the unemployment now experienced. But whether we should understand this as a process or tendency, whether we should understand it as informalization, whether we should address it as an economy (rather than as social activity more broadly defined), and whether we should say that it is something new, something never felt before, at least not like this: these are all issues I wish to place in abeyance. So I choose instead a rather clumsy putative term: *idiosyncratic forms of livelihood*.

The chapter is organized as follows. I begin with a brief comment on why, it seems to me, the in-depth ethnographic study of idiosyncratic forms of livelihood is important. So as to give the reader some sense of the kind of world I allude to in the remainder of the chapter, I then follow this with a series of vignettes from the province of Alicante in Spain. I believe that assumptions that livelihoods have never been like this before are widespread, unsubstantiated, and probably, along many dimensions, substantially false.[2] I therefore turn next to a few comments on past livelihoods in industrializing western Europe. This brings me to how we study informal activities as we find them today, and I try to query this by reflecting in the final sections of the chapter on civil society and social labour.

Studying Idiosyncratic Forms of Livelihood

Why are there so many recent studies of informal economic activities, of "new kinds" of economic relationship, or "new kinds" of industrial district, and why are they so important? Not because the capitalist economy in the West is becoming disorganized, decentred, or unregulated. That may be why some people write their articles, but it is not why they are important. Nor is it because what we are witnessing here are the bases for a new kind of non-State-mediated participatory democracy, be it in the shantytowns of Chile, the micro-credit systems of the Gramein Bank, or the co-operatives networks of small northern Italian firms.

What makes the study of idiosyncratic forms of livelihood important, and what the challenge to these studies is, is that we now lack a politically effective class analysis of most people in any given social formation. This is so whether we are talking about the so-called unemployed, workers and owners in small enterprises, youth and the aged, or supposedly orthodox workers (blue or white collar) who complement their income with other activities. Indeed, one does not have to stray too far into science fiction to imagine a major Western city where mass-production factories have been replaced by the headquarters of firms whose capital lies far away in distant climes, populated by an economically active population of hard-to-classify share-holding white-collar workers, serviced by (equally hard to classify) formal and informal service suppliers of food and cleaning facilities, all of whom turn the city over at night to "the street people."

Class analysis, of course, has fallen into disrepute. Gorz, for example, concludes that social actors of this kind "form a non-class in the sense that they do not undergo social integration . . . [through] their common work situation" (Mingione, 1991:43), and Castells and Porter (1989:31) believe that "the experience of labour and the emergence of stable class positions do not correspond to each other" in informal economies.

But even those who abandon it, favouring the study of temporary political coalitions around institutionally recognized social identities, must surely acknowledge that the principles of property and labour, by which value is produced and transformed, remain in place and are ubiquitous (even in informal economies). So whatever new times we may reach, we shall not be able to do so by abandoning entirely the trail back from cyberpunks and virtual reality through the maze that brings us up against that fundamental relationship. They remain therefore the organizing principles for the project I am engaged in here.

Life and Livelihood: Alicante, Spain

Superficially, the area of the País Valenciano to the south of the city of Alicante is not dissimilar to the Italian case. There is a long history of prosperous agriculture alongside small manufacturing which, as in Italy, is concentrated by product: Crevillente is associated with rugs, fishnets and rope; Alcoy with blankets; the towns of Castellón with ceramic tiles; and the towns surrounding Alicante with toys. But the largest such product concentration is that of shoes around Elde and Elche, in the south of the País.

Moreover, this pattern of pockets of product-specific manufacturing centres, interspersed amid prosperous commercial agriculture, goes back a long way in Valencia's history. Though, to the visitor, Valencia may appear "like Catalonia, just a little less so," retaining like Catalonia a strong sense of regional distinctiveness from Spain, speaking a version of Catalan and having a stronger tradition of commerce than the interior regions of Spain, the similarities can be misleading. Valencia's development[3] through the last century was closely tied to export agriculture, especially wines and oranges. Dependency on foreign markets and on imported agricultural inputs put Valencia sharply at odds with the persistent tariff protectionism of the Catalan bourgeoisie. Meanwhile, the demands of commercial agriculture in the region were never sufficiently great to drive up rural wages and thus eliminate artisan production; rather, the evidence suggests that stimuli for items such as packing cases and irrigation machinery often gave the impetus for development of manufacturing less directly tied to the export agriculture sector (Nadal, 1990).

There is, then, a significant history of interlocking agricultural and manufacturing production here. Indeed, the whole metaphor of the radical break, so central to modernism, seems inapposite here: be it the radical break of the migrant from rural community to urban anomie; or of the artisan master to the routinized and de-skilled factory worker. These kinds of sweeping away of the past are by no means an imagery familiar to the pluriactive household. A more familiar image would be one of the continuity of flexibility, adaptability, and transformations alike in skills, tools, and the package of households' livelihoods. To this "pre-existing mode of production" came the demands of the new international division of labour; first, and with the greatest influence, affecting local shoe production, as the production of cheap shoes moved from Italy to Spain (and thence to Brazil), but also taking in other activities.

Throughout the 1970s production structures emerged in which a family-owned firm took a contract, from just one large U.S.A. or northern European customer, thereby establishing a relationship of extreme dependency, with the buying firm sometimes providing injections of capital and getting involved in managerial decisions, yet not thereby developing principles of loyalty. The local firm then met the orders with a workforce located in its legally-registered factory, plus a much larger workforce spread out in a "putting-out" system. José, a work distributor in shoes, comes from a town of 5,000 some ten miles from Elche. He describes his induction into the job as follows:

> After I had been working at the factory for about three years, I began to take work home during the lunch break. We had an old Seat 500 then, and I'd pile in the work, rush home, leave it with the wife and try to get back to my place on the line. It was a frantic business. But that way I got higher piece rates.[4] Maria did the work downstairs in the garage. After a while, I exchanged the Seat for a second-hand van. I got more work home that way and Maria started getting her sister and a couple of friends in on the work. But the place was awful. I started having accidents at work. And anyway half the time the pieces [the women] did turned out wrong and got rejected, so I lost my rate. Other fellows were working full-time taking work from the factory and giving out [to subcontractor homeworkers]. I started getting an old bloke who'd

worked on the machine before to take my place a couple of days in the week, so I could work more with the pick-up and at the *taller* at home. Well you can see me now: I haven't been working at the factory for over two years, but its just as frantic, because now I have to get work from a whole bunch of factories, not just the one. And you have to keep them happy or they pass the consignment on to somebody else. [Question: What about the *taller*?] *Maria* [his wife]: I won't let him in there! *José* [shrugs]: It's true. She runs that place. I don't set a foot in there, except on Sundays maybe, if we have a lot of upgrading to do.

Meanwhile, in the home, we move from the initial wife's contribution through her already-established network to an extensive set of subcontracts. And the distributor and his wife are likely now to have a small part-time *taller* (workshop), employing one or two people solely to upgrade work coming through the chain. As for women lower down in the chain, they are likely to be part of an agricultural household, and as a result, under extreme pressure. In another paper (Smith, 1990),[5] I describe the situation as follows:

The demands for work on the family's own farm are erratic; the husband/father, for example, may get a day's work, and finding a task on the farm incomplete, will put pressure on his wife or daughter to put aside the home work in favour of the farm.... [Meanwhile,] work distributors, anxious to minimize the amount of travelling and contracting they have to do . . . encourage women to take large batches by paying geometrically higher rates; home working women, already under pressure from their farming husbands, may speak for excessive batch sizes with a view to off-loading some to a neighbour.

Such a complex set of social relationships is built upon a long history of extensive interpersonal networks, through which intertwined agricultural and artisanal activities were reproduced. Over time, personal claims extending outwards from immediate family, to extended family, neighbours, community members, and ultimately other "Valencianos" became an institutionalized component of everyday life in the manner well-described by Sider:

> By "claims" I refer to the rights people have or assert not just *over* other people or to take the product of their labour, or their labour itself, but *in* other people; the structured and conscious co-involvement in other lives, whether friendly, hostile, or both (1986:92).

The Franco years ensured that the tradition of municipal support for the local economy, noted for the Third Italy (Blim, 1990; Blim, 1992), has no historical basis here. An especially important institution for the channelling of claims of the kind Sider refers to, however, is the *cuadrilla* (Cucó i Giner, 1990), a group of perhaps eight to twenty people who form friendships in school, and then continue them as they grow older, extending to include their fiancées, and later, marriage partners. It can be said, without exaggeration, that these groupings constitute the body of significant others beyond the family for a person; leisure activities such as drinking in bars, going to dances, football games, and so on, take place within this group, and political identifications are almost always uniform throughout the group.

> Ana took work in a shoe factory when she was 17. She worked there nearly five years, she says, she had trouble getting to the factory if she wasn't on the day shift and she hated the authoritarian atmosphere. She quit over a dispute with her supervisor and helped her mother on her machine at home for a few months that turned into nearly a year, her mother says. Then she helped out a friend of her mother's at her house on her machine. Her mother persuaded her to get her own machine and now she works in a small glassed-in veranda off the kitchen. She works on average from 8 to 12 and from 4 to 6, except Fridays and sometimes Thursdays, when she works longer to make up on the batches to meet her quota. Ana doesn't rely on a single distributor. She picks up batches from two or three women all of whom are part of a *cuadrilla*.

> She used to take work from Pablo S. She says he was good to her because he is her father's cousin and in his *cuadrilla*, and she tried to do good work for him, she says, he had a bad mouth and short temper. "At first I was glad to have him but, you know, I didn't like it too. I worked slower for him. I was worried about making

mistakes, but I was just starting then. He was family. Anyway I got no special deals from Pablo! Once I was off two weeks and when I asked for work again, he gave me half, saying that he was using somebody else now. He teases me about not working for him when I see him in the street. It's difficult to find work this way. You have to be nice to everybody no? But it's better this way.

When competition grew from the period I have just described, through the 1980s, this already thoroughly "informalized" economy was made still more informal, and a prevalent means by which this was done was by use of regulations governing worker co-operatives.

When I returned to the field in the late eighties I found myself one day with four guys drinking in a bar on the road between Crevillente and Elche. All four men were themselves entrepreneurs, three were in shoe production, the fourth was Ricardo's (marketing) brother. The two brothers are now in the "export-import" business. Ramón, who used to run the shop, has been invalided for some time, it is unclear whether he has had a nervous breakdown or is suffering from acute ulcers, possibly both. Much of the machinery has been dispersed, but Ricardo, together with two others at the bar, is explaining to the fourth man, how to set up a workers' co-operative to provide a shell around the productive machinery that's left, after the "thinning diet" as they describe the process of stripping down the enterprise.

The pattern is a familiar one: while officially registered firms and employment figures in the industry declined, overall shoe production increased. Registered firms declare bankruptcy and close one day, opening the next, with the original shell-firm now operating entirely in a merchant capacity, leasing the old machinery either to a "co-operative" or to a now wholly illicit subcontractor shop, made up of workers who agree to reduced wages, safety, and benefits, to get the contract from their old boss.

Many of the problems in studying phenomena of this kind arise from the uncritical use of a conceptual apparatus designed for the study of "industrial society," and they run the risk of rendering invisible fundamental elements of "informal economies." Participants in this world are seen specifically as "workers" and what they do as "work." Unfortunately, what emerges from this is a very narrow productivist view of labour. Insofar as work tends to be goal-oriented instrumental action guided by norms of efficiency, so studies which filter too narrowly through the lens of "work" end up seeing social interest and consciousness in terms of instrumentalist explanations.

Yet such "work" was itself the product of a quite specific set of historical forces. The original studies of industrial society were based on the observation that people spent much of their waking hours in regimented work, which threw them together in concentrated spaces with other people, forcing them thereby to share the same experience. Apart from its regimentation, this form of work had a mystifying quality to it, masking the specific manner and degree in which these workers had the value of their labour taken away from them, and giving them an alienated sense of their relationship to the product they were involved in producing. Out of such conditions arises a situation in which people begin to share an identity with one another, as well as a perception of the world: a particular consciousness. On this basis was built the political agenda of working class parties of the early part of this century.

Meanwhile, many of the untidy boundaries of this formula quickly became lost. Increasingly, as women (and children) were displaced in factories, it came to refer only to adult males. Almost "full employment" (say, less than seven percent [of men, of course]) also became the norm to which it referred . . . and so on. Yet the core of the formula became sedimented into social science thinking; exceptions became idiosyncrasies needing explanation, while increasingly a core set of assumptions no longer called for substantiation: "And the historian who carefully verifies each level of data can all too easily underestimate these gaps and fill them in with ideas that seem so obvious that they hardly require verification" (Rancière, 1986:326). It therefore becomes necessary to go back and enquire about that world.

History and Past Livelihoods

Writing of London, J. A. Schmiechen remarked: "The small-scale and labour-intensive sector was not a survival, but a central and dynamic component of mid-Victorian growth" (1975:413). A not dissimilar observation is made of France fifty years later when, despite a period of expansion, "industrialization ... did not prove to be ... the nemesis of handicraft production. ... France remained, in large part, a nation of *petites situations*" (Zdatny, 1990:181). It was, moreover, the kind of world to which many, if not most, workers from the mass-production factory turned, not just for buying what they needed and getting services done, but also for turning a penny or two beyond the wage. And this is to speak only in terms of the individual, rather than the household yet:

> It is clear ... that few families were dependent simply upon a single, regular, weekly wage. Much employ-ment was seasonal or casual in nature, and most families derived their income from a whole cluster of different sources: from work done by the wife and the children; from begging; from the Poor Law; and from petty crime such as coal picking or poaching (Benson, 1983:3-4).

And even here the writer is lapsing into a retrospective view of "petty crime": just five pages later he is telling us that as late as 1921 coal picking was regarded much like gleaning in rural society, with mine owners "not saying anything about [their employees] fetching a bag or barrowful for their own use" (Benson, 1983:9-10). Indeed, the "picking" was part of the "wage" in many workers' eyes. We can go back a long way in the history of industry to find a tradition that workers would have a share in the product of their labour. Thus, the line separating "established rights" from "barefaced robbery" was difficult to draw; there was a close connection between "long play" and the embezzlement of materials[6] (Berg et al., 1983:2).

Indeed, what terminated such practices was the need on the part of owners to give birth to the lockout: to force dependence on the wage and the wage alone. As William Reddy (1981) recorded for nineteenth-century France, the "strike" (*la grève*) originally meant, not days of idleness, but days spent in search of work. It was the need to control labour, not just in the factory, but beyond it, that put an end to this symbiotic linkage in livelihood practices. Thus, refer-ring to the period "before the factory," Berg et al. conclude:

> There was ... a long tradition of acquiring portions of income in ways other than the wage. The failure to keep time and to respond to wages was associated with the need to engage in a whole series of extra-cur-

ricular activities yielding up various forms of non-monetary and monetary income. Industrial discipline could only succeed as these other sources of income started to dry up. Thus the importance of the emergence of restrictions on gleaning, poaching, and gathering wood (Berg et al., 1983:9).

Occupational classifications so useful for the collection of statistics may have the effect of creating rather too neat and bounded a picture, rather too still a *tableau vivant,* which ensnares the historian or historical sociologist. Factory workers may not have been just that, and even when they were, they may not have had the job for long. Students of third world rural society have often remarked that the term "peasant" should refer less to an agriculturalist than to a rural Jack (or Jill)-of-all-trades, and the same may be said for the nineteenth-century artisan, a term which almost as a part of its definition escapes statistical classification. This makes it hard to understand the artisan in class terms, so long as class is understood as in some way associated with an occupational category. There is an ad hoc-ness, an approximation, about such a life spent looking for opportunities (Zdatny, 1990:194). Both Reddy (1984; 1987), and Rancière stress that this can be especially so for those most active in political mobilization:

> The professional identities under which militants are known to their colleagues, to "bourgeois" militants, or to the police, are often only temporary stages in an otherwise rocky career. The same individual can be found self-employed in one trade, salaried in another, or hired as a clerk or a peddlar in a third (Rancière, 1983:322-3).

This is very far from an exhaustive review of livelihoods in two of Europe's most "advanced" industrial societies in the late nineteenth century. But for our purposes here, two things seem to emerge. The first is that, even in the heartlands of capitalist industry, the arena of work was no more confined to the factory than was the civil society of the worker nicely removed from the heavy hand of the bosses. The second is how familiar this all sounds for anybody who has been working in informal economies in the late twentieth century. And yet a certain core understanding of industrialization, and of the mass-collective worker, seems to have all but buried the so-called idiosyncrasies of such a world. Regulation by bosses and the need for regularity among statisticians (and statistically-inclined historians and sociologists) have worked their wiles on the recorded history of working people, and the "discovery" of today's informal economy has to be seen in this light.

Thus, rather than take the notion of labour we apply to contemporary informal economies from the core formula mentioned earlier, it would be more appropriate to place it in the context more sensitive to actual historical variations, and the same goes for notions we have of an unregulated society "beyond the reach of [State] regulation." I turn to this in the remainder of the chapter.

Informal Activities and Civil Society

What we see from these historical examples is a kind of world which circumscribed the formal processes of regulation, and this dimension of "informal economic activity" as an arena of non-institutional heterotopia is an important one. Yet, use of the term "informal" tends to underplay the emergent processes of social regulation which must inevitably play their part in the economic relationships to be found here. The informal economy is both a social space contesting dominant forms of regulation and also a constantly emerging field of regulation itself.[7] As a result, we might learn something by turning for a moment to nineteenth-century understandings of civil society.

The notion of "civil society" was originally inseparable from the history of the rising bourgeoisie in western Europe. As with the contemporary term "informal economy" vis-à-vis the formal, so civil society was a "question of listing everything that [had] been left over after limiting the sphere of the State" (Bobbio, 1989:25). However, as this negative definition attained currency, it assumed within it a more positive, constructive, attribute of civil society, as

> a group of ideas that accompanies the birth of the
> bourgeois world: the affirmation of natural rights
> belonging to the individual and social groups inde-
> pendently of the State, and which limit and restrain
> [the State's] power (Bobbio, 1989:22).

The way in which civil society here mirrors the amorphous character of current uses of informal economy results specifically from the changing nature of what civil society was being opposed to, that is the changing State; for Marx and Engels were evolving the notion of civil society against the backdrop of the absolute State, whose defining criterion, for them, was that its mode for regulating society was antithetical to the development of bourgeois society. In this early meaning, described in *The Holy Family* (1956), the fact that "bourgeois society" and "civil society" are described in identical terms in German[8] allows Marx and Engels to understand it both as a class liberating itself from the shackles of the absolute State and as a sphere, or social space in Bourdieu's terms (1991), of social interaction.

This might be nicely illustrated by the plaque outside the New York Stock Exchange, which commemorates the tree under which shares were first traded in the United States. This is because the contrast between the empty space under the tree, which only became relevant when a few stock traders hovered around it amidst the bustling and free-flowing traffic of Broad Street, and the solid granite front of today's stock exchange, serves to remind us that there could scarcely be an institution whose cliff-hanging legitimacy relies more thoroughly on its being regulated than today's Exchange.

And this was the issue for civil society as it developed in the eighteenth-century coffee houses, where the pamphlets of the much-heralded "free press" were read while bourgeois organic intellectuals engaged in "rational" debate with State officials (Habermas, 1989), toward the project of delimiting the extent to which the State could interfere in the civil world of bourgeois market society. And yet precisely those notions used to demarcate the boundaries between civil society and the State (freedom and rationality) themselves became the principles for regulation within civil society itself.

So the bourgeois class formation we are witnessing here has two critical characteristics: that it emerged in opposition to a form of regulation against which it was set; and that, in doing so, it compartmentalized functions for social reproduction into different "spaces" in the social edifice. As Polanyi put it: "A self-regulating market demands nothing less than the institutional separation of society into an economic and political sphere" (1957:71).

Indeed, the British transition to a constitutional monarchy represented the triumph of this process. The shift that was taking place in Britain, from the Great Revolution of 1688 onwards, was one in which social functions were removed from local communities and located in the State. As Raymond Firth (1956) pointed out in respect to peasant communities, actors who are too concerned with community values make bad market decisions, and this concerned the

British bourgeoisie too (Macpherson, 1984). Their solution was not to do away with the monarchic State, but to make it constitutional, that is to say to compartmentalize society into its "rational," economic, functions, characterized by "freedom," and its social functions, to be managed by the State and characterized by order (Sayer, 1987).

Gramsci's (1971: *passim*) contribution to the notion of civil society was to recognize, for the political dimension, what Polanyi recognized for the economic: that civil society itself could not survive without its own forms of regulation. Thus, for Gramsci, there were not one but two political arenas of bourgeois society, the one expressed through the State and hence a reworked version of its predecessor (a fact especially clear in England where the constitutional monarch personifies this continuity), using legitimized forms of violence (what Gramsci called "domination"); and the other emerging within civil society as a form of regulation he referred to as a bourgeois hegemony.

It is processes of this kind that elude studies of informal economies that insist on their historical novelty. Rather, any given informal economy is situated within a history of unfolding fields of regulation. We have seen, for example, how the regulation of factory workers required that control should extend beyond the factory gates into the self-provisioning strategies of families. And, subsequently, Ford's agenda included a corporate society in which consumption patterns were an inherent component of regulation. It is within the context of these competing and overlapping fields of regulation that we have to begin to understand the waxing and waning of shadow economies in western Europe. This refers to regulatory conditions external to informal economic relationships themselves. What we can see from the case of bourgeois civil society, however, is how, historically, appeals for regulating within civil society explicitly acquired legitimacy by being contrasted to that of the old State, i.e., appeals to reason and freedom. Yet this informal sphere could not remain unregulated, and the form of regulation that emerged was a result precisely of the interaction of the internal properties of civil society and its relationship to the State. Civil society was simultaneously an arena beyond the State and an arena incorporated by the (increasingly modernized) State. A similar process of exclusion and incorporation can be found in shadow economies, and I hope I can get at something of this dialectical process by use of the concept "social labour."[9]

Social Labour

By relating idiosyncratic forms of livelihood to nineteenth-century understandings of "civil society," we are prompted to move beyond a rather narrow focus on "economies." Yet to cut the rope that tethers us to the strictures of livelihood puts us in danger of floating off into the stratosphere, seeing idiosyncratic forms of livelihood only as alternative societies, exotic lifestyles, or subcultures. We therefore have to go beyond seeing the entire informal economy as an extension of the instrumentalist requirements of narrowly defined "work," without abandoning the fundamental role of labour. To do this, we have to discover both the general features of social labour and the way it has come to be defined within shadow economies as both within and against the way in which "labour" came to be defined under Fordism.

For Marx, "labour" was synonymous with human life, and thus the only starting point for social enquiry into any historical period (1970: *passim*; 1976:47). This was a rather general understanding of labour. Yet, he also pointed out that, under capitalism, that which distinguishes humans from bees, namely the ability to conceive a project before working on it, gets broken up into separate parts: mental and physical labour. So, for Marx, there were two ways of looking at social labour. One was an abstract category spanning over history, in which labour that was directed towards changing objective conditions ("transforming village into town, wilderness into agricultural clearings," for example) was simultaneously a process of intersubjective communication in which producers form "new powers and new conceptions, new modes of intercourse, new needs, and new speech." The other was the way in which these two components, material reproduction (instrumental, directed toward a single object, monological) and cultural reproduction (intersubjective, discursive and dialogical) were separated out in the capitalist factory, through means of machinery and the division of labour, in a specific historical epoch.

While Marx concentrated his attention on the kinds of compartmentalization that occurred within factories between manual and mental labour, and then in ever more detail within the manual labour process itself, Weber addressed the process of compartmentalization that occurred within cultural production in the society at large. As Habermas (1984) has pointed out, Weber noted the way in which the initially discursive and directly intersubjective elements of cultural production, relating respectively to the objective world, the normative order, and the subjective world, became "rational-ized" into compartments in modern society: science, law, and art. Moreover, because experts developed professional authority in each of these spheres, so the (rest of) society became increasingly alienated from its "cultural senses." And, just as ever more sophisti-cated machinery and more "rational" divisions of labour in material production alienated the Fordist labouring population, so, too, ever more sophisticated language and divisions of expertise in cultural production alienated the Fordist citizenry from cultural production of any hegemonic significance, i.e., in scientific discoveries, legisla-tion, or high art.

We must begin, then, by setting the specific form that social labour takes in shadow economies, both within this capitalist framework, and as a kind of labour that has developed explicitly beyond and against such a framework. Yet, much of the intellectual discourse on restructured economies and societies has remained locked in the material production component of social labour. Pos-sibly this is because social science concepts were developed for studying industrial societies in which that component was figura-tively stressed as bona fide "labour" by being physically placed in a specific social space: the factory. When various social practices in the shadow economy cannot then be read off from this very narrow instrumental view of labour, it is a mistake to declare the whole project of viewing society in terms of social labour to be unwork-able. Rather, we have to bring back a more synthetic view in which cultural production becomes an inherent part of our understanding of "social labour," and conversely, we have to understand "culture" within the same terms as we understand any other artifact of human activity (Williams, 1961; Williams, 1977).

Marx noted the way in which this kind of mental labour had been systematically taken out of the hands of workers; the stresses of industrial labour were not its unpredictability, but its monotony, and not its use of emotional and cerebral resources, but its dehumanization. Because this was so, Marx addressed these issues (Habermas, 1979), and generally speaking, industrial sociologists have followed him. But, together with the wear and tear of this material production process, the people I am concerned with face immense stresses in the intersubjective, cultural production, com-ponent of social labour that Marx did not deal with when he focused on factories. This latter component, therefore, has to be given far more weight.

After all, the process by which material production was severed from the intercommunicative components of social labour was itself a political project, aimed at the design of a quite specific mode of social regulation. If we were to reexamine the fine-grained political disputes through which this was established, we would find that a whole series of other exclusions and divisions both gave form to those disputes and then resulted from them. "Domestic spaces" in society were reformulated, a women's place in the reproduction of this regime of accumulation was carved out, "free speech" was banished from the corporation and consigned specifically to bourgeois-controlled media, and so on. The point is that these were not, as is often asserted, directly a result of their "function for the reproduction of capital." Rather, they are specific cultural forms produced by a whole series of disputes and overlapping fields of force that, in the process of their enactment, selected out from and reformulated various patterns of tradition.

In turning to the shadow economy, therefore, we have to recognize that the intercommunicative component of social labour has reemerged as an important form of potential regulation, and therefore becomes as much the arena of struggle as does the arena of material production itself. This, in turn, calls for a kind of sociological enquiry that is sensitive simultaneously to structural conditions and instrumental practices and also to the interpretative understanding of cultural production. This chapter has been an attempt to view contemporary idiosyncratic forms of livelihood through a rather more historical lens than is usual. My hope has been that, by doing so, I might provoke some rather different visions of that world. The project remains an incomplete one, however, and this chapter can do no more than provoke. I hope it has at least done that.

Notes

1. The issue of ethnographic method for the study of contemporary informal economic activity in the West is taken up more directly in Smith (1993), from which this chapter draws. Versions of this chapter, and Smith (1993), have benefitted from comments from a great many people. It was first presented at the City University of New York in March 1992, a second version was presented in Montreal at the Canadian Anthropology Society conference, and a third at the Polanyi Institute meetings in Montreal in November, 1993. Comments from many participants therein have helped me. Harriet Friedman, Winnie Lem, Enzo Mingione, Susana Narotzky, Bryan Roberts and Gerald Sider have all been greatly helpful.

2.   Studies of informal economies in the West, of industrial districts, and of new forms of economic relationships (from hierarchy and market to network), are now myriad. It is striking how rarely these studies place their object of enquiry into any actual historical setting: by "actual" I mean to distinguish such a history from the more common formulaic "history" of industrialization which is often used as a substitute. This means that assertions that "putting out" today is quite different from the past (in what sense? for whom? etc.), or that we are now entering a qualitatively *new* era of capitalism, have to be taken on faith.

3.   The nature of Valencian development over the past two centuries is the subject of intensive debate. See, for example, Lluch (1976); Giralt (1978); Aracil and Bonafé (1978); Martínez Serrano et al. (1978); Palafox (1987); and Nadal (1990).

4.   In most factories, machine workers are paid a low basic wage conditional on their producing a minimum unit rate. Units above the minimum are paid in batches, each batch being worth a geometrically greater rate than the one before. It therefore pays a worker to produce as many batches as possible.

5.   See also Sanchis (1984). For Catalonia, see Narotzky (1989; 1990).

6.   Such an observation makes a mockery of James Scott's notion of pilfering as an "everyday form of resistance" (1986).

7.   Fields of social regulation among people engaged in idiosyncratic forms of livelihood are, of course, thoroughly articulated to dominant modes of Fordist and post-Fordist regulation in the social formation as a whole. Here I focus only on the emergent character of regulation in economic practices, however informal they may be at their inception.

8.   *Bürgerliche Gesellschaft* [sine imperio] (Kosselleck, 1979:81).

9.   The relevance for a specifically class analysis of informal economies lies in the fact that civil society was simultaneously a space within society in which certain practices and relationships were supposedly given the freedom to develop, and also, through the way in which they actually developed, the formation of a class: the bourgeoisie.

References

Aracil, Rafael, & Mario Garcia Bonafé, (1978), "La no industrialización valenciana: algunos problemas," in *La industrialización valenciana: historia y problema* (Valencia).

Benson, John, (1983), *The Penny Capitalist: A Study of Nineteenth Century Working Class Before the Factory* (Dublin: Gill & Macmillan).

Berg, Maxine, Pat Huson, & Michael Sonenscher, (1983), *Manufacture in Town and Country Before the Factory* (Cambridge: Cambridge University Press).

Blim, Michael, (1990), *Made in Italy: Small-scale Industrialization and its Consequences* (New York: Praeger).

Blim, Michael, (1992), "Small-scale Industrialization in a Rapidly Changing World Market," in *Anthropology and the Global Factory: Studies in the New Industrialization in the Late Twentieth Century,* edited by F. A. Rothstein & M. L. Blim (New York: Bergin & Garvey).

Bobbio, Norberto, (1989), *Democracy and Dictatorship: the Nature and Limits of State Power* (Minneapolis: University of Minnesota Press).

Bourdieu, Pierre, (1991), *Language & Symbolic Power,* translated by John B. Thompson (London: Polity Press).

Castells, Manuel, & Alejandro Portes, (1988), "World Underneath: The Origins, Dynamics, and Effects of the Informal Economy," in *The Informal Economy: Studies in Advances and Less Developed Countries*, edited by A. Portes, M. Castells, & L. A. Benton (Baltimore: Johns Hopkins University Press).

Cucó i Giner, Josepa, (1990), "Asociaciones y cuadrillas: un primer avance al análisis de la sociedad formal valenciana," in *Identidades colectivas: etnicidad y sociabilidad en la peninsula ibérica*, edited by J. Cucó & Joan J. Pujadas (Valencia: Generalitat Valencia).

Firth, Raymond, (1956), *Elements of Social Organization* (Boston: Beacon).

Giralt, Emili, ed., (1978), *Dos estudios sobre el País Valenciano* (Valencia).

Gramsci, Antonio, (1971), *Selections from the Prison Notebooks*, edited & translated by Q. Hoare & G. N. Smoth (New York: International).

Habermas, Jürgen, (1979), *Communication and the Evolution of Society*, translated by T. McCarthy (Boston: Beacon).

Habermas, Jürgen, (1981), "Toward a Reconstruction of Historical Materialism," in *Advances in Social Theory and Methodology*, edited by K. Knorr-Cetina & A. V. Cicourel (Boston: Routledge).

Habermas, Jürgen, (1984), *The Theory of Communicative Action*, 1, *Reason and the Rationalization of Society*, translated by T. McCarthy (Boston: Beacon).

Habermas, Jürgen, (1989), *The Structural Transformation of the Public Sphere* (Cambridge: MIT Press).

Kosselleck, Reinhart, (1979), *Future Past: On the Semantics of Historical Time*, translated by Keith Tribe (Cambridge: MIT Press).

Lluch, Ernst, (1976), *La vía valenciana* (Valencia).

Macpherson, C. B., (1984), *Democratic Theory* (Oxford).

Martínez Serrano, J. A., Ernest Reig Martínez, & Vicent Soler Marco, (1978), *Evolucion de la economía valenciana, 1878-1978* (Valencia: Caja de Ahorros de Valencia).

Marx, Karl, (1970), *The German Ideology*, edited by C. J. Arthur (London: Lawrence & Wishart).

Marx, Karl, (1976), *Capital*, 1, translated by Ben Fowkes (London: Penguin/NLB).

Mingione, Enzo, (1991), *Fragmented Societies: A Sociology of Economic Life Beyond the Market Paradigm* (Oxford: Blackwell).

Nadal, Jordi, (1990), "El desarrollo de la economía valenciana en la segunda mitad del sigle XIX: ¿una vía exclusivamente agraria?" in *Pautas regionales de la industrialización española, sigle XIX y XX*, edited by J. Nadal & A. Carreras (Barcelona: Ariel).

Narotzky, Susana, (1989), "Ideas that Work: Ideologies and Social Reproduction in Rural Catalunya and Beyond," unpublished Ph.D. thesis (New York: New School for Social Research).

Narotzky, Susana, (1990), "Not to be a Burden: Ideologies of the Domestic Group and Women's Work in Rural Catalonia," in *Work Without Wages*, edited by J. Collins & M. Gimenez (Binghampton: SUNY Press).

Palafox, Jordi, (1987), "Exports, Internal Demand, and Economic Growth in Valencia," in *The Economic Modernization of Spain, 1830-1930*, edited by Nicolas Sánchez-Albornoz (New York: New York University Press).

Polanyi, Karl, (1957), *The Great Transformation* (Boston: Beacon).

Rancière, Jacques, (1986), "The Myth of the Artisan: Critical Reflections on a Category of Social History," in *Work in France: Representations, Meaning, Organizations, and Practice*, edited by S. L. Kaplan & C. J. Koepp (Ithaca: Cornell University Press).

Reddy, William, (1981), "Modes de paiment et contrôle du travail dans les filatures de coton en France, 1750-1848," *Revue du Nord*, 63, pp. 135-46.

Reddy, William, (1984), *The Rise of Market Culture: The Textile Trade & French Society, 1750-1900* (Cambridge: Cambridge University Press).

Reddy, William, (1987), *Money and Liberty in Modern Europe: A Critique of Historical Understanding* (Cambridge: Cambridge University Press).

Sanchis, Enric, (1984), *El trabajo a domicilio en el País Valenciano* (Madrid: Ministerio de Cultura).

Sayer, Derek, (1987), *The Violence of Abstraction: The Analytic Foundations of Historical Materialism* (Oxford: Blackwell).

Schmiechen, J.A., (1975), "State Reform and the Local Economy: An Aspect of Industrialization in the Late Victorian and Edwardian London," *Economic History Review*, 28, 3.

Scott, James, (1986), "Everyday Forms of Resistance," *Journal of Peasant Studies*, 13, 2.

Sider, Gerald M., (1986), *Culture and Class in Anthropology and History: A Newfoundland Illustration* (Cambridge: Cambridge University Press).

Smith, Gavin, (1989), *Livelihood and Resistance: Peasants and the Politics of Land in Central Peru* (Berkeley: University of California Press).

Smith, Gavin, (1990), "Negotiating Neighbours: Livelihood and Domestic Politics in Central Peru and the País Valenciano," in *Work Without Wages: Domestic Labour and Self-employment Within Capitalism*, edited by J. Collins & M. Gimenez (Binghampton: SUNY Press).

Smith, Gavin, (1991), "Writing for Real: Capitalist Constructions and the Constructions of Capitalism," *Critique of Anthropology*, vol. 11, 3.

Smith, Gavin, (1993), "Toward an Ethnographic Method for the Study of Idiosyncratic Forms of Livelihood in Western Europe," *International Journal of Urban and Regional Research*.

Vincent, David, (1981), *Bread, Knowledge, and Freedom: A Study of Nineteenth Century Working Class Autobiography* (London: Methuen).

Williams, Raymond, (1961), *Culture and Society 1780-1950* (Harmondsworth: Penguin).

Williams, Raymond, (1977), *Marxism and Literature* (Oxford: Oxford University Press).

Ybarra, Josep-Antoni, (1986), "La informalización industrial en la economía valenciana: un modelo para el subdesarrollo," *Revista de treball*, 2.

Zdatny, Steven M., (1990), *The Politics of Survival: Artisans in 20th Century France* (Oxford: Oxford University Press).

Chapter Two

Survival Strategies for Small Business Families in a Peripheral Local Economy: A Contribution to Institutional Value Theory

Jane Wheelock

This chapter uses a qualitative empirical study of small business family work strategies in a peripheral region of the U.K. as the basis for developing a substantive institutional analysis to examine the economic character of the entrepreneurial family.[1] Levels of self-employment in the Northern Region are the lowest in Britain, whereas unemployment remains high, so that small business survival is problematic. The British government, in common with others in de-industrializing economies, has promoted the small firm and the enterprise culture as important contributions to work force flexibility and the restructuring process. The research project posited that access to unpaid family labour and to family networks provide the small family business with an important element of flexibility, thus contributing to both family and business survival.

The empirical work identified family involvement in businesses set up during the 1980s on Wearside, northeast England. As might be expected in a regional and local economy subject to substantial de-industrialization, many of those interviewed had no prior experience of self-employment, and a number had previously been unemployed or out of the job market due to sickness or family responsibilities. Taped interviews were undertaken with two family members in each of 24 businesses; those interviewed were identified in the first instance through local support services. In seeking to relate family work strategies and small businesses, it was important for the research design that female as well as male heads of businesses should be interviewed. In the event, eight female and eight male business heads were interviewed, together with seven husband and wife teams and one family business. Businesses which had set up since the start of the 1980s were sought, and the sample included a range of business age profiles, with the youngest having been in business for a year and two months, and the oldest for a decade. Businesses were very largely from the service sector. The study focused on entrepreneurs at the smallest end of the scale, including only the self-employed and small employers, and excluding owner-controllers and owner-directors.

Substantive institutional analysis is quite different from mainstream economics, which sees itself as the "science of choice." The formal approach to economics emphasizes maximizing activity, with an axiomatic presumption of scarcity. When coupled with rationality, economics thus becomes a science of choice (Stanfield, 1982:67). Stanfield follows Polanyi (1946) in his substantivist approach which, as Waller and Jennings see it, means analyzing "the economy as an instituted process of interaction serving the satisfaction of material wants" (1990:488). Economic behaviour is therefore treated as a cultural process where behaviour is learned. The value standard of conventional economics takes a "more is better" approach, thereby promoting an econocentric culture (Stanfield, 1982:77). Analyzing the behaviour of small business families on Wearside, it was apparent that despite the widespread rhetoric of the enterprise culture disseminated by government throughout the 1980s, the market culture was not the major determinant of behaviour.

A substantive view of the economic process argues that "the economy is the instituted process of culturally patterned arrangements by which a given human group provisions itself as a going concern" (Stanfield, 1982:71). Such an approach makes considerable sense of the value system and culture of survival that lay at the heart of how small business families in northeast England behaved. Polanyi saw market society as one in which the economy is disembedded from society. "The need is to examine the relation of lives to livelihood and subordinate the economy to the lives it properly should serve ... precisely to re-embed the economy in society" (Stanfield, 1982:73). This is what this chapter hopes to do in relation to small business, whose role in economic regeneration has been so prominent in New Right policies. As Waller and Jennings (1990) point out, there are two further advantages to substantive analysis, though neither of them have necessarily been achieved in practice. The first is to address the importance of the links between market and non-market activities, which it is difficult for formalist economic accounts to include; the relations between familial institutions and the market certainly proved crucial to the survival of the small businesses studied. The second is that gender roles can be unpacked, for "reification of the market in formalist economics constitutes the acceptance of our current prioritization of gender roles as appropriate and natural" (Waller and Jennings, 1990:490).

This chapter, then, examines the "economic character" of the small business family, arguing that economic motivation must be examined in a family rather than an individual context. In relating lives to livelihood, a "familial economic unit" and its distinctive work strategy are shown to be crucial. The chapter explores the interrelations between the formal market activities of self-employed men and women, and the formal and informal work activities of their families; it sees the small business operating at the boundaries of the formal and the informal (or complementary) economies, linking the two together. This provides the value system for the entrepreneurial family, so that the satisfactions of being able to integrate the personal, the family, and the public aspects of a predominantly domestic life style counterbalance the inherent self-exploitation of the small business family. The rewards are largely not financial; it is the domestic orientation of the entrepreneurial way of life that constitutes its appeal. The market culture is thus not the model for the conduct of life in these small business families.

Those interviewed had predominantly been pushed into self-employment, with many re-creating elements of their previous employment. It is the inextricable linking of business, labour market, and domestic work in the small business family which ensures that this economic unit can achieve maximum flexibility in its work strategies. Survival is made possible by the form that flexibility takes in the familial economic unit. The links between family and business life cycles are facilitated by the constrained spatial location of the small businesses interviewed. The importance of the complementary economy for small firm survival thus transforms the disadvantages of location in a peripheral region into the means for its survival. Survival mechanisms intertwine with the formation of values in the small business family, indicating that the household is a key institution in the process of evolutionary change.

Flexibility and the Economic Unit

What then is the basis for the economic character of the entrepreneurial family? Labour is generally seen as the major resource at the disposal of the small business, while for the self-employed their capacity to work is usually their sole resource. This research posited that small businesses and the self-employed would be likely to be able to make use of the labour of other family members in addition to that of the proprietors themselves, and that this might provide an important element of flexibility within the business. But members of a family do not have just one work role; market and non-market activities must both be considered. Any family unit combines work performed to earn income, unpaid domestic work or work for self-consumption, as well as unpaid work outside the household unit such as voluntary work. Work for self-consumption includes all domestic tasks, as well as care of the young, the sick, and the elderly. It is worth bearing in mind the part that families play in providing the next generation of the work force: their role in the reproduction of labour. Unpaid work is not purely private and personal.

In the small business family, it is therefore possible that three work roles are being fulfilled: a full-time or part-time job in the formal economy, work in the business, and unpaid work in the complementary economy. Individual families need to combine work for self-consumption with work for income, taking account of the fact that the work that they do in the social economy is unpaid. Family work strategies will change, not only with the family life cycle stage, but also in response to changes in the economy (see Wheelock, 1990). In the case of small businesses, they may also change in response to the life cycle, or stage of development, of the business.

The degree of de-industrialization and economic restructuring that the British economy was experiencing at the start of the 1980s prompted an examination of the responses of individual firms to the competitive problems they were facing. Researchers at the Institute of Manpower Studies came up with a model of the "flexible firm." Evidence collected by Atkinson (1985) and his colleagues suggested that large manufacturing firms were dividing their work forces between a functionally flexible core and a numerically flexible periphery. Core employees, kept on permanent contracts, were a diminishing proportion of the work force. They were expected to become more flexible in terms of skills exercised, with reductions in demarcation between jobs. The peripheral work force was flexible in that it could be hired and fired as market conditions dictated. This numerical flexibility could be achieved through the use of part-time, frequently female, labour, whose numbers and hours could be readily varied, through the use of contract or self-employed labour, or through subcontracting to smaller firms to service peripheral needs or to meet market fluctuations.

There has been much academic dispute over whether the flexible firm is a new phenomenon which has arisen out of a crisis of Fordist mass production methods, or whether it is simply a management strategy to deal with an immediate set of competitive problems. Glancing briefly at the wider interpretation, there is an implication not just of more flexible large firms, but of flexibility in the production system as a whole, also related to more flexible technology. Economies of scale are augmented by economies of scope with new technology involving the cheapening of small batch production of customized products. Here small firms take on a crucial role. Piore and Sabel (1984) see a proliferation of small companies using new technology to compete in market niches, and establishing networks with one another as in the "industrial districts" of Northern Italy. Scott and Storper (1987) point to ensembles of flexibly specialized activities as in the Japanese system of subcontracting. This links in with shifting consumption patterns, where mass markets are saturated and demand for less standardized or more personalized products are taking their place.

It is not surprising that politicians and policy makers have seen self-employment and small business growth generally as part of the rebirth of an "enterprise culture," as crucial contributors to economic regeneration in the 1980s and 1990s. Academic and political debates have echoed one another in emphasizing the flexibility of these small units. What are the internal mechanisms for achieving such flexibility, or does it simply come about through the birth and death of individual firms? What is required is a wider examination of the organizational processes at work within the small firm in much the same way that Atkinson did for large firms.

It is by examining the contribution that family members make to the work of the small business that such a model can be developed. Given the predominance of labour as a factor of production within small-scale enterprise, flexibility in the use of family labour provides us with a key to understanding the overall flexibility of such enterprises. In the entrepreneurial family, work for the business unit and work for the family unit are closely interrelated, so that the work strategies adopted justify the use of the term "familial economic unit." We can in fact look at the monetarily rewarded aspects of the family's work (business and employment) and at its unpaid work (domestic and caring roles) and examine how far Atkinson's functional and numerical flexibility apply to each type.

Flexibility and the Business Work Role

Figure 1 provides a representation of the overall flexibility of the family economic unit, and summarizes the major aspects of functional and numerical flexibility in the sample businesses.[2] Functional flexibility within the business work role is obtained when those working within the business, including family members, have a flexible set of skills to offer and vary what they contribute according to the needs of the business. Numerical flexibility derives from the fact that the business is able to make use of work from three sources. The business owner can draw on individuals from his or her own nuclear family unit (in other words from the domestic sector), she or he can turn to the wider social economy and draw on family or friends through the voluntary sector, or she or he can go to the formal economy. In fact, many of the individuals who are originally sourced through the social economy are transferred to the formal economy in that they get paid for their work contribution to the enterprise.

Variations in the proprietor's own hours can also provide numerical flexibility. The interviews demonstrated that proprietors experienced considerable variations in their hours; some on a seasonal basis, some undertaking weekend or evening work, others finding that their work tends to bunch, thus requiring additional hours. Several have found their work loads dry up with economic recession, with one proprietor forced to take up a full-time employment contract to ride it out. In other words, proprietors make considerable variations in their hours in response to the needs of the business.

Inevitably, the flexibility available to the business proprietor through the family unit is dependent on who performs the enabling domestic, caring and income-earning roles. Neither the business unit nor the family unit can survive if these tasks are not performed. Members of the family economic unit are freed, or enabled, to contribute to work of the business depending on the functional and numerical flexibility available for domestic and caring roles. Functional flexibility occurs when members of the nuclear family economic unit itself vary the domestic or caring roles that they perform. Numerical flexibility involves either calling on family or friends from outside the household itself in an unpaid capacity from the voluntary sector, or paying individuals from the formal or the irregular economies. It may also be important for members of the household to bring in income from employment.

Figure 1: Flexibility and the familial economic unit

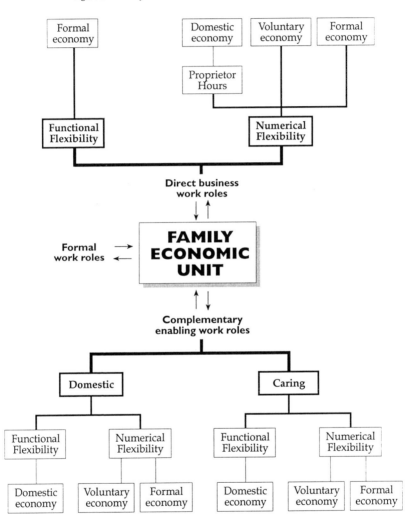

A more detailed look at one business provides a typical example of the sorts of processes at work. Although this was a sole proprietorship, husband and wife appeared to play an equal role in the start-up preparations, visiting banks, enterprise agencies and so on together. "Whenever James was going to do something for the business, then he said to me about it, you know," remarked his wife. Jenny had part-time employment as a nurse when the garage opened, so was able to work half-time in the business, acting as receptionist and administrator and learning to help with stores and bookkeeping:

> but as time progressed, we weren't making the money that we thought we might have done, so I got a job where it entailed more hours and more money.

Jenny, in other words, moved away from direct work for the business towards an enabling, income-earning role. Meanwhile, James and Jenny had identified an old family friend to take over at least part of her role in the business. The friend was ex-merchant navy, recently retired, so that he and his wife were starting to get on top of one another:

> I mean, she'd led an independent life . . . I just said, come in a couple of days a week, come in from 10 to 2 or whatever and I'll see you all right. . . . When Andy doesn't turn in . . . you really know. . . . You're backwards and forwards to the phone.

In addition, their teenage son now contributes to the business. As Jenny puts it:

> He'll go down to the garage with his dad and answer the phone, he loves that, and he goes down after school, but I wouldn't dream of saying he must go down.

An old army colleague has also kept the garage open for the occasional weekend when James and Jenny have wanted to go away. It is possible that in the long run he may become a partner in the business, injecting additional capital, and allowing James and Jenny more time together.

When looking at the numerical flexibility provided by the formal economy, there were of course a number of the businesses which had only ever involved the proprietor and perhaps a spouse in a self-employed capacity. However, relatives and (less likely) friends were frequently formally employed for periods of time within the business. For instance, Sheila, a single business owner, had her brother-in-law working with her from the start of the business in March 1989, but he obtained a government-funded Employment Training (ET) placement with her ten months later. Her sister Sally had also helped with the books on an informal basis for more than a year before getting a part-time ET placement. At the time of the follow-up telephone interview, both Ben and Sally had finished their period on ET. Ben was just setting up on the government-funded Enterprise Allowance (for the second time) himself, and his business will have links with Sheila's. She now has her brother as a replacement ET worker. Such extensive family involvement is not unusual.

There was considerable dependence on part-time labour in the sample. As the businesses started, three proprietors were working in the business part-time. In addition, 45 percent had part-time employees, and by the time of interview this had risen to over 60 percent. It was apparent from the interviews that small businesses often rely on subcontract, self-employed, freelance, or associate employees, who may well be obtained through informal networks; when business is slack there is no obligation to keep them on. Those who have taken on permanent staff have often had to let them go when business circumstances dictate. In terms of formal employment, then, small businesses appear to adopt methods of ensuring numerical flexibility similar to those of their larger counterparts.

Assessing functional flexibility is rather more complex, depending as it does on a more qualitative judgement of the variety of work undertaken by core employees in the larger businesses, or by the family unit in the case of those who do not employ outside labour on a regular basis. A number of those interviewed commented on the fact that being a small business proprietor necessitated doing a wide range of jobs oneself. Indeed, for many, the variety of the work was one of the appeals of self-employment. Setting up in business frequently needed the development of a wider range of skills than those required for employment, even when the business was in a very similar field. In particular, though proprietors often had the necessary craft related skills, they still needed to develop their business skills. In many businesses, spouses either learned together or taught each other the relevant skills.

Flexibility in Enabling Work

When a spouse takes employment in the formal economy, whether part-time or full-time, this may provide a crucial source of family income enabling the business to continue. Unpaid enabling work can be divided into two categories: the domestic work involved in the major tasks of meal preparation, cleaning, shopping, washing and ironing, and other minor tasks; and the caring roles required in relation to birth, child rearing, illness and death. To what extent is the entrepreneurial family flexible in undertaking these tasks, and how does it achieve such flexibility?

Looking at domestic roles alone first of all, most of the flexibility came from within the domestic economy, from the self-employed household itself. Interestingly, in nearly half of the households (eleven in all), domestic tasks were shared between spouses. It is important to realize that this does not imply equal sharing between husbands and wives, but rather that husbands either do, or share in, several of the major household tasks that are normally undertaken by wives.[3] In this "sharing" organization of domestic tasks, there was nevertheless substantially more flexibility than might otherwise be the case.

In seven households there was a minimum of functional flexibility in domestic tasks, with a "traditional rigid" form of organization. Domestic arrangements seemed largely to predate any business involvement that wives may have taken up, even though in two cases wives had at least nominally been involved full-time in the business. I had thought it possible that people might change their patterns of domestic work when businesses were started up, but the evidence was that it was relatively minor changes that were instigated. So, for example, some cut down on the amount of housework they did, some purchased microwaves or dishwashers to save time, while others turned to the formal economy to employ a cleaner for a few hours a week.

It is when looking at caring responsibilities that much more flexibility becomes apparent, and indeed such caring work could be very time-consuming. Caring work loads were high in the sample businesses: there had been births in one-third of the families since business start-up, while in one case step-children joined the family. All the new mothers were business proprietors except one, and she had a substantial role in the business. The step-father was also a business proprietor. Major illnesses and the death of a spouse have called for important caring functions within four small business families, where Frank and Fiona provide an interesting example, illustrating other features of the flexibility of the familial economic unit as well.

Frank had initially established his business on a part-time basis six years prior to interview, while he was still undertaking some lecturing. When the business was four years old, Frank developed a serious illness; he and his wife were able to devise strategies for coping with this within the household. Fiona already had some of the skills necessary for their bookkeeping and accountancy business, but Frank had passed on his own skills as he developed them. She was thus in a position to take over the business during the emergency period when he was in hospital:

> it was a question of actually writing to clients — making sure stuff was collected in, doing quite a lot more administrative work and taking it in to you and working through it.

Frank's illness proved to be a long-term one, possibly stress-related, necessitating permanent adjustments to the business. He strictly limited the number of clients he took on, while Fiona had a rather larger role than she had before. However, it remained a part-time commitment which she combined with her own self-employment as a lecturer. Fiona also took on more of the domestic tasks, notably cooking and shopping: "He hasn't got to think about those two and also there's less stress."

It is worth noting that for rather more than one-third of those interviewed, being part of an entrepreneurial family gave husbands the opportunity to take a role with child care which they might otherwise not have had the opportunity for. For several of the families interviewed, one of the positive aspects of running a small business was that it provided both spouses with the opportunity of participating in domestic and family life. Frank is explicit on the matter, as is his wife:

> *Frank:* It also allows us a particular life style which suits us, basically it's very much a mixture of business and home. *Fiona:* Almost indistinguishable. *Frank:* And allows me to take part in a lot of home activities, child rearing, housework and so on and it also allows me to cope with the illness we were talking about earlier.

However, three husbands did not participate in child care at all because of business pressures.

The final issue of note was the importance of the voluntary economy and of close relatives in providing child care assistance. A study of women's work on Wearside (Stubbs and Wheelock, 1991) found that families preferred to make child care arrangements within the nuclear family if at all possible, and that reliance on close female relatives was the second choice; the use of a nursery tended to be a final option. These findings are confirmed here; nearly half of the businesses rely on relatives to assist with child care: six on a regular basis, five on a more irregular one.

Lesley, who is self-employed in her secretarial services business and was pregnant at the time she was starting up, emphasizes the crucial role that regular assistance from relatives may play:

> At a very early age, C started going to her grandma's, Nick's parents in Hebburn, and without them I could not have done the business, could not have carried on. They've been a blessing.

It seems that relatives do not get paid for their services, but occasional gifts may be given instead. Lesley again:

> They'll not — they really won't take anything. [We] occasionally buy them something big like a television. *Nick:* They know they can call on us at any time and we're there for them and they're there for us, I mean that's what the family is like.

This, then, is work that remains firmly within the unpaid complementary sector of the economy, but which is crucial enabling work for the business family.

Values in the Small Business Family

When a substantive institutional analysis is used to assess the economic character of the self-employed family, the relation of lives to livelihoods becomes clear. This then shows that values are developed in a family and not an individual context. It is apparent that the family economic unit is able to make use of a wide range of strategies to ensure flexibility in the performance both of direct business tasks and of indirect enabling work. It is indeed precisely this flexibility which makes it so appropriate to extend the term "family economic unit" (which Andy Lowe [1988] used of the families he studied who ran small hotels in rural Scotland) to small businesses as a whole. Lowe argues that proprietors put the family in first place with the business second. What comes out of the Wearside study is that family and business needs are integrated with each other in the entrepreneurial family.

Families often needed to adapt to a new way of life when they set up in business, and for some this was much easier than for others. The strategies adopted in order to mesh business and family can be seen along a continuum according to the way of life adopted. At the "sharing" end of this continuum are families who tend to share social lives, business, and domestic work, and where there is joint discussion and responsibility for family work. At the other extreme is the "segregated" life style, where the business owner and his or her spouse are more independent of each other, with little contribution to the business from their other half, and the possibility of outside employment; there is probably a traditional gender division of domestic labour. In the middle of the continuum a more complementary way of life can be found. The spouse may either provide informed support for business decisions, or may take a subsidiary work role in the business, but moral support for the business from the spouse is seen as essential. The spouse is also likely to provide some form of enabling support, either through income earning, and/or through domestic or caring work.

The evidence from the interviews was that all the entrepreneurial families were adopting a more or less domesticated life style. Pahl and Wallace, in their study of complementary economic activity in two-earner working class families on the Isle of Sheppey, argue that a process of domestication was going on there. For these authors, "domestication" is "the product of a value system which puts home-centred activities as the central focus of a distinctive life-style" (Pahl and Wallace, 1985:219), with self-provisioning, and an enlarging of work within the domestic economy, flowing largely but not entirely from a home-centred value orientation. Wearside entrepreneurial families were also adopting such a value system, although in this case it derived from involvement in the business project of the family, both directly and indirectly. This meant a particularly intense form of domestic value system.

Many of the sampled business proprietors found themselves pushed into becoming entrepreneurs. The process of adaptation required of the family and the individuals in it could be very tough; nevertheless, these two dozen Wearside families took on the way of life required by the small businesses which they ran. It was a lifestyle which called for considerable integration of business, domestic, and paid work strategies. This places the family economic unit at the meeting point of the complementary and the formal economies, and integrates private family roles and public business roles. It is in this integration that the heart of the satisfactions of running a small business are to be found. The next section shows that the familial economic unit is not economically rational, and that it is precisely this domestic orientation of the entrepreneurial way of life that constitutes its appeal.

The Costs and Benefits of Flexibility for the Small Business Family

There is considerable academic debate over the extent to which industrial organization has been restructured since the 1970s, whether it be along the lines that the managerialist adherents of Atkinson's model of the flexible firm predicts or in accord with networking between small firms in industrial districts as seen by institutionalist advocates of flexible specialization. The case for flexibility in whatever form as a novel feature of the labour process and industrial organization in developed capitalism since the end of the long post-war capitalist boom remains unproved (Pollert, 1991). It seems to be widely accepted, in contrast, that the intensity of work has increased, and the study sample of small businesses on Wearside were no exception.

There was an almost universal feeling amongst the sample families that hours are either long, or very long, when a family sets up in business. These findings confirm Helen Rainbird's (1991) study where many of her (also qualitative) interviewees reported working over 50 hours a week and up to 60 or 70 hours in some cases. Interestingly, however, a third of Wearside proprietors reported working long hours before starting up in business, though self-employment was often seen to involve more evening work. Work time can impinge particularly severely on the family when it is located at home, as was the case for well over half the sample when the business was set up.

Yet, as already indicated, there were some non-monetary rewards for the patterns of work involved. For nearly half the sample, running a business meant that husband and wife could spend more time with each other, in some cases because they work with each other in the business; it could also mean more time with the family. When examining how family and personal lives get

structured by entrepreneurial work strategies, Finch's (1983) observation of family life as a series of overlapping and interacting
timetables is a useful one. As has already been indicated, it is the
flexibility of business hours that may allow proprietors more time
with children or spouses, or to cope with illness, for example.

What of monetary rewards? During the 1980s policy makers
have seen the material rewards for business ownership as of
supreme importance, concerning themselves with creating a system
of incentives that will ensure profits. Yet in the Wearside sample,
only five families saw themselves as distinctly better off as a result of
being in business, with a further six marginally so. Even when looking at this group it is worth realizing that some were receiving social
assistance benefits beforehand, so that income levels were still not
high. Seven families were actually worse off than they had been,
with four having about the same income level. Levels of income
were such that a number of business families were entitled to draw
State benefits, including family credit, free school meals or prescrip-
tion drugs, and housing benefit. For a number of businesses, a further enabling income coming into the house was essential. It is
worth noting, however, that a likely contributor to low incomes, particularly at the outset, was that nearly half of the sample stated that
they were avoiding borrowing money for the business; for many
this meant reinvesting a substantial proportion of takings, and
restricting what they took out of the business.

It is apparent, then, that even modest income rewards were
comparatively rare for the entrepreneurial families in the sample. It
would appear that while Marx talks in terms of the restlessness of
the circulation process of capital to ensure that "Mr. Moneybags" the
capitalist can accumulate, the small business proprietor (and family
members) must work ceaselessly to obtain an often meagre financial
reward. Why then are families prepared to do this? True, there are
financial features of business life which help to make the business
feel like "ours" for the families concerned, as Rainbird (1991) also
found. Fringe benefits, such as a car or a telephone paid for by the
business, can help to identify the business with the household. More
significantly, the business has assets held on behalf of the family,
and some families identify the business as a form of security for their
children.

Essentially, however, the rewards derive from the way of life;
while it is demanding, it is intrinsically satisfying for most families,
despite its problems and pressures in terms of hours of work or uncertain financial rewards. As already indicated, it is a lifestyle that

integrates family and business satisfactions and values. Personal satisfaction is gained from being in control of doing a good job, of providing a quality service, with the hope of economic rewards, but with the reality of sheer survival as a baseline. Largely, however, motivations are not individually based, but derive from a focus on the domestic values of the family economic unit.

Autonomy in a Culture of Survival

The survival of these small business families, then, is survival on the margin between the formal and the complementary economy, based as it is on the flexibility of the family economic unit and the intensification of its labour. There are some interesting parallels with Gudeman and Rivera's (1990) study of the house economy in rural Colombia. Like the peasant house, the family-based small business is confined to the periphery of competition and persists where the corporation cannot. Many of these small businesses were operating at the margin of profit and beyond the production possibility frontier. Indeed, few of the Wearside businesses relied on any form of innovation to survive. Their functioning relied on the value produced by labour.

Individual, family, and business survival, then, are bound up together through the continuing use of old forms of working, forms which rely on intensifying work. In her study of nineteenth-century Edinburgh, Stana Nenadic was examining family strategies for small firm creation and survival, and argued that "family strategies for generating income went hand-in-hand with business strategies" (1991:25). Helen Rainbird (1991) interprets the self-employment of the Warwick sample that she studied as a form of disguised wage labour, on the grounds that the majority were earning only a subsistence living and that their dependence on large companies suggested that the major flow of value was from the self-employed to large companies. Such reliance on the creation of absolute surplus value is dictated by deteriorating pay and conditions in the labour market.

The evidence indicates that this "culture of survival" amongst small businesses is quite distinct from the "enterprise culture" of policy makers. In Britain and elsewhere, governments have orchestrated the ideology of an enterprise culture. This provides a language justifying economic insecurity on the grounds that such a culture will ensure social integration. Individualism, autonomy, independence, self-help, and anti-collectivism are underlined as important qualities for this new culture (Burrows, 1991). In contrast to government revivalism, John Ritchie (1991) suggests that a pragmatic "doing the business" typifies the enterprise culture of the subject, the lives of business people themselves. But it is important to go further than this to understand the process whereby autonomy and exploitation co-exist, for it is survival that is significant for the small business proprietor in an increasingly insecure labour market. The key lies in values that are ignored by politicians who trumpet the individualism of the enterprise culture or economists who assume the individualism of a "rational economic man." These are the values of reciprocity and co-operation as an irreducible feature of human life.

Following Polanyi and Sahlins, Gudeman and Rivera (1990) see reciprocity as the obligation to give, receive, and return as a mode of integrating the inherent opposition between the self and the other. The predominant stream of thought in economics follows Adam Smith in seeing the "propensity to truck, barter and exchange" as a basic economic motivation, with the conflicting interests of self-seeking individuals harmonized through the market mechanism. Roberts and Holroyd (1990), analyzing family firms, suggest that although in boom times formally rational objectives of profit maximization and accumulation may predominate, other forms of rationality based on family and affective relations and traditional loyalties, or sheer survival, are significant during economic slumps. Certainly, the Wearside economy in the 1980s was scarcely enjoying boom conditions, and equally clear is that the business families studied were concerned with survival, in the context of a domestic, rather than a market, value system.

As I have argued elsewhere (Wheelock, 1992a), many economists make the error of starting from the individual, rather than from the household and the family. Those who do not, namely the new household economists who follow Gary Becker, persist in positing that individual household members are economic maximizers, rather than reciprocators. In the Wearside small business, the family acts as a collective worker by linking family and business life cycles. In Warwick, Rainbird (1991) saw this in terms of an "interwovenness" of lives. This holistic lifestyle provides the reward of autonomy for the family economic unit. Yet it is also the source of its exploitation through a process in which technical and affective relationships are fused (Roberts and Holroyd, 1990). Apparent autonomy for the family means real dependence for the business.

This dependence derives from operating at the margin in an attempt to survive in conditions of labour market instability. In northeast England, it is possible that the importance of the complementary economy for small firm survival transforms the disadvantages of location in a peripheral region into the means for its survival. It is a survival which relies on the destabilizing effect of low-wage competition in a region in economic decline.

At the beginning of this century, Hobson saw economic insecurity as a scourge, which adversely affected the character of working people by undermining their confidence. Drawing on Hobson, Mark Lutz (1992) goes on to argue that security of employment modifies the conscious stress on personal gain seeking and is the first essential in any shift to public and social motives. Certainly, as we approach the end of the century (and the millennium), one of the big questions facing us is how to achieve social integration in a world of insecurity. New Right policy makers and mainstream economists say that there is no dilemma: if the individual pursues his (or more rarely her) self-interest, social harmony will ensue. This ignores the fact that people want to contribute to society, as well as to their individual interest; that they want to participate in, and be a part of, their culture.

Far from pursuing their own self-interest, small-scale entrepreneurs on Wearside are actually prepared to be exploited in order to play their part in a social enterprise which has two dimensions to it. On the one hand they want to be part of a co-operative family, which, though not by any means free of gender specific roles, is based on reciprocal values. The second dimension is the need that people have to undertake purposeful work. The success of the small business form of economic enterprise for the individuals and families involved can be seen as a failure of late twentieth-century capitalism. Despite its self-exploitation, self-employment provides for personal dignity and an inherently satisfying way of life for those who stay with this option. The shortcomings of large-scale enterprise can be seen, with Tomer (1987), as a failure of big organizations to invest in the organizational capital needed to ensure effective work from their employees. Bagnasco (1990) perceives it as the outcome of the crisis of Fordism and Keynesianism, where flexible forms of organization avoid the minute division of labour and State intervention. The small business operates on the boundaries of the formal and complementary economies and links the two together. This linking process provides both the flexibility needed for the survival of the entrepreneurial family unit and the satisfaction of being able to integrate the personal, the family, and the public aspects of a predominantly domestic lifestyle.

Developing the techniques of substantive institutional analysis for the case of small businesses operating in a peripheral regional economy, it has been possible to show that values are far more complex than either orthodox economists or New Right politicians have led their followers into thinking. Such analysis has shown that values are developed in a family, rather than an individual, context. It has also demonstrated that values are formed and reproduced by interactions at the margins of the formal and complementary (or informal) economies. The economy must indeed be embedded in society, but the household and the family must also be integrated into the economy to gain a full understanding of economic behaviour. Finally, a focus on the household also means that gender issues become integrated into any analysis of the relation of lives to livelihood.

Notes

1. The research was undertaken with a grant from the Economic and Social Research Council (award no. R000 23 2524) during the winter of 1990-91. I thank the Council for its generous support. For full details of the research, see Wheelock (1991).
2. This is based on the typology of the whole economy developed in Wheelock (1990) chapter 1.
3. The classification of the division of domestic labour used here was first developed in Wheelock (1990) where details are provided in chapter 4.

References

Atkinson, J. S., (1985), "Flexibility: Planning for an Uncertain Future," *Manpower Policy and Practice*, 1 (Summer).

Bagnasco, A., (1990), "The Informal Economy," in *Economy and Society: Overviews in Economic Sociology*, edited by A. Martinelli and N. J. Smelser (London: Sage).

Burrows, R., ed., (1991), *Deciphering the Enterprise Culture* (London: Routledge).

Finch, J., (1983), *Married to the Job: Wives' Incorporation in Men's Work* (London: Allen and Unwin).

Ekins, P., and M. Max-Neef, eds., (1992), *Real-life Economics: Understanding Wealth Creation* (London: Routledge).

Gudeman, S., and A. Rivera, (1990), *Conversations in Colombia: the Domestic Economy in Life and Text* (Cambridge: Cambridge University Press).

Lowe, A., (1988), "Small Hotel Survival — An Inductive Approach," *International Journal of Hospitality Management*, 7, 3, pp.197-223.

Lutz, M., (1992), "Living Economics in Perspective," in *Real-life Economics: Understanding Wealth Creation*, edited by P. Ekins and M. Max-Neef (London: Routledge).

Nenadic, S., (1991), "Small Firms in the Late Nineteenth Century: Family Strategies for Creation and Survival," Economic and Social Research Council Small Business Initiative Researchers Meeting, University of Warwick.

Pahl, R. E., and C. Wallace, (1985), "Household Work Strategies in Economic Recession," in *Beyond Employment: Gender, Household and Subsistence*, edited by N. Redclift and E. Mingione (Oxford: Blackwell).

Piore, M., and C. Sabel, (1984), *The Second Industrial Divide* (New York: Basic Books).

Polanyi, K., (1946), *Origins of our Time: the Great Transformation* (London: Victor Gollancz).

Pollert, A., ed., (1991), *Farewell to Flexibility* (Oxford: Blackwell).

Rainbird, H., (1991), "The Self-employed: Small Entrepreneurs or Disguised Wage Labourers?" in *Farewell to Flexibility*, edited by A. Pollert (Oxford: Blackwell).

Ritchie, J., (1991) "Enterprise Cultures: A Frame Analysis," in *Deciphering the Enterprise Culture*, edited by R. Burrows (London: Routledge).

Roberts, I., and G. Holroyd, (1990), "Small Firms and Family Forms," BSA Conference Paper, University of Surrey.

Scott, A. J., and M. Storper, (1987), "High Technology Industry and Regional Development: A Theoretical Critique and Reconstruction," *International Social Science Journal*, 112, pp.215-32.

Stanfield, J. R., (1982), "Towards a New Value Standard in Economics," *Economic Forum*, 13 (Fall), pp.67-85.

Stubbs, C., and J. Wheelock, (1991), *A Woman's Work in the Changing Local Economy* (Aldershot: Avebury).

Tomer, J. F., (1987), *Organizational Capital: the Path to Higher Productivity and Well Being* (New York: Praeger).

Waller, W., and A. Jennings, (1990), "A Feminist Institutionalist Reconsideration of Karl Polanyi," *Journal of Economic Issues*, 25, 2, pp.485-97.

Wheelock, J., (1990), *Husbands at Home: the Domestic Economy in a Post-industrial Society* (London: Routledge).

Wheelock, J., (1991), "Small Businesses 'Flexibility' and Family Work Strategies," Sunderland Polytechnic Business School Research Paper.

Wheelock, J., (1992a), "The Household in the Total Economy," in *Real-life Economics: Understanding Wealth Creation*, edited by P. Ekins and M. Max-Neef (London: Routledge).

Wheelock, J., (1992b), "The Flexibility of Small Business Family Work Strategies," in *Small Enterprise Development: Policy and Practice in Action*, edited by K. Caley, F. Chittenden, E. Chell, and C. Mason (London: Paul Chapman).

Chapter Three

Family Strategies and Social Development in Northern and Southern Italy

Enzo Mingione

amily strategies have a different impact in different regions of
Italy. This chapter provides a theoretical framework for looking at the different results of family strategies in northern and
southern Italy. A relatively high dose of "familism" and "par-
ticularism" is typical of the Italian (Paci, 1992) and other variants of
modernization (Mediterranean, Chinese, etc.). At the same time, in
no case can industrial development be understood without devot-
ing great attention to the adaptation and change of reciprocity networks and to family and kinship strategies, which have maintained
their crucially important role as the fundamental socio-organizational context for the biological reproduction of humankind. As factors that are adapted and resurgent in innovative ways within
modernity, these complex mixes of reciprocal loyalties greatly condition individual economic behaviour and strategies.

The Social Embeddedness of Economic Behaviour:
A Theoretical Basis

The starting point for this chapter is a critique of the economistic
market paradigm, typically adopted in various different approaches
of sociology and economics which aim to simplify the interpretation
of the transition to industrial society. Individualism and the competitive utilitarian behaviour of *"homo economicus,"* the atomized
individual striving for the maximization of immediate benefits, have
always been highly inadequate criteria for understanding industrial
societies. The assumption of atomized individual utilitarianism has
been used for the formal operationalization of the macro-oriented
social sciences, particularly economics. But this has highly distorted
our understanding of complex social realities, where human

behaviour continues to be influenced by ascriptive and optional collective loyalties as well as by non-monetary and also, to a large extent, non-utilitarian goals and relationships.

The market is not by itself a socio-regulatory factor.[1] As explained by Polanyi (1957; 1977), the diffusion of individualism is a socially disruptive force which does not directly generate new organizational rules, but activates various forms of social reaction. This belief is in part present in the sociological tradition, even if often underestimated and overshadowed by the idea that modernization follows a single parameter, imposed by market competition and by social organizations based on immediate common interest, rather than a set of variants resulting from complex interaction between different social mixes and new opportunities for competition which are always embedded in various contexts of sociability. The main distorting factor in the sociological tradition has been the use of the dichotomy between *Gemeinschaft* and *Gesellschaft* as a pure opposition between a model of traditional society and one of modern social life.

This radical opposition has overshadowed the reality of complex innovative adaptation of social arrangements, wherein both principles of reciprocity and principles of association continue to co-exist. Weber (1947:136-37) introduced the idea that there are only two socio-regulatory factors: reciprocity[2] (collective before immediate individual interests) and association (common interests immediately defended by an organizational structure, i.e., interest groups). In the reality of social life they always intermingle and are continually changing, bringing about a set of variants of industrial development which are neither linear nor evolutionary nor properly understandable within purely dualistic typologies. The persistent, varied, and changing importance of reciprocal factors is generally underestimated by social scientists; this leads to a vision of contemporary social history in which the differences, variants, and specificities arising out of various combinations of social mixes have been almost totally ignored. This criticism partially applies also to recent contributions in institutional economics[3] and in economic sociology.[4]

The assumption that economic action is not individualistically atomized, but rather embedded in socio-institutional structures (Granovetter, 1985) and constrained by power relations (Hirschman, 1970; Hirschman, 1977; Hirschman, 1982) is certainly a major step forward compared to the mainstream approaches in economics and sociology. But it does not get to the heart of the question: the fact that industrial societies are based on "systems of social integration" founded on the complementarity between forms of institutional regulations and associative organizations on the one side and the role of adapted reciprocity oriented networks on the other (Mingione, 1991; Sayer and Walker, 1992).

What is required for the interpretation of the different, and over time, changing modalities of social organization systems subjected to the pressures deriving from industrialization, and thus also from the diffusion of competitive individual behaviour, is an intermediary theoretical tool that can explain the mixes of associative and reciprocity factors characterizing the various cases. Such a tool will allow us to criticize unilinear evolutionistic interpretations of economic growth (Rostow, 1960), understand the fundamental reasons for the different variants, and take into due consideration the role played by systems of reciprocity. The already existing conceptual tool which comes closest to this intermediary theory of social integration systems is that of hegemony, though it is not the same because it underlines the features of political domination rather than the socio-organizational mix.

The concept of hegemony makes it possible to explain the variety of, and changes in, specific modes of political domination (socio-political regimes) over complex combinations of social classes in diverse contexts. Marx emphasizes the fact that the modes of social control do not end with the general supremacy of the bourgeoisie over the proletariat but are, rather, expressed in complex variable forms, as was already apparent in his historical-political works. Gramsci (1966) highlights, in the specific case of the formation of the unified Italian State, the way in which the system of hegemony entailed one mode of social integration in the North (based on modernization and industrial development), and another in the South (based on the persistence of an agrarian regime). Underpinning this system was an alliance between the innovative northern bourgeoisie and the southern landowners which remained in force until the Second World War.

An important final point is that the innovative adaptation of some modes of sociality, among them family entrepreneurship and communal solidarity, may be a fundamental feature in long-term variants of industrial development rather than a sign of backwardness. The specific features from the innovative adaptation of already existing modes of sociality are not only inherited but also more or less manipulated by different hegemonic regimes; they are resistant over time to pressures in various phases of the historical process of worldwide industrialization, which has obviously had different effects in different social contexts.

Western industrial history went through a long period (from the first half of the nineteenth century to the late 1960s) which could be defined as the age of divided societies. During this period associative organizations grew in importance, as was reflected in the institutional regulation of economic life, but their importance was also overemphasized by social scientists (Parsons, 1951; Parsons and Bales, 1955). In fact, it is also true that during the phase of divided societies, and even in the more associative-oriented cases (Grieco, 1987; Morris, 1990), reciprocity networks maintained and developed a great vitality, starting with the family. Throughout the industrial revolution in the advanced countries, the family benefitted not only from the quantitative increase in available resources and the continuous improvements in the means of long-distance communication (Goode, 1963) but also from the demographic change resulting from the prolongation of life, which in general made possible the contemporaneous presence of three generations.

The era of divided societies, called the age of Fordism in its mature stage, has come to an end; more complicated mixes of old and new reciprocal networks with associative interest groups are now emerging. This is what I mean by "fragmented societies" (Mingione, 1991). From the standpoint of long-term historical trajectories, social history in the last few centuries can be seen in terms of a three-stage discontinuous development: from *segmented*[5] to *divided* to *fragmented* societies.

There are at least three major areas in which the present transition is producing important tensions affecting the systems of social integration and the hegemonic balances of each society. First, the employment structure is moving rapidly towards a fragmented polarization between high-income and low-income (irregular, part-time, temporary) forms of paid employment. Running parallel to this is the decline of the "job for life" employment system. The possible consequences of this transformation differ depending on the modes of social integration of the emerging forms of the division of labour, which range from the polarization between work-rich and work-poor social contexts (Pahl, 1984; Morris, 1990) to various forms of redistribution within households, communities, social groups, and so on. Second, contradictions exist between the present trend towards a new, more radical, phase of globalization, and the increasing importance of local, sectional, and particularistic interests (ethnic, kinship, and friendship oriented). Third, political instability is being induced by the decreasing capacity to govern the new complexity by means of the associative political order that matured within the system of national democracies, as definitively consolidated in the Fordist-welfarist age.

For these and other reasons, in every industrial society the reciprocity-based side of social mixes has become more visible, and consequently also more interesting for macro social scientists, even though they have often been taken by surprise by the abrupt end to a long period when standardization, high growth rates, tendentiously egalitarian welfare programmes, and institutional conflicts over redistribution seemed due to continue indefinitely. The attention given to the informal economy and the study of family strategies has paved the way for this "surprise discovery."[6] Starting from studies on informal and domestic work and on family strategies, it has been possible to understand better the variety of models of development by also taking into account the importance of social factors and relations previously considered typical only of backward regions, exotic groups, and strictly subsistence economies.

In what follows, I focus on the difference between family strategies and informal relations in northern and southern Italy.[7] My main aim is to show the importance of these factors in shaping the different systems of social integration in advanced industrial societies. Obviously, these two cases do not exhaust a typological range which is increasingly diversified. In this light, the analysis of the Italian case should be considered as a contribution to an open debate.

As already mentioned above, Gramsci (1966) explains the historical division into two models of the modes of social integration in Italy in terms of a hegemonic strategy that made compatible both industrial development in the north and social control over a vast area still characterized by the domination of large landowners and their intermediaries. For reasons explained in the third section of this chapter, this two-tier model reappeared after the Second World War, though in a new form. It is precisely the persistence of this dual mode of social integration over a long period which allows us to see Italy as divided into two distinct cases, rather than as one of the variants of industrial development with wide regional imbalances.

Northern Italy: A Partially Successful History of Modernized "Familism"

During the years following the end of the Second World War, Italy became clearly divided into three different areas rather than two. In the North-West, large industrial and financial concerns became highly concentrated and vertically integrated, attracting a considerable wave of working-class immigration from the South. The Centre and North-East were characterized by slow growth, relatively high socio-geographical stability, and the consolidation of co-operative family farming and of small industrial concerns mainly oriented to local markets. In the South, agrarian reform and the economic policies of the central State dismantled the agrarian system of socio-political domination, setting off a wave of outmigration, chaotic urbanization, and the spread of a modern system of monetary consumption increasingly supported by external resources.

In the early 1970s, the first and third Italys appeared quite different from one another. The North-West was characterized by a numerous working class employed in large manufacturing concerns and living either in metropolitan cities or in single-industry towns and districts. The chaotic economic growth of the previous decades had not been matched by sufficient development of housing and provision of welfare services. The average income was more than double that of the rest of the country, but the quality of life was affected by poor standards and deficiencies in education, housing, health, local transport, and infrastructure.[8]

The third Italy had remained a less developed area, and it was still characterized by a rate of employment in agriculture more than double that in the industrial triangle (15 percent as against 7 percent). The high degree of social stability, accompanied by a constant slow growth of local markets, favoured the development of co-operative agricultural and food industries and of small industrial ventures. Social stratification was centred on family businesses, where the divisions between employers and employees were not pronounced. The social division of labour was often interlinked with the family and kinship organization, where unpaid family help played an important role. The large majority of firms, when involved in export-led growth, later almost entirely regularized employment conditions for family helpers and other previously irregular workers in order to avoid excessive taxation (EEC, 1989). The quality of life benefitted from the high degree of social stability and from a consequently less fragmented local political back-ground.[9]

Apart from the differences between them, the first and the third Italys already showed important similarities in their systems of integration of the social division of labour. These similarities became crucial factors later on and marked out convergent paths which have led to an almost complete homologation of the two regions. One of these similarities was due to the fact that households and kinship networks retained their crucial strategic economic role, even in the case of working-class families in large cities. Another was the diffusion of modernized productive households ready to adapt to new conditions and able to provide social integration for the increasingly diversified and complex form of flexible employment (Paci, 1978; Paci, 1992). A third was the paternalistic and decentral-ized style of the social relations between capital and labour (Magat-ti, 1991) which proved very open to local resources and innovative opportunities. This became a crucial success factor as soon as the Fordist conditions of mass production were substituted by the search for flexibility, vertical disintegration and subcontracting chains, socio-economic networking, and new forms of complex economic organization.

The household system, and kinship and local networks, have developed a highly important role for various reasons. On a nation-al scale, the cohesion of the family was bolstered by the absence of a divorce law up to the beginning of the 1970s and by strict laws regulating inheritance and family assistance (Saraceno, 1976; Acquaviva et al., 1981). Even after the introduction of divorce, abor-tion, and more egalitarian and modern family laws, the cohesion of the family structure was not undermined (Barbagli, 1990). The fiscal system, openly in favour of family farming and small craft enterprises and tolerant towards tax evasion by the self-employed and small units, has protected family businesses. The persistence of peasant-worker arrangements (Villa, 1986), the development of sub-contracting networks, and later on, of moonlighting and of tem-porary employment of family members, have reinforced the economic importance of the family as the crucial centre for social integration, micro-distribution of resources, and strategic decision making. Extensive income pooling, high rates of saving, and a collective solidaristic responsibility for the life chances of every member of the family have been magnified by the persistent deficiencies in the public welfare system and by serious housing problems.

The working class, largely composed of recently migrated families from the South, obtained a relatively comprehensive system of social security, job tenure, and family wage during the 1960s and early 1970s. This, however, involved almost exclusively adult male breadwinners and was poorly complemented by the insufficient development of welfare services provision. As a consequence, a system of social relations became established with the nuclear family household at its core, supported by kinship, neighbourhood, and workmate networks. Formal and informal resources were maximized towards home ownership and the education of, and the creation of better employment opportunities for, children. Both demographic practices of households (an increasingly older marriage age, delayed childbearing, falling birth rate, cohabitation of adult children with parents) and economic strategies (income pooling, informal support between kinship networks, a high saving rate, high investment in home ownership, maximizing of formal and informal resources[10]) confirm this familism physiognomy of the Italian working class.

For obvious reasons, similar strategies remained typical of the large group of productive households present in the North-West and of the extreme openness to economic innovation. Family farmers used the available social resources in order to activate a model of relatively affluent and advanced part-time agriculture which was strongly integrated into the growing agribusiness complex (Brusco, 1979; Mottura, 1990). Off-farm employment opportunities for family members were exploited, both to supplement declining farm revenue and to keep up with technical and organizational innovations. Children were sent to good schools and their professional competence used for both innovative farming techniques and improving agribusiness as well as in local economic and financial networks.

In manufacturing and services the development of a more flexible model, centred on family business, produced a huge growth in the number of firms rather than increasing the size of existing ones. In some less dynamic cases, parents, in order to cope with an expanding business, would call rather early on their children to work with them, giving rise to a relatively high dropout rate from school. In other cases, common in the more dynamic and metropolitan contexts, parents not only invested in and encouraged long-term and specialized educational training for their children, but also provided the resources for starting up new businesses or for restructuring and transforming their own firms. This led to a double model of intergenerational social mobility: one that was centred almost exclusively on the promotion of children through direct use of family resources, contacts, and networks; the other centred also on better educational attainments and increasingly oriented to technologically advanced and innovative specializations. This dual model has also been noted among the working class (Martinotti, 1982; Bagnasco, 1986). The children of the last generation of migrants from the South found great difficulties within an educational system that was rather inclined to discriminate against them. Consequently, with the help of the family, they would more often end up in unskilled self-employed or wage-work jobs (Negri, 1982). On the contrary, the children of local workers and of long since integrated southern migrants have, in general, more opportunities to achieve high educational qualifications and to end up in well-qualified white-collar jobs or in more sophisticated advanced consultancy and professional self-employment.

This duality in family mobility strategies has led, in the long run, to divisions in the system of social stratification between the stronger innovative firms and the more traditional firms which are vulnerable to economic downturns, and between individuals in highly paid and safe careers and others condemned to less secure jobs. However, the mobility strategies of northern Italian families has matched rather successfully the post-Fordist transformations of the employment structure. The youth unemployment rate increased in the late 1970s (Altieri, 1991), reflecting the longer waiting times before finding a job and the increasing supply of female labour. However, in the mid-1980s the rate fell, and a considerable number of unskilled and poorly paid jobs, with uncertain tenure prospects, attracted immigrants from developing countries (Macioti and Pugliese, 1991; Mottura, 1990).

The house-holding system has changed considerably in order to socially integrate the new division of labour. Marriage and childbearing have been delayed to a relatively late age, and children have prolonged living with parents until their late twenties.[11] During this prolonged cohabitation, children can afford to look for a good job, a search which in most cases reaches a successful conclusion due, among other causes, to a favourable labour market. The rapid increase in the rate of employment for married females and in moonlighting activities by adult males has contributed, together with the relative stability of the Fordist and small enterprise employment system, enough resources for families to support their children's employment prospects. At the same time, this very process (that is, the allocation of a number of insufficient income jobs to married women and moonlighters) prevents a situation arising in which the concentration of temporary and poorly paid jobs among particular social groups creates a new broad area of social disadvantage. In other words, in northern Italy the diffusion of work-poor households, a phenomenon noted by Pahl (1984) and Morris (1990) in the U.K., has been extremely limited.

The situation outlined above is sufficient for a preliminary conclusion to be drawn on the interface between family strategies and the model of development, at least along two crucial lines. First, family strategies are, in all cases, important factors in the model of development. They not only call our attention to the forms of social integration underlying economic development, but also to non-monetary and informal resources and their use, together with monetary and officially recorded resources, in promoting individual welfare and social mobility within and between generations. Second, the case of northern Italy shows that a relatively high degree of familism is not, at least under certain conditions, incompatible with economic growth and success within an advanced free market economy.

Family Strategies and the Social Economy of the Mezzogiorno

After 1945, the southern agrarian regime came under attack from a vigorous peasant revolt and became inconsistent with moves to include Italy in the new prospects for industrial development in the West. At this time the majority of the southern population was trapped in serious rural poverty, the productivity of agriculture was low, and industrial production was weak and backward. The main socio-economic ingredients in the transformation of the South in the period that followed included agrarian reform and a wave of land sales by landlords, leading to the constitution of an unstable class of micro family farmers (Rossi Doria, 1956), considerable State investment in public infrastructures, a period of high private investment in residential construction (Sylos Labini, 1964) accompanied by a chaotic urbanization process, and two decades of intensive migration. Starting in the late 1950s, outmigration accelerated and the governments of the time initiated industrial development policies which mainly aimed at decentralizing heavy petrochemical and steel works to the South (Becchi Collidà, 1978).

What this part of the picture does not tell us is how the social integration mechanisms became transformed and how the new hegemonic strategy was implemented on the southern front. To cut a long story short, the agrarian socio-political regime of integration became progressively replaced by a new one that was not based on industrial wage-work, entrepreneurship, and diffused market competition. In fact, this system of interaction was growing too slowly to provide an immediate substitute for the discontinued agrarian system of integration. During the transition phase in the 1950s, familism and clanism were particularly visible (Banfield, 1961) before being weakened by the acceleration of urbanization and outmigration trends. However, the foundation of the new system of social integration mainly involved the recycling of the local intermediating notables (Graziano, 1974; Graziano, 1980; Donolo, 1978; Gribaudi, 1980) within the new political party structure with its increasing capacity for patronage-based redistribution of central State resources.

This change provided the means to modernize consumption behaviour in a context where regular wage-work, innovative entrepreneurship, and dynamic family farming remained sporadic. The transformations in employment compensated for the huge decline in agricultural jobs through outmigration, an increase in precarious work in building and private services, and steadily growing employment in public administration (Piselli, 1989; Mingione, 1989a). The possibility of finding a job depended either directly (public administration) or indirectly (building and services through State contracting) on the degree of integration into the political party patronage system. Within this system, both professionalism (*Beruf*) and entrepreneurship were overshadowed by the domination of the clientelistic process of resource redistribution (Jedlowski, 1990). Family strategies became restructured within a vast network of particularistic competition to obtain a share of resources, through local party bosses, in exchange for political consensus.

The system gave the impression of creating development as long as it was complemented by outmigration, the relocation in the South of large manufacturing plants, and increasing State expenditure. Towards the mid-1970s all three conditions came to an end. The gap between North and South began to grow again, and the conditions of life in the South rapidly deteriorated (*Inchiesta*, 1990; Triglia, 1992). This process, however, has not been accompanied by social conflict and political instability. On the contrary, the consolidated dependence of the southern population on centrally redistributed resources through political channels reinforced consensus towards the government (Piselli, 1989).

Another important phenomenon on the southern social scene in the last few decades has been the dramatic expansion of criminal organizations, led by the exponential growth of the drug business. The patronage-oriented system of social integration, the employment structure strongly characterized by black labour market activities and youth unemployment, and poor legal protection for all forms of social interaction are extraordinary fertile ground for the growth of crime.

In the last fifteen years, the southern population has been engaged in achieving the same strategic goal as the northern population: to promote social mobility under the complicated conditions of the post-Fordist age (characterized by de-industrialization and increasing fragmentation of the employment structure). From this point of view, the North and the South are similar: children live with their parents until a relatively advanced age; marriage and child-bearing are frequently postponed; the family and kinship structure invests an important share of its resources in order to support young people during a fairly long period of unemployment; and working opportunities are found in most cases through the help of reciprocity networks. Despite the similarity, all this happens in radically different social contexts and with quite different outcomes.

The modern industrial working class, with secure jobs paying a family wage, constitutes a tiny minority. Its political and social influence is limited, squeezed as it is between two heterogenous social groups typical of this context: the middle classes, integrated in and locally managing clientelistic operations; and a large diversified group of semi-proletarian precarious workers, concentrated in building and small traditional private services. The usual composite nature of the urban middle class here undergoes a hierarchical reorganization due to the dominance of political patronage operations, controlled by a stratum of professionals already engaged in political careers. At the other end of the social ladder, that of the semi-proletariat, we also find a composite aggregate of subjects, who substantially depend on obtaining something through redistribution based on patronage; either a job, a subsidy, a pension, or inclusion in a welfare programme, etc.

The participation rate of southern women is persistently low, particularly in the case of urban working-class or semi-proletarian women (*Inchiesta*, 1992). This is the result of the combination between the need for long hours of domestic chores in order to compensate for the deficiencies of welfare provision on the one hand and the absence of employment opportunities on the other. This means that multiple-income families are quite rare, particularly among the low-income majority of the urban population. This is also the stratum most severely hit by the other crucial employment phenomenon: youth unemployment. In the South, the numbers and the rate of youth unemployment have increased steadily, involving nearly half the generation between the ages of 15 and 30. This period of unemployment is generally very long, more than four years on average, and creates particular difficulties for low-income families with many children in the 15-30 age group. A positive outcome is not at all certain, moreover, especially for young females who may never experience any form of official employment, or poorly educated males who may be condemned for life to precarious employment and thus to poverty (Altieri, 1991; Calzabini, 1992; IRES-CGIL, 1992; Pugliese, 1993).

Even more than in other peasant societies in Europe, a tradition of extended or multinuclear families is almost completely absent here. This is explained by, among other things, the fact that family farming was sporadic until the period following agrarian reform (Piselli, 1989). Thus, a limited number of extended cohabiting families derive neither from cultural custom nor from a family business strategy, but is due, rather, to the absence of services or to a constraint produced by the housing market, i.e. the difficulty of finding separate housing for new nuclear families (Carboni and Zanchettin, 1990). Furthermore, the capacity to provide economic support and social solidarity among non-cohabiting family members has been seriously weakened by migrations and chaotic urban growth and made even more problematic by the serious deficiencies in local and interregional transport and communications. The large majority of households are nuclear families, which are relatively more isolated than in the North from extended kinship support (Signorelli, 1989; Siebert, 1989; Mingione, 1989b). They are, on average, still much larger than in the North for two concomitant reasons: the birth rate has been declining only recently and from higher levels; and the constitution of single-person or couple households remains less likely for economic (insufficient income) and socio-environmental (the difficulty of being supported by non-cohabiting relatives) constraints (Signorelli, 1989; *Inchiesta,* 1992). This also means that southern families are supporting on average a higher number of children, which makes the goal of intergenerational upward mobility more difficult *per se.* These are more or less the sociodemographic conditions that southern family strategies have to take into account in the face of the present youth employment crisis (Cavalli, 1990).

In confronting the socio-economic post-Fordist transformation, southern families are roughly divided into two composite groups: the middle class, which is well connected and runs the patronage system; and a diversified majority group composed of a tiny manufacturing working class, a large group of precarious workers, a group of unskilled workers in public administration and in private services, and an area of quasi-proletariat with complex mixed working and family profiles. Unlike in the North, family businesses are less dynamic and highly dependent on State patronage operations; those that are better connected with patronage hierarchies form part of the middle class, while others that are only marginally supported by clientelistic connections belong to the quasi-proletariat. Both types have no chance of creating employment opportunities with their own resources, but instead strictly depend on the patronage redistribution system (Piselli, 1989).

The middle class has fewer children per family, and they are more and better educated on average. The capacity to select the best schools and to invest more money in education is particularly effective here. At the opposite end of the social scale, there is a large group which is already in, or is falling into, serious poverty (Spanò and Morlicchio, 1992). The father's work in agriculture, building, or private services is low-wage, insecure, and often informal. The mother is a full-time housewife working very hard in the house in order to compensate for the lack of income and welfare services. There are many children, all of them early dropouts from school and officially unemployed. The males find temporary work from time to time, but are unable to find an acceptably secure, lasting, and adequately paid job unless somebody in the support network manages to break into the patronage system. Alternatively, young males may be involved in organized crime; in this case the "fortune" of the family depends on how long they are able to survive and stay out of prison in order to provide financial resources sufficient to upgrade the standard of living. The females may not even be officially registered as unemployed; they spend the years before marriage in domestic work for the family and in rare moments of unofficial employment.

Under these conditions, it is clear why southern family strategies are largely unsuccessful in matching the post-Fordist employment transformation and also why the consensus towards the ruling class is reinforced rather than weakened. In the South, the only realistic opportunities of acceptable employment, other than involvement in organized crime, depend on the redistribution of resources from the central State. It is not so important that the competition for jobs is free, and that only a minority which is better integrated into the political networks obtains good results. What conditions social behaviour is the pervasive monopoly of the clientelistic system. This conditioning also affects family businesses, entrepreneurship, and advanced economic ventures to a large extent. These initiatives, even in the best cases, are not adequately supported by the local market which is weak and distorted. Therefore, they cannot survive long without the support of the local and central authorities. This proves to be a vicious circle: the more success is conditioned by favours from the clientelistic elite, the less normal entrepreneurial, professional, and innovative strategies are implemented. Consequently, economic behaviour further increases its orientation towards complying with the rules of patronage.

Within this picture, familism and the support of reciprocity-based networks are not in themselves the limits to economic development or to market economy success. It is, rather, the system of social integration based on the dominance of patronage redistribution which diverts social behaviour away from any of the possible alternatives of rational and professional allocation. As we have seen, family strategies are trapped in this system of social integration as one of the dependent variables. It could be said that southern familism is the product of the transformation of the social integration system in recent decades, certainly not the original cause of its orientation.

On a different front, that of the role of informal work within the various models of industrial development, the experiences of the North and the South may be useful for comparative considerations. The widespread belief that the third Italy's successful model of flexible industry is based on a high level of informal activities is mistaken. A high level of particular typologies of irregular work in small enterprises did accompany the industrial transformation that took place between the 1960s and 1970s, only then to drop back to a normal level in the following period. In the South, on the contrary, the underdevelopment of the region continues to be characterized by a very high level of "black" labour and unregulated activities which in no way indicate the existence of resources for development; they are, rather, symptoms of the failure to develop. It is now apparent that the concept of informal work spans a typological range of highly diverse experiences and cannot, therefore, constitute a general theoretical tool for understanding the socio-economic transformations in the post-Fordist age. It represents, instead, a field of analysis that needs to be opened up once again, after decades of neglect, in order to bring into focus all the possible modes of individual, family, and social strategies.

In the case of northern and southern Italy, the paths of transformation and of adaptation to post-Fordist conditions have been quite different. In this respect, it is possible to make some brief concluding observations that link up with several ideas put forward at the beginning of this chapter on the crisis of the Fordist social equilibrium and the impact of new mounting tensions.

Italy is at present going through a serious politico-institutional and social crisis. It may be assumed that it is a more radical and violent form of transition than that which is also characterizing the other industrialized countries, for reasons that are indicated in all of what has been said above. The hegemonic structure that characterized the social, economic, and political order of post-war Italy was grounded in the effectiveness of the clientelistic political system as the nub of social integration in the South and in its simultaneous compatibility with the model of economic development adopted for the country as a whole. It has been the falling away of this compatibility that has opened up a profound crisis of "hegemony," which is all the more serious in as far as it risks forming a vacuum in the social integration of the South that cannot be immediately counteracted.

The system is now being subjected to a violent attack from the outside precisely because it is no longer compatible with the new requirements of the single European market, of global socio-economic equilibrium, and of the post-Fordist restructuring of industrial societies. However, while elsewhere the specific forms of social integration have adapted, although with difficulty, to the new conditions and consequently managed to delay further the "hegemonic' crisis, the South risks suffering a collapse similar in extent to that of the regimes in eastern Europe. The market, which is not suitably regulated by a long historical, social, and cultural tradition, does not represent a solution in this case either; it is, rather, a factor aggravating politico-social instability (Mingione, 1991). In this sense, what is now happening in Italy, and in the South in particular, can be used as a basis for comparative considerations on the modalities of the "hegemonic" crises characterizing the passage from divided to fragmented societies.

Notes

1. Although the idea that the market is in itself one of the main socio-regulatory factors is still very widespread, it is rarely discussed in critical terms; see, for example, Lange and Regini (1987:12-22). I have expressed a different position in Mingione (1991:21-24) when criticizing Polanyi's idea that exchange, like the other forms of integration, i.e. reciprocity and redistribution, is also in need of a supporting structure of social relations.

2. Weber does not mention reciprocity, but calls this category of factors "communal" (Weber, 1947:136). For an explanation of the reasons why I prefer the term "reciprocal" to "communal," see Mingione (1991:24-29).

3. See Aglietta (1979); Boyer (1979; 1986); Boyer and Mistral (1983); du Tertre (1989); Lipietz (1987); and Block (1990).

4. See Roberts et al. (1985); Lash and Urry (1987); Bagnasco (1988); Magatti (1991); and Sayer and Walker (1992).

5. The term "segmented" is taken from Durkheim's (1984) definition of pre-industrial societies as characterized by the prevalence of "mechanic solidarity" in stable and closed communities, not particularly affected by social and geographical mobility.

6. See Ferman and Ferman (1973); Pahl (1984); Redclift and Mingione (1985); Ferman et al. (1987); Portes et al. (1989); and Offe and Heinze (1992).

7. The assumption that Italy can be divided into two cases has been debated since the 1977 publication of the important work by Bagnasco on the *Tre Italie,* which introduced the idea that Italy should be seen as being divided into three sub-systems, rather than into North and South according to the conventional dualistic approach. These sub-systems are referred to as the first Italy (the North-West, better known as the industrial triangle, delimited by the three cities of Milan, Turin and Genoa), the South or Mezzogiorno, and the Third Italy (the Centre and North East). In a recent special edition of *Inchiesta* (1990), several authors have argued for a return to the classical dualistic vision.

8. See Boffi et al. (1972); Bagnasco (1977; 1986); Martinotti (1982); and Perulli (1981).

9. Bagnasco (1977) provides a comprehensive documentation showing that the population of the third Italy is better serviced, both in terms of local and central (education, health, long-distance transport) provisions.

10. See Barbagli (1984); Saraceno (1986; 1988a; 1988b); Livi Bacci (1980); Melograni (1988); and Federici (1984).

11. Recent surveys on youth unemployment show that a large majority of young males, but also a fair number of females, live with their parents until they find a secure tenured job, up to an average age of 27-28; a considerable minority (from one quarter of females to more than a third of males) do so into their early thirties (IRES-CGIL, 1992).

References

Acquaviva et al., eds., (1981), *Ritratto di famiglia negli anni ottanta* (Bari-Roma: Laterza).

Aglietta, M., (1979), *A Theory of Capitalist Regulation: The U.S. Experience* (London: Verso).

Altieri, G., ed., (1991), *Tra Nord e Sud,* Collana IRES (Roma: Ediesse).
Bagnasco, A., (1977), *Tre Italie: la problematica territoriale dello sviluppo italiano* (Bologna: Il Mulino).
Bagnasco, A., (1986), *Torino: un profile sociologico* (Torino: Einaudi).
Bagnasco, A., (1988), *La costruzione sociale del mercato* (Bologna: Il Mulino).
Banfield, E. C., (1961), *Le basi morali di una società arretrata* (Bologna: Il Mulino).
Barbagli, M., (1984), *Sotto lo stesso tetto* (Bologna: Il Mulino).
Barbagli, M., (1990), *Provando e riprovando* (Bologna: Il Mulino).
Becchi Collidà, A., ed., (1978), *Lavoro, sussidi, Mezzogiorno* (Milano: Angeli).
Block, F., (1990), *Postindustrial Possibilities* (Berkeley: University of California Press).
Boffi, M., S. Cifini, A. Giasanti, and E. Mingione, (1972), *Città e conflitto sociale* (Milano: Feltrinelli).
Boyer, R., (1979), "La crise actuelle: une mise en perspective historique," *Critique de l'économie politique,* 12-13.
Boyer, R., (1986), *La Flexibilité en Europe* (Paris: La Découverte).
Boyer, R., and J. Mistral, (1983), *Accumulations, inflation, crise* (Paris: PUF).
Brusco, S., (1979), *Agricoltura ricca e classi sociali* (Milano: Feltrinelli).
Calzabini, P., ed., (1992), *La disoccupazione: più de vista* (Napoli: Liguori).
Carboni, C., and L. Zanchettin, (1990), "Famiglia, mercato del lavoro e marginalità sociale," *Inchiesta,* pp.111-25.
Cavalli, A., ed., (1990), *I giovani del mezzogiorno* (Bologna: Il Mulino).
Donolo, C., (1978), "Mutamenti nel blocco sociale dominante nel Mezzogiorno," in *L'economia italiana tra sviluppo e sussistenza,* edited by A. Collidà (Milano: Angeli).
Durkheim, E., (1984), *The Division of Labour in Society* (London: Macmillan).
Du Tertre, C., (1989), *Technologie, flexibilité, emploi* (Paris: L'Hartmattan).
EEC, (1989), *Underground Economy and Irregular Forms of Employment: Synthesis Report and Country Monographies* (Bruxelles: European Economic Community).
Federici, (1984), *Procreazione, famiglia, lavoro delle donne* (Torino: Loescher).
Ferman, L. A., and P. R. Ferman, (1973), "The Structural Underpinnings of Irregular Economy," *Poverty and Human Resources Abstracts,* 9, pp.13-17.
Ferman, L. A., S. Henry, and E. Hoyman, (1987), "The Informal Economy," *Annals of the American Academy of Political and Social Science.*
Goode, W., (1963), *World Revolution and Family Patterns* (New York: Free Press).
Gramsci, A., (1966), *La Questione Meridionale* (Roma: Editori Riuniti).
Granovetter, M., (1985), "Economic Action and Social Structure: The Problem of Embeddedness," *American Journal of Sociology,* 91, 3, pp.341-510.
Graziano, L., ed., (1974), *Clientelismo e mutamento politico* (Milano: Angeli).
Graziano, L., (1980), *Clientelismo e sistema politico* (Milano: Angeli).
Gribaudi, G., (1980), *I mediatori* (Torino: Rosenberg e Sellier).
Grieco, M., (1987), *Keeping it in the Family: Social Networks and Employment Chance* (London and New York: Tavistock).
Hirschman, A. O., (1970), *Exit, Voice and Loyalty: Responses to Decline in Forms, Organizations, and States* (Cambridge: Harvard University Press).
Hirschman, A. O., (1977), *The Passions and the Interests* (Princeton: Princeton University Press).
Hirschman, A. O., (1982), *Shifting Involvements: Private Interests and Public Action* (Oxford: Martin Robertson).
Inchiesta, (1990), "Tre Italie o un nuovo dualismo?" 88-89.
Inchiesta, (1992), "Donne del Sud," 96.

IRES-CGIL, (1992), *Caraterristiche e tipologia della disoccupazione in Italia: sperimentazione di strumenti di analisi e valutazione* (Roma: IRES).

Jedlowski, P., (1990), "Nuovi ceti nel Mezzogiorno: fra clientelismo e professionalità," *Inchiesta*, pp.126-39.

Lange, P., and M. Regini, (1987), *Stato e regolazione sociale* (Bologna: Il Mulino).

Lash, S., and J. Urry, (1987), *The End of Organized Capitalism* (Cambridge: Polity Press).

Lipietz, A., (1987), *Mirages and Miracles: The Crisis of Global Fordism* (London: Verso).

Livi Bacci, M., (1980), *Donne, fecodità e figli* (Bologna: Il Mulino).

Macioti, M. I., and E. Pugliese, (1991), *Gli Immigrati in Italia* (Bari: Laterza).

Magatti, M., (1991), *Mercato e forze sociali. Due distretti tessili: Lancashire e Ticino Olana* (Bologna: Il Mulino).

Martinotti, G., ed., (1982), *La città difficile* (Milano: Angeli).

Melograni, P., ed., (1988), *La famiglia italiana dall'ottocento a oggi* (Bari: Laterza).

Mingione, E., (1989a), "Note per un'analisi delle classi sociali," in *Società, politica e cultura nel Mezzogiorno*, edited by R. Catanzano (Milano: Angeli).

Mingione, E., (1989b), "Tipologie familiari e transformazioni economiche," *Critica Marxista*, 4, pp.151-69.

Mingione, E., (1991), *Fragmented Societies: A Sociology of Economic Life Beyond the Market Paradigm* (Oxford: Blackwell).

Morris, L., (1990), *The Workings of the Household* (Oxford: Polity Press).

Mottura, G., (1990), "Nel futuro che s'apre le mattine. Considerazione sulle imprese, i lavori e i territori delle nuove agricolture italiane," *Inchiesta*, pp.38-50.

Mottura, G., and E. Pugliese, (1975), *Agricoltura, Mezzogiorno e mercato del lavoro* (Bologna: Il Mulino).

Negri, N., (1982), "I nuovi torinesi: immigrazione, mobilità e struttura sociale," in *La città difficile*, edited by G. Martinotti (Milano: Angeli).

Offe, C., and R. G. Heinze, (1992), *Beyond Employment* (Oxford: Polity Press).

Paci, M., ed., (1978), *Capitalism e classi sociali in Italia* (Bologna: Il Mulino).

Paci, M., (1992), *Il mutamento della struttura sociale in Italia* (Bologna: Il Mulino).

Pahl, R. E., (1984), *Divisions of Labour* (Oxford: Blackwell).

Parsons, T., (1951), *The Social System* (Glencoe, Ill.: Free Press).

Parsons, T., and R. F. Bales, (1955), *Family Socialization and Interaction Process* (New York: Free Press).

Perulli, F., (1981), *Parentela ed emigrazione* (Torino: Einaudi).

Piselli, F., (1989), "Parentela, clientela e partiti politici," in *Società, politica e cultura nel Mezzogiorno*, edited by R. Catanzaro (Milano: Angeli).

Polanyi, K., (1957), "The Economy as Instituted Process," in *Trade and Market in the Early Empires*, edited by K. Polanyi, C. Arensberg, and H. Pearson (Glencoe, Ill.: Free Press).

Polanyi, K., (1977), *The Livelihood of Man* (New York: Academic Press).

Portes, A., M. Castells, and L. A. Benton, (1989), *The Informal Economy: Studies in Advanced and Less Advanced Countries* (Baltimore and London: Johns Hopkins University Press).

Pugliese, E., (1993), *Sociologia della disoccupazione* (Bologna: Il Mulino).

Redclift, N., and E. Mingione, (1985), *Beyond Employment* (Oxford: Blackwell).

Roberts, B., R. Finnegan, and D. Gallie, eds., (1985), *New Approaches to Economic Life* (Manchester: Manchester University Press).

Rossi Doria, M., (1956), *Riforma agraria ed azione meridionalista* (Bologna: Il Mulino).

Rostow, W., (1960), *The Stages of Economic Growth* (Cambridge: Cambridge University Press).

Saraceno, C., (1976), *Anatomia della famiglia: struttura e forme familiari* (Bari: de Donato).

Saraceno, C., (1986), *Età e corso della vita* (Bologna: Il Mulino).

Saraceno, C., (1988a), *Sociologia della famiglia* (Bologna: Il Mulino).

Saraceno, C., (1988b), "La famiglia: i paradossi della costruzione del privato," in *La vita privata. Il Novecento*, edited by Aries and Duby (Bari: Laterza).

Sayer, A., and R. Walker, (1992), *The New Social Economy* (Oxford: Blackwell).

Siebert, R., (1989), "I mutamenti delle relazioni familiari," in *Critica Marxista*, 4, pp.171-85.

Signorelli, A., (1989), "Famiglia, lavoro, potere: le transformazioni culturali," in *Società, politica e cultura nel Mezzogiorno*, edited by R. Caranzaro (Milano: Angeli).

Spano, A., and E. Morlicchio, (1992), "La povertà a Napoli," *Inchiesta*.

Sylos Labini, P., (1964), "Precarious Employment in Sicily," *International Labour Review*, (March), pp.268-285.

Triglia, C., (1992), *Sviluppo senza autonomia* (Bologna: Il Mulino).

Villa, P., (1986), *The Structuring of Labour Markets* (Oxford: Clarendon Press).

Weber, M., (1947), *The Theory of Social and Economic Organization* (New York: Free Press).

Part II

The Community Versus the Market: The Ups and Downs of Practices of Resistance

Chapter Four

The Sou Sou Land Possibility: Survival and Community Mobilization in Trinidad and Tobago

Ivan Laughlin

Today's language, accumulated with that of yesterday and utilized as a medallion on the necklace of Caribbean islands, effectively becomes a millstone submerging the region in a sea of hopelessness, dependence, conformity, irrationality and fragmentation. Yesterday's language was third world, developing, under-developed and less developed; today's language is trade liberalization, a new world order, sustainable development, globalization, and structural adjustment. Homogenization of humankind is the agenda; the direction continues to be as always from without, never from within. The great human strength derived from cultural diversity is now threatened by that medallion of destruction; creative energy, so much of which still lies dormant in the Caribbean people, fails to find a relevant environment in which to be unleashed.

Due To a Lack of Interest, Tomorrow Has Been Cancelled Indefinitely

For so many of our young people there is no sense of future; there is only today. In my country of Trinidad and Tobago, a piece of graffiti appropriately describing the condition appeared some years ago in an urban area fringing the capital city of Port of Spain: *due to lack of interest tomorrow has been cancelled indefinitely*. Yet the political and economic strategies being pursued at the official level continue to have no sense of engagement with the population. These strategies and policies continue to reflect a lack of belief in the capacity of the people to exercise bold initiatives, and the people instinctively recognize that reality.

Unless regional groupings possessing similar cultural roots can find the self-knowledge, the self-confidence, and the purpose occasioned by development strategies appropriate to their special circumstances, then the concept of a global village is nothing more than a farce. The reality in the Caribbean is that all developmental decisions are rooted in the cultural imperatives of other civilizations. Hence political and economic transformation can only be effective to the extent that community viability exists, and community viability begins first with the human environment, with people. If the human spirit can only glimpse a future of hope and possibility, then we open up opportunities for innovation and enterprise. Ultimately, then, we return to the basic requirements of community, in a sense to its three first principles: *people* with a capacity to exercise control over their own lives; *land* with a capability to be used to sustain life and production; and *shelter* to provide a place that is definable and offers security. The transformative vision therefore begins in the realm of those basic tenets of community. In giving tangible expression to those necessities, we help to engender courage and to extend the horizons of hope, which are the fundamental underpinnings for psychological and social transformation.

So often in the process of national development in the Caribbean today, people are relegated to mere statistics in the methodologies of economic and physical planning. There is a signal failure to discover the kind of developmental environment that can allow the creative energies of our people to be unleashed. It is not that there is a lack of political will: everywhere there is evidence of it. But to the extent that the political will is captured within the framework of existing development strategies we cannot approach the frontiers of relevant transformation. Undoubtedly the situation demands bold initiatives, even calculated risks, if we are to fundamentally address the requirements of the people of the region, but the prevailing economic and physical development programmes and policies continue to be wholly inadequate to the needs of the human environment. However, it is also important to look to the unofficial side, because alongside the severe economic and social problems that confront the region can also be seen the powerful desire of the human spirit for survival. Whether it be in Jamaica or Guyana, Haiti or St. Lucia, Trinidad and Tobago or Santo Domingo, there is abundant evidence of people courageously struggling to create habitats that can provide for their basic needs: the Sou Sou Land Possibility is one such expression of survival.

The Sou Sou Land Perspective: The Beginning

Trinidad and Tobago is a twin-island country, located at the southern end of the Caribbean archipelago, with a population from a wide diversity of ethno-cultural backgrounds. Here, as throughout the Caribbean, there are no indigenous peoples; unlike most of the Caribbean, however, the dominant groups are of African and Indian descent, as well as those of European, Lebanese, and Chinese extraction. It is a country whose colonial past has known Spanish rule, during which the land was settled by French immigrants and worked by African slave labour. British colonization followed, during which indentured labour from India was introduced after Emancipation in 1838. At Emancipation, the population was some 50,000; today it is just over a million. So in a sense we are a new country, with a significant percentage of the population having come from the Caribbean and beyond over the past 100 years because of the promise of economic opportunity, first in sugar and cocoa, and then in the petroleum industry. As a result, we are a volatile, restless people not yet rooted in our environment (Trinidad much more so than Tobago, whose colonial history was somewhat different). Yet we possess latent, creative capabilities not quite fully explored. The steel band is a striking example of that creativity; born in the African-dominated areas of the city in the latter part of the 1930s and nurtured during World War II, it is the major innovation in musical orchestration in this century.

It is important to note that this creative expression was unleashed in an environment of the heightened political awareness of the 1930s and of economic self-reliance generated by the blockade imposed by the international conflict. The experiences of that period of Caribbean history show that strategies for transformation are not pre-ordained. They need to emerge out of processes that stimulate the imagination of the population and allow us to engage the realm of the unknown: to try to discover that which has not yet been discovered. In Trinidad and Tobago one such process has been emerging over the past ten years, since 1983. It was initiated not by governmental action but by a non-governmental, non-profit, land reform initiative called Sou Sou Land. Sou Sou comes from the patois meaning literally "penny by penny." It is a traditional form of banking among village folk in Trinidad and Tobago, developed as an indigenous method of saving by the former slaves within the plantation system; there are counterparts throughout the region. Essentially, a fixed number of participants would pool savings, usually in fixed, equal amounts on a regular basis, weekly or monthly. Each participant would then in turn, at the same intervals as deposits are made, draw their "hand" (the lump sum of what their overall deposits would be). The process is democratically organized, there is no interest accruing to the participants, and the fundamental ingredient for success is trust in the promoters. The "hand" is usually used for a variety of domestic purposes. In the Sou Sou Land initiative the "hand" is land.

Sou Sou Land began literally by accident. Some ten years ago, responding to the predicament of a group of his landless constituents, opposition politician John Humphrey took a positive, humanitarian, and courageous approach to find affordable land on which these people could settle with their families. As he himself recounts the origin of the project:

> On that Sunday afternoon in late 1983 when I met with nineteen "squatting" families who were my constituents, all of whom were to be rendered homeless by court order within twelve hours, I did not know it, but Sou Sou Land was emerging. I was able to negotiate with the owner of the land to postpone demolition of the houses to enable me to find another settlement area. A tract of idle State land was located where over 100 "squatters" had settled, and I obtained the support of the settled community to add nineteen houses. I thought the location suitable since there had never been demolitions in the area. However in a matter of days, the demolition squad of the Ministry of Housing and Resettlement moved in.

> Not wanting to jeopardize the security I retreated but did not surrender. A programme had been initiated for a group of "squatters" in San Fernando where monies were collected to purchase land with the intention of settling the "squatters" on their own land. When I presented this idea to my constituents they mandated me to locate land which they would buy as a community. I found an abandoned estate of 117 acres and after visiting the estate with the "squatters," they agreed to each buy one acre and rally relatives and friends who needed land to take up the rest of the estate.

At that point I visited my colleague, Lennox Sanker-singh, a barrister-at-law, to assist in the legal work required. He did much more: Lennox and I conducted meetings, collected funds and kept records. We designed a system to assure proper control. We were seeking 117 applicants with the intention of confining our efforts to this one project. The response to what we were doing was overwhelming. Hundreds of land-less people, on hearing about our efforts, came to the weekly meetings. In one month there were 1,000 applicants.

Sou Sou Land Limited, a non-profit company, was formed to offer what seemed a relatively simple service to help the landless solve their problem. I was asked to undertake the responsibilities for the conceptual planning and land surveying; others joined to form a technical team for the exercise. By 1986, 1,200 hectares of land were purchased, spread over thirteen projects in Trinidad and Tobago involving the investment of some eighteen million Trinidad and Tobago (T.T.) dollars, provided by twelve thousand participants. In the Sou Sou Land programme, the prospective settlers deposited their money to Sou Sou Land Ltd. in affordable instalments. The company purchased and developed the estates in a process that involved interaction and collaboration with the settlers; at the end of the exercise they received their parcels of land, ready to organize their own shelter. The process was therefore financed by the investors, and its success depended on the trust placed in the personnel who conducted the business of the company.

Sou Sou Land is in fact a home-grown response to the provision of basic human needs born out of the particular historical conditions that have shaped this part of the world. The "oil boom" in Trinidad and Tobago between 1973 and 1983, with its unprecedented inflows of revenue, reinforced land development, infrastructure standards, development zoning, and development procedures at the official level; it also served to inflate development costs and make shelter acquisition prohibitive to those at the lower end of the income ladder. It is debatable whether such standards, zoning, and procedures are relevant at any time in societies such as ours. The point is that during the oil boom, official land development policies, together with a demand for construction materials which outstripped supply, and the dominance of the profit motive fuelled by the flow of money, caused land prices to soar well out of the reach of a significant section of the population. By 1983, therefore, for Sou Sou Land to provide land for the landless meant first of all that the company had to proceed without official approval and in contravention of the rules and regulations governing land development, although every effort was made from the outset to bring the Sou Sou Land strategy to the attention of political and professional interests. We argued that if the laws were not serving the public interest, then they must be amended and adapted to it. Regulations that were largely irrelevant and not applicable needed to be reviewed as a matter of urgency. In effect, the Sou Sou Land initiative was raising issues related to the "social contract" and saying that prevailing economic and physical development approaches were detrimental to the well-being and dignity of large sections of the population.

By November, 1986 the Sou Sou Land trust was at a critical stage, since the shelter component of the settlements was beginning to take shape. The government of the day and the planning authorities were in conflict with Sou Sou Land for reasons that were both political and technical, and the scale of the land reform exercise demanded a rapprochement for the benefit of the participants.

The Quantum Leap

On December 15th, 1986, the country elected a new party, the National Alliance for Reconstruction (NAR), with an overwhelming majority, after thirty years of rule by the Peoples' National Movement (PNM). Through the election victory of the NAR a national statement was made about the Sou Sou Land concept, which was a major plank of the NAR's campaign platform, in which it was proposed to be used as a basis for its land reform initiatives. John Humphrey was appointed Minister of Works, Settlement, and Infrastructure; I was asked to head the National Housing Authority (NHA) and to use that as the vehicle for implementing the New Settlements Program based on the Sou Sou Land concept. A new NHA board was appointed, incorporating a wide range of expertise, including some of us who were involved in the Sou Sou Land enterprise.

Knowing full well that the Sou Sou Land concept was based primarily on the participation of people in the overall development process, and realizing that the country, particularly in the urban areas, lacked a culture of decision making as a result of political emasculation and dependence, the implementation procedure demanded sensitivity and patience. It was therefore necessary to set up strategies to bring the people into the decision-making process. Such strategies cannot be devised by simply establishing bureaucratic or administrative structures, or by asking people to indicate whether they support one development programme or another. They must emerge from an active process in which tangible aspects of the development thrust can be brought before the community in many different and relevant programmes and projects. Such a process is what the human settlement approach provides.

Sou Sou Land, at the non-governmental level translated to the national level, required a quantum leap that was sensitive to the prevailing political, economic, and social situations. Accordingly, the overall approach had to make sense of the Sou Sou Land experience with its shortcomings, its mistakes, its potential, and its community mobilization focus, but the fundamental message was that the process of national reconstruction had to be gradual. That is the essence of the Sou Sou Land approach. There are no overnight solutions, but once relevant strategies are set in motion, and creative energies are released in the process, then there is a chance of finding relevant solutions to the issues of economic, social and political transformation. There are no textbook prescriptions; it is simply a commonsense approach to finding, by our own efforts and exertions, solutions to the problems we face.

In the NHA, we had to set in train a number of strategies that could take account of the serious limitations of previous housing and settlements policy as well as the limited resource capability of the Authority. Essentially, the settlements approach combined urban renewal, village expansion, sites and services programmes, squatter regularization, and community rejuvenation. It is not my intention in this chapter to assess the government's settlements programme; much political water has flowed under the national bridge since December 1986, and this has had significant adverse effects on the Sou Sou Land trust at both NGO and State levels. I resigned from the NHA and the official settlements programme in early 1988. The overall programme was slow in being implemented, losing much of the enthusiasm generated by the initial thrust in 1987; moreover, it was not captured in the wider context of a human settlements approach so crucial for achieving maximum impact on the fundamental issues of job creation and community viability. Additionally, the long drawn out negotiations for IDB funding, and the conditions of such funding, had an adverse impact on the programme. However, the quantum leap served to place the Sou Sou Land approach to land reform on the national agenda and this, coupled with the activities of Sou Sou Land Ltd., has caused the concept to receive international recognition.

The NGO Initiative

Today there are three Sou Sou Land actors on the national stage:

Sou Sou Land Ltd.: Now forging the community development aspect of the projects and at the same time struggling for financial viability. The government's parallel programme drew some participants away from Sou Sou Land Ltd. projects because of superior locations. This, coupled with the experimental nature of the original initiative, has put the company under financial stress.

Public Sector Settlements Program: Incorporating squatter regularization, sites and services projects, urban renewal, and village expansion on State lands. The role of the State in this programme has been defined as that of facilitator, in an attempt to achieve the essential ingredient of the Sou Sou Land concept with the participation of the communities in the overall process. Unfortunately, this programme is not being undertaken in tandem with agricultural diversification, and the reorganization and redistribution of State lands is not a priority thrust of the government; consequently, the potential far-reaching effects of the programme have been severely diluted.

Non-governmental organizations (NGOs): A number of community organizations have emerged over the past six years, with the objective of fostering community viability with land as the base. These organizations are credit unions, co-operatives, and community based organizations, and they are mobilizing their human and financial resources for achieving land and property ownership and rational living environments for their membership. I work with a number of these groupings in Trinidad and Tobago, all of which have the potential to generate a new approach to economic and social development.

It is through this last and most recent frontier of the Sou Sou Land initiative that a new arena in the private sector has begun to take shape. Some refer to it as "the third sector" or "the people's sector" since it has in effect developed out of the informal sector. The categorization is not important; the essential reality is that this new initiative has been nurtured by Sou Sou Land, and has thrown onto the national stage an important option for the process of nation building. In effect the Sou Sou Land initiative has raised fundamental issues about the development process and it is important that some of these be identified. By focusing on land for the landless, it has highlighted the crucial phenomenon of dispossession, a widespread reality in the Caribbean and beyond, wherever colonization has existed. Land use, land ownership, land rationalization: in a word, *land* is the primary consideration, the basic requirement for relevant development to be undertaken.

The critical importance of *directly involving people* in the development process to inform both planning and implementation is also a pillar of the Sou Sou Land approach. Because the focus is on living environments, primarily on land and shelter, the affected populations recognize the importance of their involvement, and community mobilization is paramount. This leads to the growth and development of NGOs and community-based organizations (CBOs) based on the prospect of community viability. The direct involvement of the citizens has also served to activate the women in the communities, and they have become a decisive factor in the success of the respective projects.

In a departure from the practice of separate approaches to urban and rural development, the Sou Sou Land perspective provides for relevant linkages between the two approaches. It thus creates, in a context of growing economic hardship, the possibility for rural development to be pursued outside the urban centres, thereby enabling urban renewal to be undertaken.

It is people in the informal sector who have been primarily engaged in the Sou Sou Land process. It is estimated that in the Caribbean, fifty to sixty percent of the population is involved in this sector. The recognition of the creativity and enterprise contained therein has activated new sources of finance and investment, and when the focus is on land and shelter the formal financial operators cannot ignore the new investment possibilities. The experience in Trinidad and Tobago is that governmental budgetary action has served to create financial mechanisms in the formal mortgage market which make finance available to those much lower down the income ladder than was previously the case. Additionally, some commercial banks and credit unions have been actively opening up their loan facilities at special interest rates to those involved in the various settlement projects.

The CBOs generated by the Sou Sou Land approach have precipitated the advent of human settlements practitioners employed by the CBOs to provide the technical requirements for the settlements. This means that the common sense of the community can now be enhanced by access to new development technologies and the practitioner can be informed by the voices of the community.

I will now briefly describe some of the projects I am involved in, and which illustrate the benefit of a human settlements approach as a basis for engaging the population in the task of discussing the relevant strategies for transformation. A great deal of my work is centred on spontaneous settlements or squatter communities, which comprise some fifty thousand families by official figures. These settlements are, in effect, self-help achievements in terms of the provision by residents of appropriate infrastructure and basic shelter. In such a context, that process of self-help utilizes unconventional methods of housing construction and housing finance.

At the end of the day the squatter has a house with a value which cannot be translated into collateral in the formal market because he/she does not own the land on which his/her house sits. In the informal arrangements, the squatter has the option of selling the house (usually at a price that bears little relationship to the formal market). However, where there is a programme of squatter regularization, the squatter has the option of selling both the house and the claim to the land on which the house sits at a price that approaches the formal market value. The regularization of squatter communities, where the physical conditions allow for such regularization, has the effect of bringing existing housing stock into the formal arena. This is achieved by the involvement of the residents in the exercise of mobilizing the community, organizing and upgrading the land use and infrastructure, providing for communal needs, and purchasing their individual parcels. That constitutes a process of human settlement activity whereby the individual squatter is able to move from ownership of a dwelling with no formal collateral value to ownership of a property which allows for access to finance in the formal market. The squatter can therefore finance construction related to renovation and expansion of the existing shelter. Moreover, the squatter regularization process serves to develop community cohesion and foster community viability.

There are three such projects which serve to illustrate the possibilities. The first is Wallenvale — Sangre Grande in East Trinidad, an estate owned by the Trinidad Co-Operative Bank adjoining the rural town of Sangre Grande, occupied by some 400 residential squatter families and twenty-five agricultural small farmers. The project has been in progress for nearly three years utilizing the Sou Sou Land method of self-financing, with community-elected street representatives to interface with the technical team and the bank's officials. To date seventy percent of the community have made their financial commitment to the programme and infrastructure upgrading is in progress using construction crews from the community.

The second project is the La Seiva Village Co-Operative in Maracas Valley, an old settlement dating back to 1930 which has expanded significantly over the past fifteen years to a population of 350 families. They have formed a housing co-operative to undertake the activity of regularization in a context in which the ownership of the land incorporating the settlement cannot be verified. It is an unusual situation, requiring special legal methods to have the land ownership issue settled; this has been a major problem for the residents over the years. Utilizing the Sou Sou Land approach, the community was mobilized to form the co-operative, with an overall estimated investment in their housing stock of over twelve million T.T. dollars (three million U.S. dollars). There is therefore a legal entity that is undertaking the task of acquiring ownership.

The third undertaking is the Cachipe and St. Mary's Farmers' Co-Operative in Moruga, which is an integrated project involving agricultural and residential squatting on State lands. The farmers' co-operative is the spearhead of the endeavour, involving eighty residential squatters and over one hundred farmers; after a considerable length of time they have been able to negotiate special arrangements with the government to carry out the project. This particular venture, in a depressed area of the country, is significant because it focuses on village expansion in an environment of economic opportunity. Based on the Sou Sou Land approach, it is a genuine attempt at human settlement development.

In all these schemes the womenfolk play a decisive role, and there are always expressions of economic enterprise to create income for the financing of the exercise. Another project is in Bon Accord, in the small sister island of Tobago which has a population of just over fifty thousand. Unlike the other three projects, this one is linked to the formal sector although not an integral part of it, as it is being undertaken by the Mount Pleasant Credit Union, which has a membership of five thousand representing about thirty-five percent of the adult population of the island. Over the past few years tourism has become the main economic thrust in Tobago; obviously it is mainly large corporate entities and wealthy individuals who can afford to capitalize on opportunities in the marketplace. Just under three years ago I encouraged the Credit Union, with whom I had been involved on another project, to purchase a strategic property of 112 hectares (277 acres). At considerable sacrifice the purchase was made and the project is now under way, comprising residential, handicraft, small-scale industry, recreation, education and cultural activities. Adjoining is a homesteading area of small farms based on organic agricultural production, a nature reserve and a small naturalist tourist centre. All of this adds up to an integrated settlement, financed by the Credit Union Bank, in a quantum leap for the membership and management, which points to new directions for the overall credit union movement in the country.

The Sou Sou Land Possibility

The experience of the past ten years in which I have worked with the Sou Sou Land approach suggests that, within the different undertakings, the experience of survival provides important lessons for the process of political transformation and economic diversification. This is nothing new in the Caribbean, for in the colonial period the village, whether urban or rural, was always the nexus for the survival of the people. What is important about the Sou Sou Land initiative is that, in addition to the struggle for survival by communities themselves, the concept and approach is also struggling to survive against a regional political and technocratic elite who continue to hold to the conventional physical and economic strategies of development.

The fact is that we are in the throes of a major societal crisis in the Caribbean. The imperatives of survival are telling us that we must engage the realm of the unknown, we must take risks, not blindly but with courage and the knowledge provided by our experience of survival and achievement over the past five hundred years, and it is in that context that certain basic issues arise. Human settlement development needs to emerge as a prime strategy for rational development; housing and shelter cannot be dealt with in isolation or designated as a single sector. They need to be viewed as components of human settlement; therefore, in dealing with their provision, the focus is on the development of community viability. In so doing, the involvement of people in the overall exercise becomes fundamental, and the possibility arises for generating hope.

This is especially the case in economies where foreign exchange is in short supply or non-existent, where funds for capital expenditure are limited, where unemployment is high, growing, and concentrated among the young who constitute the bulk of the population and where, therefore, settlement and housing development are stimuli for job creation.

Human settlement suggests a holistic approach involving people, land, finance (usually in limited supply), infrastructure, and shelter. It is an approach that requires integration, co-operation, and co-ordination; therefore, the need for community is paramount. It is a process in which the psychology of the individuals involved could begin a transformation occasioned by possibilities not previously considered. Creative energies, long bottled up by the daily need to survive, then have the opportunity to be unleashed. This can be the beginning of a journey into that realm of the unknown where new enterprise and appropriate endeavour can be expressed. In the former colonial world, we have been so subjected to concepts of development whereby we are designated undeveloped or underdeveloped that there exists a major problem of perception at the level of the formal sector. So often "becoming developed" is seen as having to follow the process utilized by the industrialized world.

The formal education and training to which professionals, technocrats, and planners are subjected generate a frame of mind, a way of seeing, that usually cannot fathom the *modus operandi* of what has been called the informal sector, because that sector cannot be encapsulated into components of development. Survival carries with it the inherent realities of flexibility, spontaneity, and even unorganization (as opposed to disorganization), and there is a signal failure to appreciate these crucial aspects of the informal process. Incrementalism is the underlying philosophy: self-help is a major ingredient. As long as we persist with the conventional categories of dividing mankind into first, second, or third worlds, or into developed, developing, or underdeveloped societies, then we are doomed to the never ending socio-economic whirlpool of dependency and stagnation, unable to generate relevant and sustainable development. This is because all these categories deny the individuality of peoples or nations, and place psychological shackles on the former colonialized world by setting the form of development pursued by the industrialized world as the standard.

For us in the Caribbean, our historical experience suggests that human settlement as an operative strategy has the capacity to provide the basis of a sensitive vision of development. Such a strategy incorporates shelter and housing, but also embraces all aspects of the living environment, such as land development and land use, productive economic activity (especially food production), infrastructure development, and the provision of social services. The human settlement strategy, focused as it should be on the involvement of people, provides a possibility for an internal dynamic. In so doing, the imagination and commitment of the population can be engaged, thereby creating positive psychological and physical conditions for community viability, and for purpose and commitment in the task of sustainable transformation. Viewed from that larger perspective, the possibility of a vibrant internal developmental dynamic can emerge. Then the strategies of political and economic transformation can come from within and generate psychological conditions in which we can deal with the rest of the world from a position of confidence.

The Sou Sou Land possibility opens up a fresh vision of Caribbean human settlements opportunities. It can provide for *community cohesion*: the opposite tendency to the contemporary urban situations of ongoing fragmentation. The "village" once again begins to reassert itself, whether it be the urban village or the rural village, built around purpose, involvement, and self-help, thereby generating hope. It tends to *social needs,* to uplift the quality of life by addressing the provision of health and sanitation, education for living focusing on skills, recreation, and entertainment. It offers *economic opportunities,* in that the programmes ultimately must be self-financing; therefore the settler has to pay the appropriate price for the land including the land value which is usually subsidized, the cost of professional and technical services, and the cost of infrastructure upgrading. In such circumstances there is an incentive for the family to search for ways and means of generating income, and so economic opportunities can begin to be discovered from within the community itself.

Sou Sou Land also promotes *infrastructure upgrading,* by the incremental provision of access roads, drainage, water supply, and waste disposal. The communities become fundamentally involved in the upgrading exercise, linking as necessary and as possible with governmental agencies related to self-help and to village upgrading programmes. There is also *property ownership,* as in the final analysis the programmes afford the settler the opportunity of becoming a property owner with secure land tenure in an environment of an improving quality of life. This objective of ownership has the capacity to create a positive psychological condition in the potential recipient, and the future can then be approached with purpose and enterprise.

We also see *improvement to housing* as the incremental process of squatter regularization opens up new opportunities for the financial market. In the first instance the settler usually makes payments drawn from the informal financial sector to establish participation, but as the overall scenario unfolds, there is the need to access the formal market, which has to organize its conditionalities in the light of this entirely new market opportunity. The critical issue here is collateral, because the settler already has a building with a market value and the land purchase is always at a price below market; hence the property (house and land) value on the open market is substantially higher than what the settler requires to complete the purchase. The potential exists, therefore, for loan funding to allow for the land purchase and the improvement to the housing.

Another benefit is the *expansion of rental accommodation,* as spontaneous settlements are often in close proximity to urban centres and offer a unique possibility for the provision of much-needed rental accommodation. In the process of improving their housing, the settlers can provide additional space for rental purposes; this increases their income flows to meet their loan commitments while alleviating the need for government involvement in the provision of rental accommodation.

Small scale farming is also encouraged; identified as homesteading, this is an essential component of village revitalization. In a situation of economic crisis, it allows for the basics of shelter and food to be available and for surpluses to be marketed. In such circumstances, an entrepreneurial environment can be created for the growth and development of community co-operatives which can provide technical services and liaise with government and non-government agencies, as well as managing agro-industry and marketing. In addition, homesteading makes it possible for farming to be more organic, thereby reducing the excessive pollution caused by the modern day overuse of toxic chemicals in agricultural production.

The human settlements perspective, giving rise as it does to an environment of possibility, may very well be one of the catalysts that can unleash the creative energies of the Caribbean people. The perspective can then lay the basis for economic and social transformation, opening up new tendencies in the political process, and suggesting relevant developmental strategies aimed at achieving sustainable transformation. There is obviously no single answer, but the paradigm as outlined is a search for a human environment that can precipitate discovery. The Sou Sou Land approach has made its errors along the way, but because it is addressing the fundamentals of human settlement, it is a dynamic process. If sensitively pursued, it is an unfolding story that opens up new frontiers of human settlement development, embracing people, land, limited finance, and shelter as a basis for generating viable living environments in which communities have control over their affairs and can organize their future.

Chapter Five

Middle Class, Social Networks, and the "Neo-Liberal" Model: The Case of the Chilean School Teachers 1973-1988

Larissa Lomnitz and Ana Melnick[1]

W e have used anthropological methods to illustrate the effects of neo-liberal economic policies of structural adjustment on a sector of the middle class which until recently has been associated with the modernization process in Latin America: public sector employees. Our research aimed to cast light on the fate of this sector of the middle class, with special emphasis on survival strategies based on social networks. The hypothesis was that members of this social group have been among those most affected by the neo-liberal policies of structural adjustment, since not only did their standard of living deteriorate, but also their class identity was threatened.

Introduction

A group of primary and secondary school teachers in Chile were studied; they constitute the empirical reference, and their fate shows the effects of neo-liberalism more clearly than that of other groups for two reasons. First, as teachers, belonging to the middle class and employed in the public sector, they exercise one of the most representative functions of the welfare State. The teacher is the most conscious reproducer of the State ideology, and his/her role in society is the basis of his/her symbolic construction as a member of the middle class. Second, the Chilean case is particularly instructive since official policies centred on the destruction of the welfare State after the 1973 military coup d'état, and the implementation of a correspondingly neo-liberal policy following the elimination of such possible sources of resistance or negotiation as labour organizations and political parties.

Of course, neo-liberal economic policies are not only to be found in Chile; but Chile offers possibly the only example where the measures required by the model were implemented so rapidly and in such a way that the population had no real possibility of offering any resistance. For this reason, the Chilean case is particularly interesting with regard to what actually happened to the people who experienced this process. What has the social and human cost been?

The Role of the State in Latin America: A Brief Account of Recent History

In Latin America, the State assumed a very active role in the model of growth and partial modernization implemented during the years following the Second World War:

> (The State) expanded and assumed new and varied functions — job creation, capital accumulation, the creation of public enterprises, the provision of social services (health, education, housing, social security). It also supported private enterprise by means of subsidies, protection, and credit (Sunkel, 1988:9-10).

All this was done on the basis of the industrial development already achieved and the surplus generated by traditional exports. However, these were not enough to sustain growth and fulfil all the functions the State had assumed and that society was coming to demand more and more. "As the surplus ran out, the governments increasingly resorted to inflationary financing and later to taking out loans from foreign sources, the latter process reaching a feverish climax during the 1970s" (Sunkel, 1988:9-10). The spectacular level of foreign borrowing came to an abrupt end in 1982, when the foreign debt crisis curtailed the State's accumulation and redistribution role. At that point, not only was a source of credit lost but the need to send large remittances abroad emerged.

The policies of economic adjustment were the response to this situation. On the one hand, they included reducing imports and attempts to increase exports with the aim of generating income in foreign currency; these policies implied reducing income, consumption, investment, employment, and salaries. On the other hand, the public sector as a whole was cut back by dismissing public employees, keeping salaries down, reducing expenditure on social services, eliminating subsidies, decreasing public investment, and privatizing public enterprises while attempting to increase government revenues (Sunkel, 1988).

Chile was not in any way different from the rest of Latin America in this respect. Since the crisis of the 1930s, the State had been conceived as the body responsible for promoting development, as a fundamental factor in the process of saving and investment, and as the corrector of social inequalities: the welfare State. The growing demands made on this welfare State, and the will to satisfy them, went beyond its possibilities. They provoked the crisis of 1973 among other things.

Soon after assuming power, the military government began to implement a neo-liberal economic policy, among whose main postulates was the reduction of the role of the State in development and distribution. These functions were now assigned to the market. The concept of the "subsidiary state" was established, replacing that of the welfare State. According to this concept, the State should limit itself to defining the rules of the game and the financing of administration and defense, with some social expenditure aimed at compensating for the effects of the market on those living in extreme poverty.

The Effects of the New Model in Chile

The passive role of the State led to a reduction in public investment of more than 50 percent between 1974 and 1982. At the same time, the State's diminished role led to a decline of 31.5 percent in the number of public employees between 1975 and 1981; the numbers remained stable after 1982. As a result of the new policies, per capita public social expenditure fell 13 percent between 1970 and 1986. During the same period, the following reductions in public expenditure occurred: education 28.9 percent; health 37.8 percent; and housing 38.6 percent. Per capita consumption fell 17 percent from 1973 levels, and average purchasing power went down 15 percent compared with 1970. In 1980, 15 percent of the work force was unemployed, more than double the historical figure; by 1982, the figure was 30 percent.

Although there are no studies to show how much of this deterioration was assigned to the middle classes, there are some indicators that suggest that this group was one of the most affected. First, there was the massive dismissal of public employees. Then, the average education among the unemployed in the area of Gran

Santiago tended to rise, including levels considered to be characteristic of middle-class status, while the percentage of unemployed with low educational levels declined, as can be seen in Table 1.

Table 1: Educational Level of Unemployed in Gran Santiago (%)

	1970-73	1974-76	1977-80	1981-82
Illiterate	2.5	3.7	2.6	2.2
Primary	57.4	58.6	51.0	43.5
Secondary (9th to 12th grade)	29.6	27.8	35.4	42.5
Special Education	6.6	6.0	6.5	7.2
University	4.0	3.9	4.4	5.0

Source: Riveros, 1984.

An index constructed by PREALC-ILO in 1987 of the single salary scale of the Chilean public sector, referring to those institutions that use a single scale, measures the evolution of the gross salaries received by public employees, including basic pay and other benefits required by law. The results show that at best the salaries paid to public employees between 1974 and 1986 did not rise at all. In general, whichever indices are used, it is clear that real wages fell dramatically between 1973 and 1986. Salaries never reached 1970 levels, not even at the highest point in 1981; in 1986 they were still 15 percent below the 1970 level (Garcia and Uthoff, 1988).

An employment survey carried out in Gran Santiago showed that 30 percent of the active population worked in the informal sector (Schkolnik and Teitelboim, 1988). In this context, the survey's authors found the case of pre-school and primary teachers particularly surprising: at the time of the survey many were employed as servants, factory workers, or salespersons, while others had opted to set up small commercial enterprises. All these data would seem to indicate that a certain percentage of the so-called informal sector comprised members of the middle class who had lost jobs in the public and private sectors; the middle class had to adopt survival strategies in the face of the new economic reality. How do these survival strategies use social resources, or social capital?

The Use of Social Capital

This chapter puts special emphasis on the idea of social capital, following research on the use of social networks in complex societies (Lomnitz, 1971; Lomnitz, 1977; Lomnitz, 1982; Lomnitz, 1988; Lomnitz and Pérez Lizaur, 1987). A study of the Chilean middle class carried out in 1968 found a system of reciprocal exchange of bureaucratic favours. On the one hand, this marked a level of equality and belonging to the same class; on the other hand, it operated as a system of solidarity for the conservation of status. In other words, social relations represented an important economic resource (Lomnitz, 1971). In later studies on the informal sector and upper classes in Mexico, it was established that while reciprocal exchange social networks were represented within each group, the structure of the networks themselves (size and composition) and the type of favours exchanged (goods and services) varied according to the needs of each group or class. The evidence from this current study clearly suggests that, in the context of a dictatorship, the implementation of neo-liberal policies in Chile meant for many groups the destruction of the social networks found in 1968.

The typical member of the middle class studied in 1968 was either a public servant, a private employee, or a liberal professional. His/her access to the State apparatus depended to a large extent on his/her *network of political, social, and family connections.* These networks operated a system of reciprocity which consisted of the continuous exchange of favours; an ideology of friendship and social closeness motivated the exchange. Favours tended to be bureaucratic and usually consisted of preferential treatment in dealing with red tape and/or priority access to one the services offered by the State, ignoring the rights and priorities of third parties. This system consisted of a tacit dyadic contract, or a chain of such contracts between persons linked by mutual friends who acted as intermediaries. It is important to note that the initial favour was granted without any specific idea of how it would be returned; the required reciprocity was held in reserve for future use, should the need arise.

Types of Favours

The most frequent way of obtaining a job was by using contacts, particularly in the public sector. Looking for a job entailed mentally examining all of one's personal relationships, until one hit upon a friend with some link to the personnel department of the specific agency where employment was sought. In the same way, when a vacancy required candidates, a list of relatives and friends would be gone over until the appropriate person was found.

Bureaucratic favours represented the most frequent use of the system. Such favours included the expedition of certificates, licences, permits, passports, and numerous other types of documents. Obtaining these would normally entail a considerable waste of time and bothersome red tape procedures. These favours had varying importance and included import licences, customs facilities, exemptions from military service, and loans.

In the same way, the network was used to get places for children in prestigious public schools. Middle-class parents are very aware of the value of a good school for their children, since their school friends represent important and lasting social connections. The school is a source of friendship which extends the area of social interaction outside the family, and which may go beyond barriers of class, sex, and national origin. A friend who helps to get a child into the desired school would thus elicit considerable gratitude and would provide a highly valued favour. Similarly, social introductions to influential people and/or potentially useful contacts were also thought of as very special favours.

Rules of Reciprocity

The commitment to reciprocity acquired on receiving a favour tended to be stronger than any written or legal document. In spite of its importance, the reciprocity element was not mentioned openly. Also, a person who was never in a position to reciprocate stopped asking favours if he/she wanted to maintain a relationship of equality. Similarly, a person with experience in the use of this system would try to measure his/her requests, to avoid taking on too many obligations and "owing favours" to undesirable people. However, an established relationship would not last if the persons involved did not exchange favours from time to time. If the relationship was to be maintained, it had to be periodically activated, even if only with small favours. By asking for such favours, the friend was given to understand that he/she too could ask for a favour when he/she wished. Another rule of reciprocity was that gifts and payments of any sort were excluded; to offer either of these would be taken as a personal insult, since the exchange of favours is between equals.

To summarize, the use of the system required a lot of tact and a discerning eye. Friends whose resources and possibilities were inferior to one's own should not be asked for anything beyond their capacity. Furthermore, they should be given the chance to reciprocate, otherwise their pride would prevent them from asking for future favours. On the other hand, a powerful contact should not be bothered with trivial requests: the services sought should be in accordance with rank.

The *degree of familiarity* or social distance between the persons exchanging favours could lead to variations in the rules of reciprocity described above. Approaching a relative or an intimate friend was not the same as approaching someone who had been reached through other contacts (see Figure 1, scale of "confianza" — confidence). In all cases feelings of friendship and of common liking ("simpatía") were essential; in any case, the category of "friend" or of "relative" comprehended many degrees of social distance.

Who Were Members of the Network?

Essentially we are talking about personal relationships between individuals who considered each other to be on the same social level. As a result, according to one of our informants, contacts were sought among relatives, members of the same political party, friends, acquaintances of the same social level, friends of friends, work companions, members of a Masonic lodge, or, in general, people sharing the same intellectual aspirations, the same political ideology, or similar interests in life. This list included people who thought of themselves as equal in terms of the middle-class ideology of friendship.

Why was the use of this system limited to the middle class? Each class has different resources and needs. The middle class was in the position of offering and receiving favours of a bureaucratic type. A member of the working class could not reciprocate this type of

Figure 1: Scale of favours by degree of "confianza"

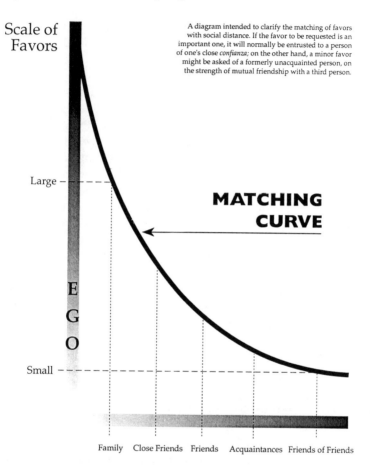

Scale of Favors

A diagram intended to clarify the matching of favors with social distance. If the favor to be requested is an important one, it will normally be entrusted to a person of one's close *confianza*; on the other hand, a minor favor might be asked of a formerly unacquainted person, on the strength of mutual friendship with a third person.

Large

MATCHING CURVE

E G O

Small

Family   Close Friends   Friends   Acquaintances   Friends of Friends

Scale of Confianza

favour, and a member of the upper class would not be prepared to undertake such an exchange, for recognizing equality with a member of the middle class would be considered degrading. As a result, when two individuals from different social classes are concerned, the exchange would take on a different form, because the elements of reciprocity within the context of sociability characterizing the system were lacking.

These situations can be described by simplified models of exchange. The ideal model, equality of access to the services run by the State, operates in effect in exchange for the payment that State employees receive for their work; as a result, the model does not include the existence of the exchange of favours, since theoretically they are unnecessary. A system of informal exchanges which coexists with others can also be represented. According to this model, the combination of friendship and services only occurs between equals. With other social classes the nature of the exchange changes, since the element of friendship and the symmetry of resources does not enter into the situation. With the lower classes, the "favour" is returned with loyalty and gratitude. With the upper classes, it is reciprocated through graft: the receipt of corrupt payments.

The system of the exchange of favours described above can be interpreted as an expression of solidarity aimed at the survival of a social group. A member of the middle class should seek the largest possible number of friends located strategically in the different levels of both the public and private sectors. It was, therefore, absolutely necessary to extend the prime network of relatives, incorporating friends, relatives of friends, and friends of friends. Thus, each member of the middle class is at the centre of an extensive network of personal relationships interconnected by ties of both family and friendship.

Values and Attitudes

Most of our informants revealed a certain ambivalence towards the use of their networks. They tended to be reticent when talking about the personal benefits they had obtained, especially when these were of a financial, political, or legal nature; they spoke far more freely of bureaucratic favours. However, the majority agreed that any informal exchange system should not exist in an ideal society. This ambivalent attitude appears to be based on the underlying conflict between the ideology of class solidarity and of responsibility for one's own kind, and the liberal ideology of free enterprise historically adhered to by the middle class. Although the universality of the rules and the ideology of free enterprise based on individual merit are recognized, in practice government officials found themselves sought out by relatives and friends, and felt they could not let them down. For this reason, friendship and group solidarity often took precedence over individual merit.

The struggle for existence was competitive, but it tended to be fought for in groups and not individually. Thus, the fact of losing did not affect the individual's self-image, as might be the case if success depended exclusively on personal merit. On the other hand, the ideology of friendship is egalitarian: "anyone can have friends." Having at our disposal this study on Chilean middle-class networks prior to the coup allowed us to appreciate quite well what happened to those networks in the wake of the changes brought about by the military coup. However, we first discuss what the implementation of neo-liberal economic policies meant for the group that was studied: the teachers.

The New Situation: The Privatization of Education

Before the 1973 coup, the teaching profession in Chile was well established. While teachers' salaries were never high, a succession of democratic governments committed to the idea of the welfare State had enabled teachers to consolidate their position in society. They had active professional organizations with important links with the government, their working conditions and job security were good, and there were sound teacher training courses at university level. After 1973, the rules of the game changed abruptly and completely. The teachers' union (Sindicato Unico de Trabajadores de la Educación) was abolished, as were other organizations representing the profession, and many teachers were dismissed from their posts for political reasons. The first concrete loss for the profession as a whole was job security. Then, in 1973, the new government decreed that the appointments of all public employees were "temporary." In other words, public employees could be dismissed whenever the government saw fit.

Towards the end of the decade, the idea of privatizing the State began to materialize. Decentralization of the administration of education, transferring it to the municipalities, was followed very soon afterwards by privatization: ad-hoc private corporations were constituted for this purpose. Teachers found themselves transformed into employees of these private corporations and subject to labour laws which deprived them of their job security and other rights and privileges that they had previously held.

The biographies of this study lead us to infer that, while the majority of teachers always began their careers with ups and downs, sooner or later each one did achieve job stability. Both older and (less surprisingly) younger teachers had complex occupational histories, which had been economically precarious and sometimes unstable as well. But the instability for older teachers was always temporary. Once they got themselves established in their posts, like all members of the middle class they lived with some economic difficulties, but they had job security. As well as suffering a deterioration in their working conditions, teachers also lost their access to the State apparatus. The institutional change meant that middle-class political parties lost control of public administration; these parties were the representatives of the type of State that had sustained the growth of the middle class. Public administration became controlled instead by another sector of the same class, the armed forces, which was involved in other social networks, traditionally separate from the political and civilian networks.

The deterioration of the teachers' conditions of work necessarily affected the quality of education. While few data are available on this point, there are some indications that what is a reasonable inference is also a fact. Two systems of evaluation were implemented during the 1980s. The first was designed to measure pupil performance (Program for Evaluating Educational Results — Programa de Evaluación del Rendimiento); it was discontinued in 1983 and the results were never published. The second, known as the System for Measuring the Quality of Education (Sistema de Mediación de la Calidad de la Educación) published anything but encouraging results in 1989. The study revealed that in none of the subjects evaluated were more than 57 percent of the proposed objectives achieved. It also compared the results obtained in private fee-paying schools and the municipal schools; pupil performance in the latter was clearly worse than in the former (*La Epoca*, 1989).

The Networks

Networks have in the past played an important role in the survival of the middle class, both before and after the coup. What the 1989 study revealed is that important changes took place in the structure and use of the network during the military government; this will be discussed later. In our 1989 study we found that the occupational histories of all our informants, their living conditions, and how they dealt with everyday expenses and with emergencies, fully confirmed the use of networks.

For example, a 32-year-old married biology teacher said: "I have worked in six schools, in one of them permanently and in the others for periods of time. For one of the jobs I answered an advertisement in the newspaper, but I got all the others through personal contacts." Two of our informants got their first teaching jobs through their mother who was a teacher herself. Another got her first job thanks to a contact made for her by her sister, also a teacher. Access to employment also frequently involved teachers from whom the informants had received their training in the past, fellow students, colleagues or ex-colleagues, or new acquaintances in the field of education, all of whom represent part of the social network of the informants. Regarding the housing problem, even in the description of family life in the more distant past there are instances in which the informants have lived in the house of relatives, or "allegado". Later, this solution became almost universal.

The constant presence of these contacts reveals the existence of what was described above as a system of the "reciprocal exchange of favours" (or social networks). The model presented, containing a horizontal axis (representing the contacts) and a vertical one (representing the types of favours), covers a wide range of possibilities. Thus, analysis of our interview material reveals the nature of the changes in the model found in Figure 1, operating in two ways. First, on the horizontal axis the network has become very limited; in fact it has been reduced to the nuclear family and friends (for certain kinds of favours). Acquaintances are only mentioned with respect to getting a job or rented accommodation. Second, on the vertical axis the change obviously refers to the type of favours. Whereas previously favours were usually of a bureaucratic sort, today they are largely concerned with physical survival.

In the first case, it is interesting to note that politics do not appear in the networks used; especially since we are dealing with the teaching profession. Teachers as a group have always been associated with some political position or grouping, either formally or informally; this is a product of their belonging to the public sector. After the military coup in 1973, the political parties lost all control of public administration, which explains the absence of any mention of this element in the use of networks by our informants. A new factor appeared that might be called the "military network." The armed forces in Chile have always functioned as an enclave, for reasons which we do not need to analyze here. Various studies have shown that they have their own social networks, and that traditionally this has not encouraged contact with civilians. Only two of our informants referred to use of the military network; in both cases, the contact was a very close relative.

In other words, a source of social capital has disappeared, that of the political parties, without really being replaced by another, since the respective civilian and military social networks are so separate. It used to be relatively easy to ask a political contact for a favour or to find someone with access to the required person or agency. At the same time, the military have employed a discourse which suggests that they are not willing to grant favours, that they are "incorruptible." Finally, even with the right contacts, the fact of an authoritarian military government means that both those who ask the favour and those who grant the favour act in fear. Reticence is also explained by the fact that an element of trust, of intimacy ("confianza"), enters into the exchange of favours. In order to request a favour, one has to be sufficiently familiar with the person one is going to ask or with the potential source of the favour. Before asking for the favour, an automatic evaluation is made of the degree of "confianza" one has with the person who is in the position to help. Hence, the nuclear family becomes the most important source of help. In the words of a 24-year-old single female elementary teacher: "In my experience at least, nobody escapes the help of his or her parents." All this is not to say that such a network does not exist; it exists for some, as can be seen in the cases we have summarized. But, since its use is far more limited, the impossibility of using political contacts appears as a net loss for the immense majority of the members of the middle class we have studied.

In the second case, the change on the vertical axis of our network model, this can be observed in the continuous mention of favours being received (or granted) connected with the physical survival of the informants. One of the male teachers, for instance, explains how he has been able to survive: "During quite a long period of time my father-in-law used to send us and his son in the north a box of provisions: sugar, flour, oil; the most expensive things I would say." Another female teacher plans to put her son into a school, and says "I will spend at least ten thousand dollars, and then he can go have lunch with my mother. My mother will help us once again." Help with food also appears in this response from a 40-year-old philosophy teacher, mother of three children and separated from her husband:

> On one of the occasions that I was out of work I was giving a course in continuing education for teachers, and my colleagues decided to give me a present. I realized something was going on because they asked me

> to leave the room, because they were going to discuss something that I could not listen to. They decided, by majority vote, to give me a food basket. I think it was a majority decision since some of them seemed very embarrassed when the food basket arrived . . . I was very touched by the fact that everything came from their own homes. However, I did notice that some of them were very perturbed; they did not know whether I would be offended. Some of them felt it was not really the right thing to do. In fact, for me it was one of the most sensitive gifts I have ever received; that is, it was a projection of the feeling of solidarity.

The particular personality of this woman allowed her to receive this gift without feeling ashamed, but the "perturbation" that she perceived in her colleagues undoubtedly reflects a far more generalized sentiment among the middle class when the need for material help in something as basic as food is made manifest.

Our informants also talked about the help they received in relation to the care of their children. This help usually came from the mother of one of them or from a sister or a sister-in-law. Regarding this question, the family network appeared as almost the only possible source of assistance or, at least, the only one our particular subjects sought to use. Only in one case did the informant mention a neighbour who sporadically looked after the children for her, and this favour was reciprocated by the informant. Health care, particularly in the case of children, is another type of favour required of the network.

Where money is concerned, most of the demands are channelled through the family, especially if there is an emergency requiring large sums. To "get to the end of the month," a colleague or a friend can be asked to help. The majority rejected the idea of going to a bank, since interest rates are high and they were afraid of not being able to pay back on time. Here there is a strong element of reciprocity, one of the features of the use of the networks. The impossibility of reciprocity inhibits any request, since the situation would no longer be one of the exchange of favours between equals, which is what characterizes the use of networks in the middle class. Particularly revealing was the recurrent reference to the housing problem. Many teachers were forced to move to the house of close relatives, mostly parents (sometimes also friends). This was due to the combination of low salaries and the high cost of rentals.

At any rate, the type of favours we have summarized here are very different from those described for the middle-class networks before the coup. The favours described by our informants in this study are closer to the type that appeared in a study of the marginal poor in Mexico (Lomnitz, 1977). These two changes in the coordinates of the model reveal a serious decline in the status of teachers, a sector of the middle class that was forcibly privatized by the new economic model, in the sense that it was thrown onto the labour market with a considerable loss of privileges.

Conclusions

The implementation of the neo-liberal model, applied to Chile under the political conditions deriving from the military government, affected three basic aspects of teachers' lives: their working conditions, their social resources, and the symbolic representation of their role in society. Regarding the first point, teachers moved from the public sector to the private sector, in the sense that they became subject to the latter's labour laws at a time furthermore when such legislation was becoming more stringent. This placed the teachers in a position where their previous job security virtually disappeared. They were suddenly obliged to negotiate their work contracts as individuals, following market laws. The dismissal of large numbers of teachers meant that a veritable "reserve army" was created. Competition for jobs in the field of education was fierce, which pushed salaries down, forcing the teachers to work double and sometimes triple time, without the opportunity for any sort of protest since the channels for the defence of the profession had been restricted. There was no more collective bargaining aimed at establishing salary scales and levels. Apart from this, the growth of private education was encouraged through subsidized private schools, which meant "education as a business." In this sense, the "administrators" of education, be they of municipal or private subsidized schools, benefitted from the extension of the working day and the number of pupils in each grade. For the teachers this meant that it became impossible to prepare their classes properly or to improve, or at least maintain, the quality of their teaching. In this respect it is important to point out that continuing education courses for teachers had to be paid for by the teacher, and few could afford them.

In addition to the above, the reduction of public expenditures basically affected the middle class, the class to which the teachers belonged, since social spending was focused on the groups in the most extreme poverty. The opportunities for health care, housing, and education for the middle classes and their children were all reduced. Thus, the working conditions of the teachers suffered as a result of a lack of job stability, the possibility of arbitrary transfer from one school to another, the deterioration of salaries, the loss of seniority and of raises every three years, the increases in the number of class hours and in the number of children in the classroom, and finally, the absence of any defence by a professional association or union.

Regarding social resources and their use, the loss of stability meant that compared with the past, independently of how precarious their economic situation had previously been, it became necessary to turn to very close and trusted family members for favours directly related to physical survival. This is more akin to the survival networks found among the urban poor in Mexico, who faced chronic job insecurity and whose incomes derived from a system of social security based on their family and neighbourhood networks (Lomnitz, 1977). These exchange networks were necessarily small, given the limited resources of the members, and for the same reason, the favours were used to deal with urgent and constant needs: small loans, food, accommodation, child care, and information about jobs. We found the same type of favours in this study, and in the same type of network of family and close friends. The teachers found this situation disturbing, as our interviews showed. They were somewhat unwilling to talk about having to resort to this type of help and about the favours received, in view of their quality.

Previously, during the 1970s, while people also turned to family and friends in emergencies, the networks were wider; this social class also had professional associations and unions to express their demands, they had access to political parties, and through these to public administration as well. Whether the persons were public officials, or friends of fellow members of the same political party, the fact is that they possessed resources that could be exchanged and could thus keep their exchange network active. At the same time, they could conserve their middle-class status by being able to exhibit its symbols, such as bureaucratic employment, better housing, and higher education, etc. None of the teachers we interviewed mentioned this type of contact or favour. However, we assume that this system of exchange still operated, but that it was another segment of the middle class that had access to it.

In the past, the use of these networks was considered to be normal; it was perceived as the fruit of a positive ideology of altruism and solidarity. People spoke with pride of the favours that had been granted, associating them with positive qualities expressing friendship and generosity. The system was a reflection of class solidarity.

This type of network was totally absent in our study of the teachers. With respect to the symbolic representation of their role, the effect of the economic model on the teachers is seen with all its force with the transfer of the schools to the municipalities and the dependence of the teacher on the mayor, a sort of "boss" figure. The weakness of the teachers' position as salaried workers is manifested in this relationship. They have to negotiate with this person and obey his/her instructions, even when they are inadequate from the educational point of view; they realize that they cannot show their discontent as they may well lose their jobs. In addition to, and even as a consequence of, a deterioration in working conditions, there is the loss of status of "teacher": when the ruling value is one expressing the sentiment that "so much you earn, so much you are worth," the feeling that the teacher's role is not much appreciated by society is reinforced. In the triangle formed by the administrator, the educator, and the pupil, the weakest side is the educator. Administrators run the show as they please, and their decisions cannot be appealed. Pupils provide the subsidy that the State pays on their behalf. The teacher, on the other hand, means expenditure and is expendable.

How all this affects the teachers can be understood by remembering that they had always thought of themselves as part of a group of civil servants responsible for the transmission of collective values. The new system questions this traditional role by removing teachers from this group, turning them into isolated individuals in the marketplace, and by atomizing the educational system, varying the content and quality of courses as a function of the resources available in each concrete instance. Previously, the latter was unified by ministerial guidelines and the professional organizations had opportunities to participate in the formulation of educational policies, from which the teachers have now been excluded. The final conclusion is that, in the three aspects analyzed — living and working conditions, social resources and symbolic representation of their role — the balance for the teachers is definitely negative.

Note

1. The authors would like to thank Jeanne Grant for translating this chapter from Spanish. A more extensive treatment of the research presented in this chapter can be found in Lomnitz and Melnick (1991).

References

Garcia, Alvaro, and Andras Uthoff, (1988), "Aspectos Distributivos de la Política Económica de Chile: La Necesidad de Pagar la Deuda Social," Santiago de Chile, PREALC.

La Epoca, (1989), May 17.

Lomnitz, Larissa, (1971), "Reciprocity of Favours in the Chilean Middle Class," in *Studies in Economic Anthropology*, edited by G. Dalton (Washington, D.C.: American Anthropological Association, Monograph Series 7).

Lomnitz, Larissa, (1977), *Networks and Marginality* (San Francisco: San Francisco Academic Press).

Lomnitz, Larissa, (1982), "Horizontal and Vertical Relations and the Social Structure of Urban Mexico," *Latin American Research Review*.

Lomnitz, Larissa, (1988), "Informal Exchange Networks in Formal Systems: A Theoretical Model with Special Emphasis on the Soviet Union's Informal Economy," *American Anthropologist*, 90, 1, pp.42-55.

Lomnitz, Larissa, and M. Pérez Lizaur, (1987), *A Mexican Elite Family 1820-1980* (Princeton: Princeton University Press).

Lomnitz, Larissa, and Ana Melnick, (1991), *Chile's Middle Class: Struggle for Survival in the Face of Neoliberalism* (Boulder, Col.: Lynne Rienner).

Riveros, Luis Alberto, (1984), "Distribución del Ingreso, Empleo y Política Social en Chile," Santiago de Chile, CEP, Working Paper 25.

Schkolnik, Mariana, and Berta Teitelboim, (1988), "Encuesta de Empleo en el Gran Santiago: Empleo Informal, Desempleo y Pobreza," Santiago de Chile, PET, Working Paper 6.

Sunkel, Osvaldo, (1988), "Perspectivas Democráticas y Crisis de Desarrollo," Santiago de Chile, mimeo.

Chapter Six

Beyond the Market in a Market Economy: The Kibbutz Experience

Menachem Rosner

The collapse of the communist political and economic system and the economic and social crisis in many western countries has created a new interest in experiences that go beyond the market and the State. The development of the kibbutz communities and movements in the State of Israel, especially in the pre-State period, present a unique experience of both a high degree of internal autonomy and of compartmentalization between de-commodified internal relations and active participation in the Israel market economy. The first kibbutz was created in 1910 and 125,000 adults and children now live in 260 communities, organized in two major federations and a smaller religious federation.

Kibbutz ownership is both communal and social; communal ownership is comprehensive, including both the means of production and the means needed for consumption, education, cultural activities, etc. The "communal household" is responsible for the direct satisfaction of many needs and there is only a small personal monetary allocation. The basic principle is: "From each according to his abilities, to each according to his needs." Ownership is indivisible among the members, and the members get limited ownership rights by belonging to the community and through their work and participation and not through personal capital investment.

The ownership rights of the individual community are limited by the principles of *social ownership*. According to these principles, the bundle of ownership rights is divided between an individual kibbutz community that has all the "usufruct" rights and the federations of kibbutz communities. Social ownership is an expression of the commitment to the larger ideological goals, both national and social, of the kibbutz federations and of the Israeli labour movement, and is intended to counter "group egotism" and a narrow economic orientation. Participatory democracy in the kibbutz is both an ideological goal in itself and an important means of promoting members' commitment to the kibbutz community and its different work organizations. Since communal ownership excludes direct material incentives, such a commitment is a central condition for ensuring collective economic motivation.[1]

The social structure is an outcome of the different stages in the creation and the development of a kibbutz. For most kibbutzim, the creation of the community was the result of a long educational process, which started in the socialist-Zionist youth movements in the Diaspora and later in the cities of Israel. This process continued through periods of training for collective life at special farms in the Diaspora, in older kibbutz communities, and even, in a certain framework, in the Israeli army. Consequently, most members joined the kibbutz not as individuals and couples, but as small cohesive groups. Within the kibbutz communities, each with an average of about 350 adult members, there is therefore a series of cohesive sub-groups created by a common past in youth movements, member-ships of the same age group among the kibbutz-born, membership of work groups, etc. These have an important function in exercising informal social control and in strengthening the commitment to the kibbutz.

The important role of different small social groups in creating commitment to the kibbutz community is only one aspect of the social structure of the kibbutz. The membership in different groups overlaps, creating a rather dense social network mitigating conflicts and enforcing solidarities. In addition to this group structure, the institutional and role patterns of the kibbutz social structure are also rather unique. The institutional structure is comprehensive, since most of the members work in the community and have the oppor-tunity to satisfy most of their material, cultural, and social needs in its framework.

The role structure is also multi-functional and members exercise in the same community framework their different social roles as workers, family members, office-holders, etc. Initially, a relatively low level of role differentiation prevailed both in work organiza-tions and in other institutional frameworks. Currently, processes of professionalization are creating a more horizontal differentiation, while vertical hierarchical differentiation is still limited due to rota-tion rules and overall egalitarian and democratic values. Identifica-tion with kibbutz ideology plays an important role both in the decision to join a kibbutz and in the commitment to the kibbutz community.

The Economic Crisis and the New Kibbutz Concept

Although the socio-economic and institutional structures of the kibbutz communities passed through many changes during the 80
years of their development, the similarity to the "commune" ideal
type was preserved. It is only recently that an alternative conception
of a New Kibbutz has been suggested (Harel, 1988). The supporters
of this new concept consider it the only way to adapt the kibbutz to
the conditions of a post-industrial society and to attract new members from the outside. In the terms of this alternative theoretical
framework, it seems that its implementation might move the kibbutz communities away from the "commune ideal type" and
towards the market type, by introducing market mechanisms inside
the kibbutz community.

From the beginning, the kibbutz economic units (agricultural
branches and factories) have sold products in the framework of the
Israeli market system, and most goods and some services used in the
kibbutz community were on the market. But there was a clear dividing line between the market mechanism regulating transactions
with the outside and the internal communal mechanisms. During a
long period, starting in the 1920s, a complex institutional framework
was built as a buffer mechanism between the kibbutz and moshav
communal and co-operative communities and the outside market.
Nationwide secondary co-operatives were created both for marketing the agricultural products of these communities and for purchasing most of the supplies needed. In addition, the nationwide kibbutz
federations developed specific institutions to provide different services and economic functions needed by the communities, such as
construction, insurance, marketing and export of industrial
products, etc. Since the 1960s, a large network of regional
enterprises were created, owned co-operatively by the communities
of a specific region.

The main function of the regional enterprises was the process-
ing of agricultural products, to minimize the number of intermediary stages between the producer and the consumer usually
performed by the market. The main aim of these co-operative buffer
institutions, which were a part of the overall Israeli labour economy,
was to minimize the exploitation of the producer by the market. But
they also created sociological boundaries between the normative
system of the market and the internal norms of the kibbutz. The
New Kibbutz Concept is an attempt to weaken these boundaries by

introducing market mechanisms in different spheres of the kibbutz social system.

The starting point for the diffusion of the New Kibbutz concept was the severe economic crisis that developed in 1985, whose outcomes are still felt. The main expression of the crisis was the formation of a large debt, accompanied by high interest and capital payments, which weighed heavily on ongoing economic activities. The crisis came after 15 years of unprecedented growth and expansion of the kibbutz economy, based on the higher productivity of kibbutz agriculture and industry. The kibbutz communities, whose members are only three percent of the Israeli population, produced forty percent of the agricultural and nine percent of the industrial output.

In 1990, a financial aid package for the indebted kibbutz communities began to be implemented, based on an agreement between the government, two major credit banks, and the kibbutz federations. The package included rescheduling of long-term debt, partial debt remission, and relatively low interest rates. As a result of this aid, which is only in its first stage, and of other internal measures, the economic situation of a large part of the communities is improving. Some communities, including almost all those belonging to the small religious federation, have not been hurt by the crisis; of the others, a minority is still in a critical situation.

From "Commune" Towards "Market" and Hierarchy

The basic assumption of the New Kibbutz conception is that the crisis can be overcome only by allowing market forces and profit considerations to have priority over social and value-related considerations, and through promotion of greater individual autonomy in all aspects of kibbutz life, especially by the increase of consumer freedom in the area of consumption and need satisfaction.

The suggestions for giving higher priority to profit considerations were presented in a more detailed form by outside economic advisors, under the general heading of *separation between business and community*. The basic idea is that overall management of the economic activities of the kibbutz should be based on market principles, while the implementation of the egalitarian and democratic principles of the kibbutz should be confined to the community. This model is presented as an alternative to the present kibbutz conception, according to which the economic activity is an integral part of the kibbutz community.

The explicit goal of the "separation" is to "liberate" the economic units from the limitations and principles of the kibbutz. To achieve this "liberation" the suggestion is to open the option for the economic units to get their labour and capital from the general market and not mainly from inside the community. This holds first of all for labour, and the suggestion is to open the option of employing hired workers. The traditional opposition to the employment of outside hired workers was based both on ideological arguments, such as the avoidance of exploitation, and on the negative experience of kibbutz factories employing large numbers of such workers. In the last twenty years there was a permanent decrease in the percentage of hired workers, due also to the introduction of advanced technology (Leviatan, 1980; Rosner, 1988). According to the suggested separation, the management of economic units should not only have the option to hire workers from the outside but also to hire and fire kibbutz members. Up to now, the process of work place choice by kibbutz members, and work allocation to them, went through a long procedure of negotiations with the aim of satisfying both personal aspirations and community needs. Now it is suggested that the manager of every economic unit should decide if he wants to employ a certain person or not. If a member cannot find suitable employment inside the kibbutz, he should seek it on the outside labour market on condition that his income, which will go to the kibbutz treasury, will not be below the kibbutz standard of income.

It is suggested that the market principle should also hold for the supply of capital. Up to now, it has been mostly the kibbutz treasurer and not the economic unit that was responsible for the mobilization of capital from the outside. Now it is suggested that the larger units, especially larger factories, should become autonomous financial entities or "profit centres," with the right to decide which parts of their income and profits to invest and which to transfer to the kibbutz community. The suggestion is to separate two parts of the income transferred from the economic unit to the kibbutz: salaries, according to the number of members working in the factory, and dividends.

In the kibbutz accounting system up to now, labour costs for kibbutz members working in the different productive branches were calculated on the basis of average consumption expenses. Differences in skill, managerial responsibilities, etc. were not taken into account. The New Kibbutz conception suggests a separation between a calculation of the salaries in the economic units and the income distribution by the kibbutz community. According to this suggestion, the salaries should be calculated as shadow wages on the basis of the general labour market and should therefore be unequal. But this differentiation should remain secret and should have no impact on the distribution inside the community. When the economic situation of the different units enables payment of dividends to the community, such dividends, or a part of them, would be added to these salaries.

Finally, the New Kibbutz concept also suggests the possibility of investment of private capital in kibbutz economic units, especially factories, as an expression of financial autonomy. This idea is related to the difficulties, because of the debts of the past, in obtaining equity capital or bank loans for investment.

The New Kibbutz concept inevitably implies changes in *managerial authority*, i.e., in the internal organizational structure of the kibbutz economic unit. The general direction is a transition from the self-management principle of organization, that can be seen as a component of the "commune" ideal type, towards a "hierarchical" ideal type. A large body of research, partly based on international comparisons, has been devoted in recent years to the differences between the organization of kibbutz industry and economy, and conventional hierarchical patterns (Tannenbaum et al., 1974; Bartolke et al., 1985; Leviatan and Rosner, 1980).

The basic assumption of the kibbutz self-management concept is the right of the kibbutz member to participate in all areas of kibbutz life, including decision making and management. While in practice there have been deviations from this normative principle, as analyzed in the studies noted, there was a consensus about the need to implement them. The New Kibbutz concept presents a normative alternative. The most basic feature of this alternative is that members' status in the economic units be based, not on their membership in the community, but on two specific social roles. As members of the community, they have only ownership rights, similar to those of shareholders in a company.

Usually, the main expression of shareholders' rights is the election of the board of directors by a meeting of the shareholders once a year; a similar procedure is suggested by the New Kibbutz proponents. This is the alternative to the actual involvement of the kibbutz general assembly, which at present in most kibbutzim convenes once a week or once every two weeks. At present, the kibbutz assembly elects the general manager of the factory, approves the production and investment plans, and is the ultimate authority on all matters; it is specifically involved in issues concerning the supply of labour, such as employment of hired workers, permanent and temporary employment of members, professional training, etc. The "separation" concept suggests that the board of directors and plant management will have the authority to decide on most of those issues. For example, the plant manager would be appointed by the board.

The new concept replaces the *self-management* principle, based on both political and motivational participation. Instead, *participatory management* is based on motivational participation only, without the formal authority of the workers' assembly. It also suggests applying the rotation principle only for unsuccessful managers, and removing limitations on the term of office for others. In general, these suggestions point to a transition to the "hierarchy" ideal type as conceived by Williamson (1991) and others, originally found in the Weberian concept of the ideal type of bureaucracy.

While these components of the New Kibbutz concept deal mostly with the economic and occupational structure, another important part of this conception deals with changes in the distribution of income in the kibbutz community. The suggested basic change is a transition from distribution according to need, to distribution of an *equal salary*. Related transitions to achieve consumer freedom are from direct distribution of goods and services to distribution of money, and from communal responsibility for need-satisfaction to individual responsibility and autonomy.

Following the economic crisis, there were demands to limit or even abolish the free goods system, because it created opportunities for "free riding." An example of the free goods system is the cafeteria system in the dining room, where one is free to choose among different types of food without limitations on quantity. Another argument for replacing the free goods system with the distribution of money was that, as a response to the lower standard of living, it was important to increase personal preferences in how to spend a shrinking budget. The main arguments against these changes were that they will create commodification inside the kibbutz, and that monetary and calculative relations between the members and the community will replace relations based on identification and trust. Other arguments were that, in spite of the equal distribution of the monetary salary, it would lead to inequality by legitimizing outside sources of money, such as gifts and inheritances from relatives, etc.

In the framework of the New Kibbutz conception, two versions of an extension of the money distribution system were suggested. The first was for an inclusion of additional areas in the personal monetary budget, but without touching basic kibbutz institutions such as the communal dining room, the educational structure, and the health services. The second was a more extreme version in which the kibbutz institutions and services lost their monopoly status, and the kibbutz member could choose between the kibbutz institutions and the outside market. For example, kibbutz members would have to pay for their meals in the dining room; for this purpose they will receive an additional amount of money, but they will be free to decide how to use it. While the first, limited, version of the enlarged personal budget would reach 40 percent to 45 percent of per capita consumption expenditures, the second, extended, version would include the majority of per capita consumption expenditures and would express the transition to the "equal salary" system.

In short, in terms of the market-hierarchies-communes paradigm, the New Kibbutz concept favours a transition from the "commune" towards the "market" in the areas of economic activity and consumption and towards "hierarchies" in the areas of organization.

As stated above, the advocates of the New Kibbutz concept presented it as a way to adapt the kibbutz to the conditions of a post-industrial society and to attract new members, but the main rationale for the specific proposals was that they will enhance economic efficiency and personal autonomy by opening the kibbutz towards the market and by strengthening hierarchical control. Opening towards the labour market, by employing non-members inside the kibbutz and giving members the opportunity to work outside, should make the allocation of labour more efficient. The creation of a board of directors should improve the professional quality of managerial decisions, so that it will be possible to avoid poor investment decisions, etc., and could facilitate joint ventures with private capital. In the sections that follow we will explore two related questions: Will the transition to the market and hierarchy steering mechanisms lead to higher economic efficiency? Is this transition an expression of a more basic social change towards decommunalization?

Inconsistencies and Efficiency

According to the assumption on which the New Kibbutz is based, a transition towards market and hierarchy should enhance the efficiency of the kibbutz community and its organizations. But the New Kibbutz concept is only a partial transition; there is no wage system, there are no material incentives for workers, and the distribution is based on equal sums of money. This is remote from the market principle of a differentiated wage system based on the marginal productivity of labour. In a similar way, kibbutz members' ownership rights are very different from those of shareholders. They do not have the option of *exit,* and they cannot sell their shares, since members do not buy shares when entering the kibbutz. As mentioned, ownership in the kibbutz is communal and social, and not individual. But it is not only the partiality of the transition that creates inconsistencies in the New Kibbutz model. A major inconsistency exists between the system of *distribution,* based largely on an equal monetary salary (the extended comprehensive consumption budget), and the unequal, differential *contribution* by work, office holder, etc. The New Kibbutz concept maintains the separation between contribution and distribution of rewards, on which the principle "from each according to his ability, to each according to his need" is based. But instead of a particularistic distribution according to needs, which matches the commune ideal type, equal monetary distribution is suggested.

The suggested changes in the status of kibbutz members in the economic organizations, so that they might have to compete with workers from outside, coupled with the strengthening of hierarchical authority, could have a negative impact on members motivations and commitment. According to a number of studies (Tannenbaum et al, 1974; Leviatan and Rosner, 1980), motivation is based mainly on opportunities for self-realization in work, social cohesion, and participation in decision-making; research comparing kibbutz members and hired workers in kibbutz plants presented evidence of the higher commitment and motivation of kibbutz members (Rosner and Tannenbaum, 1987a).

On the other hand, the initiators of the New Kibbutz concept did not propose the introduction of conventional material incentives. They suggested only a symbolic differentiation of salaries for accounting purposes. It does not seem accidental, therefore, that as a way of overcoming some of the above-mentioned inconsistencies, a limited connection between contribution and material rewards was suggested by different economic advisors and was tried in some kib-butz communities. National conventions of the two major federa-tions representing kibbutz communities resolved, by an overwhelming majority, that even partial payment for work is not compatible with kibbutz life and with membership in the kibbutz movement.

More general problematic effects of the implementation of the New Kibbutz concepts are related to the suggested separation between kibbutz economic organizations and the community. The intrusion of the market and hierarchy principles in kibbutz economic organizations might create a basic incongruity between two different and opposed types of social relations and norms of behaviour. While social relations in the community are direct and interpersonal between equals, stressing social cohesion and approval by peers, and based on trust and solidarity, the intrusion of both market and hierarchical principles might lead to formalization and impersonality. Hierarchical control and sanctions and a calcula-tive approach might lead to suspicion and conflicts. Recent studies have shown that even before the suggested separation, employment of larger numbers of hired workers in kibbutz plants led to the intro-duction of hierarchical and bureaucratic forms and norms of organ-ization. In many cases this transition resulted in discrepancies between the expectations of kibbutz members working in these plants, based on community norms and social relations, and the new hierarchical structure and relations (Palgi and Rosner 1980).[2] To con-clude this analysis, it seems questionable whether the imposition of market and hierarchical governance mechanisms will enhance ef-ficiency or reduce transaction costs.

A Step Towards Decommunalization?

Turning to the second question, we must ask whether the develop-ment of the New Kibbutz concept is part of a more general process of decommunalization of the kibbutz and of loss of its identity. Such a process happened in many communal societies in the past (Kanter, 1972; Oved, 1988). It would also be similar to the process of "co-operative degeneration" of many producer co-operatives in the dis-tant past, and also recently (Meister, 1974). On the other hand, there are also disagreements about the possibility of defining the com-munal identity of the kibbutz. Cohen (1976) stated the difficulty of answering the question of whether the kibbutz will preserve its essential characteristics, since kibbutz values are secular, not transcendental, as in many religious communal movements.

In spite of this doubt, it seems that the following theoretical definition of this essential identity is accepted by most kibbutz scholars and leadership: "The allocation of resources to satisfy the differential needs and goals of individuals is unconditional and not dependent on the mobilization of resources from each of them" (Ben-David, 1973). The agreement with this definition seems also to be the reason for the strong opposition of the kibbutz federation, noted above, to any connection between work and material rewards. Even partial payment for work or office holding is a clear deviation from this definition. Opinions are more divided about other components of the New Kibbutz concept. Some are seen as compatible with the kibbutz identity, while others are perceived as endangering it, since they might lead to a connection between contribution and material rewards.

The Implementation of Changes

The degree of implementation in the different kibbutz communities of the changes suggested by the New Kibbutz concept can perhaps serve as a criterion to differentiate between changes compatible with kibbutz identity and changes deviating from it. We can assume a larger diffusion of changes compatible with this identity, and a limited option of those deviating from it.

In Table 1, the results of two recent surveys are presented, one based on reports by informants from 135 communities dealing with changes introduced in 1990, the other based on 208 communities (77 percent of all kibbutz communities) representing the situation in 1991. The questionnaire referred to thirty specific change proposals. Figure 3 presents a comparison between the percentage of kibbutz communities that have already implemented a specific change proposal or at least have decided on it. The data were collected almost five years after the beginning of the kibbutz economic crisis, and more than three years after the public presentation of the New Kibbutz concept. Many kibbutz communities have created special change committees, and several have gone through the change process with the help of outside economic and organizational advisors.

We will present data on eleven changes that have been discussed above. Some of the changes are related to consumption (C), and others to separation between economy and community (S). The respondents provided information about the degree of implementation of each proposal.

Table 1: Implementation of Change by Kibbutz Communities

	Area	1990	1991
Extension of individual monetary budget	C	54	59
Inclusion of home electricity budget in individual monetary budget	C	26	44
Board of Directors in factory	S	23	37
Employment of hired workers to replace kibbutz members who want another occupation	S	20	29
Economic units as profit centres	S	18	26
Partnership with private capital	S	12	21
Abolition of rotation for successful managers	S	8	7
Separation of economy from community	S	7	7
Calculation of differentiated shadow wages	S	6	6
Inclusion of at least a part of the food budget in personal monetary budget	C	9	8
Payment for additional work hours	S	2	2

(1990: n=135 communities; 1991: n=208). Source: Getz, 1991.

Only one of the change proposals presented in Table 1 has been implemented in more than 50 percent of the communities. The largest diffusion of changes has been in the area of consumption. While 59 percent of the communities extended the individual monetary budget, only 9 percent decided to open the option of choice between private provision of food and communal provision in the dining room. A larger number of communities decided to abolish the provision of electricity according to needs and to transfer the budget to the family. The diffusion of the "separation between economy and community" changes has been slower, and there are wide differences within this category. Although 37 percent of the communities decided to create a board of directors in their factories, and 26 percent decided to organize economic units as profit centres, only 7 percent decided to implement the general concept of separation, and only 6 percent decided to use a differentiated "shadow-wage" accounting system.

There appear to be different interpretations of both the board of directors and the profit-centre proposals. The fact that only a small number of communities have adopted the overall concept of separation of kibbutz economy from community probably shows that there were other, more pragmatic, reasons for the implementation of these proposals. As to forming a board of directors, one of the reasons seems to be to create a more professional control mechanism for the strategic decisions of plant management. It seems that, in many cases, the authority of the new institutions was defined in a way that would not impinge on the authority of the kibbutz institutions. In other cases, the creation of the board of directors might be connected with partnership with private capital. In most of these partnerships, the majority of voting shares belongs to the kibbutz community. There are also differences among communities as to the interpretation of the "profit-centre" proposal. While some of them stress mainly the change in the accounting system, so that the members of the work branch will be aware more quickly of the economic results of their unit, others put more emphasis on the intention that economic criteria should dominate social and value related criteria.[3]

One of the more dangerous developments, from the point of view of the kibbutz identity, is the legitimization given to an increase in the employment of hired workers. There is already some statistical evidence of such an increase after a long continuing decrease, especially in the first years after the crisis. The above-mentioned legitimization is related not only to the opening towards the market but also to a certain gap in the occupational structure, especially in the type of industry in many communities and the occupational expectations of kibbutz youth (Rosner, 1990). Many efforts have been invested in improving the quality of industrial work, introducing new technologies, and using a socio-technical approach (Rosner, 1989). But, in spite of these efforts, in many communities the gap continues to exist, and it is possible that the basis for the above-mentioned legitimization was the need to respond to the aspirations of younger members. On the other hand, it is well known that the employment of hired labour was an important component of processes of decommunalization of intentional communities and co-operatives in the past.

Three general conclusions can be drawn from the data presented in Table 1. First, the more far-reaching proposals of intrusion of market and hierarchical principles have been implemented by less than ten percent of the kibbutz communities. Only a few communities have introduced some form of connection between work and material rewards. A much larger number of kibbutz communities have discussed such proposals and rejected them by large majorities. Second, the percentage of communities implementing the more far-reaching changes did not increase between 1990 and 1991. The findings of 1991, based on 77 percent of the communities, seems to reflect accurately a certain differentiation between the large majority of communities, mainly implementing changes relevant to their specific situation without commitment to the New Kibbutz concept, and a minority experimenting with more far-reaching changes that are sometimes contrary to basic kibbutz tenets.[4] Third, between 1990 and 1991 there has been an increase in the percentage of communities implementing certain changes connected with the concept of separation between community and economy, most of them without approval of the concept. There has been also a certain increase in the transition towards a comprehensive personal monetary budget.

These findings do not point towards a more general process of decommunalization. As assumed, it seems that the rate of diffusion can serve as a criterion to differentiate between changes deviating from the basic kibbutz identity and those that are compatible with it. There might surely be other factors explaining differences in the rate of diffusion, such as the length of time needed for the implementation of far-reaching changes. However, the finding that between 1990 and 1991 there has been almost no increase in the number of communities introducing such changes seems to show, at least, that time is not the most important factor. What is the importance of ideological factors, compared with more pragmatic economic or social considerations in the initiation of these changes? We can offer only partial answers to these questions.

It seems that the small group of communities that implemented the more far-reaching changes can be characterized by some of the following factors: a lack of ideological consensus and weakening of the kibbutz ideology; a high percentage of members leaving and social instability; and a low standard of living. There seems to be no direct relationship with the economic situation of the community. At this stage we cannot measure the impact of the intrusion of the market and hierarchy mechanisms on these communities, and cannot know if they will be able to maintain their communal identity. Longitudinal comparative research is needed to give more definitive answers to these questions.

But what about the majority of communities that did not introduce more far-reaching institutional changes? Are there no trends of decommunalization in these communities? In some of them, there seems to be legitimation of an increase in the employment of hired labour, which on the basis of past experience might point towards decommunalization. Recent research findings point also towards normative changes, even when no organizational change took place. Larger percentages of members than in the past express utilitarian and calculative attitudes, and there is less confidence in the future of the kibbutz (Palgi and Sharir, 1990). These normative changes might be in part a reaction to the economic crisis, but they might also be an outcome of the New Kibbutz concept and ideology.

The discussion around the New Kibbutz concept continues. Within the communities, the discussion centres more on specific change proposals than on overall concepts, but more comprehensive alternative change concepts have also been presented. Some opponents of the New Kibbutz use the term "kibbutz renewal" to define their concept. They agree about the need to adapt different features of the traditional kibbutz to changing conditions in Israeli society, and to the challenges of advanced production and information technology. But, according to this conception, there is no need to give up the commune transaction mechanism to meet these challenges. On the contrary, the basic kibbutz socioeconomic structure offers favourable conditions both for the introduction of new technologies (Rosner, 1989; Rosner and Putterman, 1991) and for adaptation to a post-industrial society (Block, 1990). Growing opportunities for self-realization and self-development in the framework of a communal society should be the goal of the kibbutz, not a higher living standard per se. The opportunities that cannot be created in a single small community could be created through stronger cooperation between kibbutz communities, as an alternative to simply opening the kibbutz to the capitalist environment. Contrary to the priority of changes in the organizational and economic structure in the New Kibbutz concept, the alternative concepts stress the need for ideological re-orientation and for a revitalization of the Gemeinschaft-type social structure.

Hybridization or Compartmentalization?

What can we generalize from the kibbutz experience about the relationship between commune, market and hierarchy mechanisms? Are there possibilities for co-existence between those opposite principles and ideal types, of developing new hybrid types? Are these lessons for co-operatives and other types of third-way organizations? A comparison between the past kibbutz experience of market economic activity in Israel and abroad and the New Kibbutz concept illustrates the difference between two types of such co-existence. In the past there was awareness of the need to establish clear boundaries between external market activity and the internal organization of the kibbutz economic sector. Special organizations were created to serve as buffer mechanisms between the kibbutz economy and the market. Currently, the concept of separation between economy and community is an attempt to open these boundaries.

There are similarities in these two types of relationships between market and kibbutz and Wolfe's analysis of the relations between market, State, and community; one suggested type is market or State "imperialism" (Wolfe, 1989). The attempts to commercialize family relations are an extreme example of such an intrusion. The other type suggested by Wolfe is that of compartmentalization, defining strictly the boundaries between State, market and community. The boundaries established in the past by the kibbutz can be approximated to such compartmentalization, by defining the community against the intrusion of the market. There is both theoretical and empirical support for the assumption that this compartmentalization, based on conformity to the community ideal type, has contributed to the economic and organizational efficiency of the kibbutz, or at least has not diminished it (Rosner and Tannenbaum, 1987b; Leviatan and Rosner, 1980).

The kibbutz experience in the past showed that it was possible, on the basis of the commune ideal type, to achieve economic success in a market economy, at least in the conditions of Israel. Even during the crisis period, many kibbutz industrial plants performed better than similar non-kibbutz plants (Rabin, 1991). Is it possible to develop a hybrid form between commune and market, one that might not weaken the traditional bases of individual commitment and community integration, therefore also weakening its economic efficiency? Are different hybrid types possible?

The development of the organizational structure of kibbutz industrial plants shows a basic difference between two types of hybridization, i.e. between the commune and the hierarchy type. In a first stage of industrialization, there were attempts to develop a more conventional hierarchical structure, especially in plants employing hired workers. As mentioned above, this structure had a negative effect on kibbutz members' commitment and morale. As a result of such failures, new organizational forms were developed. While a certain hierarchical differentiation was maintained to fulfil coordination functions, the basic communal principles prevailed and the usual hierarchical privileges were abolished; social control was performed mainly by the peer group, and the employment of hired workers decreased (Tannenbaum et al., 1977; Leviatan and Rosner, 1980; Bartolke et al., 1985).

It is possible that when compartmentalization prevails against the trends of market intrusion, a similar limited hybridization between commune and market principles might develop, avoiding an increase in monetary and calculative relations while increasing personal autonomy and self-realization. But what about other third-way organizations? A recent article suggested a typology of such organizations (Rosner, 1991). Non-utilitarian multi-functional communities, similar to the communal ideal-type, were presented as one polar type. On the other pole, unifunctional organizations based mainly on utilitarian motivations would be located, as exemplified by ESOP and many conventional co-operatives.

It seems that for communities and organizations that are close to the commune type, compartmentalization might be necessary to maintain both their economic efficiency and the commitment of members. On the other hand, the experience of American Z-type organizations, which were initially close to the hierarchy type, points to the possibility that the intrusion of commune-type elements enhanced their efficiency in conditions both of high uncertainty and of need to adapt to new technologies. This might surely be true also for similar third-way organizations, even when they are close to the utilitarian pole.

However, there seems to be a basic difference between hybridization through intrusion by the market and hybridization through intrusion by the commune mechanism. In a capitalist market society, the intrusion by the market is a spontaneous development, even without the purposive policies of privatization. The introduction, or even the preservation, of commune-type elements in communities and organizations depends on purposive and intentional action. The ways of applying the possible lessons of the kibbutz experience therefore seem contingent on the specific economic, social, and political conditions and depend on the readiness of organizational socio-political actors to initiate such actions.

Notes

1. Empirical research has shown strong correlations between measures of commitment to kibbutz production units and their economic efficiency (Leviatan, 1980). The attitudinal measures also predicted future behaviour of kibbutz members. The percentage of kibbutz-born, with high commitment to the kibbutz, leaving the community during five years after the measurement, was significantly lower than the average (Rosner et al., 1990).
2. A more general analysis of the negative impact of the introduction of market mechanisms on voluntary action is presented by Ware and Goodwin (1990).
3. Differences in the interpretation of the profit-centre concepts are also frequent among conventional firms. Eccles (1985) found that profit-centre types ranged from mandating internal exchange on a cost basis, to allowing profit centres full exchange autonomy with either inside or outside suppliers.
4. A possible explanation of the limited diffusion of the overall New Kibbutz concept might be related to the above-mentioned inconsistencies of the concept. As Williamson stated: "Many hypothetical forms of organization never arise, or quickly die out, because they combine inconsistent features" (1991:270).

References

Bartolke, K., W. Eschweiler, D. Flechsenberg, M. Palgi, and M. Rosner, (1985), *Participation and Control* (Spardof, Germany: Verlag Rene F. Wilfer).

Ben-David, Y., (1973), "Changes and Continuity in the Kibbutz: Research and Theory," *The Kibbutz — Interdisciplinary Research Review*, 1.

Ben Porath, Y., (1980), "The F-Connection: Families, Friends and Firms and the Organization of Exchange," *Population and Development Review*, 6, 1.

Block, F., (1990), *Postindustrial Possibilities* (Berkeley: University of California Press).

Cohen, E., (1976), "The Structural Transformation of the Kibbutz," in *Social Change*, edited by G. D. Zollschan and W. Hirsh (Cambridge: Shenkman).

Eccles, R., (1985), *The Transfer Pricing Problem: A Theory for Practice* (Lexington, Mass.: Lexington Press).

Getz, S., (1991), *Changes in the Kibbutz* (Haifa: Institute for Research on the Kibbutz and the Cooperative Idea, University of Haifa).

Granovetter, M., (1991), "The Old and the New Economic Sociology: A History and an Agenda," in *Beyond the Market Place*, edited by R. Friedland and A.F. Robertson (New York: Aldive de Gruyter).

Harel, Y., (1988), "The New Kibbutz: An Outline," *Kibbutz Currents*, 2, pp.2-5.

Hirschman, A.O., (1970), *Exit, Voice and Loyalty* (Cambridge: Harvard University Press).

Kanter, R.M., (1972), *Commitment and Community* (Cambridge: Harvard University Press).

Krausz, E., ed., (1983), *The Sociology of the Kibbutz* (New Brunswick, N.J.: Transaction Books).

Leviatan, U., (1980), "Human Factors and Economic Performance in Kibbutz Plants," in *Work and Organization in Kibbutz Industry,* edited by U. Leviatan and M. Rosner (Darby, Penn.: Norwood Editions).

Leviatan, U., and M. Rosner (eds.) (1980), *Work and Organization in Kibbutz Industry* (Darby, Penn.: Norwood Editions).

Meister, A., (1974), *La participation dans les associations* (Paris: Les éditions ouvrières).

Oved, Y., (1988), *Two Hundred Years of American Communes* (New Brunswick, N.J.: Transaction Books).

Palgi, M., and M. Rosner, (1980), *Psychological, Social and Organizational Effects of Self-Management in Kibbutz Industry* (Haifa: Institute for Research on the Kibbutz and the Cooperative Idea, University of Haifa).

Palgi, M., and S. Sharir, (1990), *Public Opinion Survey* (Haifa: Institute for Research on the Kibbutz and the Cooperative Idea, University of Haifa).

Rabin, A., (1991), *A Comparison Between Kibbutz Industrial Plants and Industrial Corporations Traded on the Israeli Stock Market, (1986-1989)* (Tel Aviv: Kibbutz Artzi Publications).

Rosner, M., (1988), "A Crucial Decade: Recent Developments in the Kibbutz Movement, 1977-1987," in *Encyclopedia Judaica Yearbook* (Jerusalem: Keter Publishing).

Rosner, M., (1989), "High-tech in Kibbutz Industry: Structural Factors and Social Implications," in *The Social Implications of Robotics and Advanced Industrial Automation,* edited by D. Millin and A. B. Reele (North Holland Press).

Rosner, M., (1990), "Berufsausbildung, Beschaftigungsstrukturen und Berufliche Erwartungen in Israel und im Kibbutz", in *Jugend in Israel und in Der Bundesrepublik,* edited by W. Melzer, W. W. Ferchhoff, and G. Neubauer (Weinheim and Munchen: Juventa Verlag).

Rosner, M., (1991), "Worker Ownership, Ideology and Social Structure in 'Third-Way' Work Organizations," in *Economic and Industrial Democracy,* 12, 3 (August), pp.369-85.

Rosner, M., J. Ben-David, A. Avnat, N. Cohen, and U. Leviatan, (1990), *The Second Generation* (Westport: Greenwood Press).

Rosner, M., and L. Putterman, (1991), "Factors Behind the Supply and Demand for Non-alienating Work and Some International Illustrations," *Journal of Economic Studies,* 18, 1.

Rosner, M., and Shur, S., (1984), "Structural Equality: The Case of the Kibbutz," *International Review of Sociology,* series II, 20, 1-3.

Rosner, M., and Tannenbaum, A., (1987a), "Ownership and Alienation in Kibbutz Factories," *Work and Occupations,* 14, 2, pp.165-96.

Rosner, M., and Tannenbaum, A., (1987b), "Organizational Efficiency and Egalitarian Democracy in an International Communal Society: The Kibbutz," *The British Journal of Sociology,* 38, 4, pp.521-45.

Tannenbaum, A., B. Kavcic, M. Rosner, M. Vianello, and G. Wieser, (1974), *Hierarchy in Organizations* (San Francisco: Jossey and Bass).

Thompson, G., J. Frances, R. Levacic, and J. Mitchell, eds., (1991), *Markets, Hierarchies and Networks* (London: Sage Publications).

Ware, A., and R. Goodwin, (1990), *Needs and Welfare* (London: Sage Publications).

Williamson, O.E., (1991), "Comparative Economic Organizations: The Analysis of Discreet Structural Alternatives," *Administrative Science Quarterly,* 36, pp.269-96.

Wolfe, A., (1989), *Whose Keeper?* (Berkeley: University of California Press).

Part III

Mapping New Citizenship Practices

Chapter Seven

Citizenship and Social Change: Beyond the Dominant Paradigm

Maurice Roche

The conception of citizenship, particularly social citizenship, which prevails in the contemporary Western social formation has implications for structural change in this formation. *Social citizenship* refers to those rights and duties of citizenship concerned with the welfare of people as citizens, taking "welfare" in a broad sense, to include such things as work, education, health, and quality of life. In the mid to late twentieth century in Western capitalist society, conceptions of social citizenship tend to be intimately tied up with the development of, and lately the crisis of, the welfare State. In the late 1970s and 1980s, these conceptions, and the welfare State systems to which they are tied, have been seriously challenged by two sets of social forces, those of ideological change and those of social structural change. A main theme of my previous research on rethinking citizenship (Roche, 1992a; Roche, 1990b; Roche, 1987), and also in this chapter, is that these conceptions of social citizenship need to be rethought in terms of these sorts of challenge.

Introduction

There have been various ideological and political challenges emanating from the new social movements (e.g., internationalism, ecology, feminism, etc.). But undoubtedly the greatest challenge has been posed by the rise to power in the 1980s of the New Right and neo-conservatism in Britain, the U.S.A., and elsewhere. In some of its variants, the New Right denies the existence of social rights, while in others it displaces social rights by emphasizing social duties. But in all of its variants it aims to see public expenditure on the welfare State controlled and cut and the role of the State in welfare de-emphasized. The resurgent Right's influence continues in the 1990s through Prime Minister Major's version of Thatcherism and the new moderation in the Labour Party in the U.K. and through President Clinton's combination of interventionism with populist moralism in the U.S.A. These challenges alone suggest that we need to take stock of the concept of social citizenship, to see what reality and relevance it has for the 1990s and beyond.

There are two main implications of these ideological challenges for popular understandings of social citizenship in the modern period. First, across the political spectrum and in a variety of ways, popular awareness of the need to give a new emphasis to social duties in addition to the conventional stress on rights is growing. Second, there is the need to extend social duties into previously relatively uncolonized non-State spheres of civil society, particularly into the family, but also into society's ecosphere and into society's historicality (inter-generationality, heritage, etc.). In these ways, the new historical situation we are popularly perceived to have entered in the West means that the long revolution since the Enlightenment, of the creation and expansion of what appeared to be relatively "duty free" citizens' rights, has drawn to a close. Citizens' obligations and responsibilities, both within civil society and in citizen-State relations, are likely to be seen as equally as important as rights in current and future ideological debate, political renewal, and new institution-building.

In addition, and perhaps more importantly, the period from the mid to late 1970s to the present has been one of great and continuing structural change in the economic, political, and cultural foundations and frameworks of Western society. It has become fashionable, when discussing contemporary social change, to focus on the cultural changes associated with post-modernism, such as cultural fragmentation, esthetic and moral relativism, consumerism, and hedonism. These changes are implicitly and explicitly critical of the idea of citizenship, and no doubt have had a significant influence on the discursive context within which the new ideological challenges to citizenship have been developed (Roche, 1990b; Roche, 1994). However, for the purposes of the discussion here, the two sets of changes which I consider to be of greatest importance are *post-industrialism* and *post-nationalism*.

The term "post-industrialism" can be used to refer to the shift from industrialism to a high-technology and services-based formation in the contemporary capitalist economy (Roche, 1992a:ch.7). The term "post-nationalism" can be used to refer to the configuration of three main trends and phenomena. First, there is the phenomenon of economic globalization. This refers to the emergence of a distinctive and predominating transnational level in the contemporary capitalist economy, namely (a) global markets and flows of capital and labour, products and marketing, (b) the multinational form of corporate organization and of production process organization, and (c) generally international economic interdependency, particularly between the advanced industrial societies. Second, there is the phenomenon of political transnationalism. This refers to a renewed wave of development of political, legal, and administrative institutions at the international (e.g., UN) and transnational (e.g., E.C.) levels. Finally, there is the phenomenon of the emergence of transnational and global level social problems of awesome scale and complexity, requiring international, and indeed transnational, forms of response; these include social problems relating to environmental degradation, poverty, migration, and so forth.

In the late twentieth century, post-industrial and post-national vectors and forces of structural social change continuously generate and compound profound new social problems in contemporary societies. An important example for social citizenship here is the emergence of structural unemployment and underemployment, alongside the beginnings of an historically significant, and probably irreversible, structural erosion of nation-States' capacities to regulate these and other aspects of their economies. These changes are to be distinguished from growth-recession cycles, although they may well be connected to long waves in the international economy connected with cycles of technological innovation, new capital formation, and the "creative destruction" of old forms of capital investment.

The implications of structural change for social citizenship are generally those of stimulating awareness among politicians, policy makers, and the public about three main issues. First, there is the need to construct new social rights, such as new employment and income distributional rights (Roche, 1992a: ch.7). Second, there is the need to extend and institutionalize social rights in new post-national political formations, such as those involved in the European Community-European Union discussed later in this chapter. Finally, there is the need to connect traditional and new social rights more clearly with obligations and responsibilities. My analysis suggests that change-induced problems will increasingly set the agenda for contemporary and future citizenship-oriented politics along these sorts of lines.

In exploring the origins and causes of the new agenda facing contemporary citizenship politics, particularly social citizenship politics, this chapter focuses, for reasons both of priority and space, on the structural changes indicated, rather than on ideological or cultural change. It is divided into three main sections. The first section introduces some features of the post-1945 conventional wisdom about the nature, development, and social context of citizenship, the *dominant paradigm,* through a discussion of some key themes in the sociology of citizenship. In the second section, some of the general changes associated with the development of a *post-industrial* political-economic pattern and their implications are noted. In the third section, some features of the *post-national* change associated with various processes of "globalization" are illustrated by reference to the development of social citizenship in the European Community-European Union. The conclusion draws some of these themes together in a conception of the new problems of structural and moral complexity facing the traditional conceptions and institutions of citizenship in advanced Western societies.

The Sociology of Citizenship and the "Dominant Paradigm"

Citizenship and the Social Context: Some Key Issues
Sociological conceptions of the social context of citizenship need to provide an understanding of, or at least to contain explicit basic assumptions about, at least three types of issues (Roche, 1987; Roche, 1990b). These issues arise from social contexts which I refer to as the phenomenological context, the structural context, and the historical context. In the phenomenological context, the main issue is: What is the nature of what we might call "the citizens' community," or the citizens' intersubjective "lived world"? In other words, what is the nature of the subjectivity and sociality involved in citizenship? What are the social skills, resources, and powers needed for its exercise? What are the main norms and values of life in the citizen community? Most importantly, what rights and duties do citizens acknowledge as regulating inter-citizen and citizen-State relations? In the structural context the main issue is: What is the social structural context of citizenship and the citizen community? That is, what cultural economic and State systems underpin them and influence their capacity to develop, both in enabling and disabling ways? Finally, there is the historical context. The main issues here are: How has citizenship and its community and its context come to

be what it is? How is it currently changing, and what are its likely future lines of development?

Differing answers to these three sets of issues and questions help to distinguish between modern ideological-normative and sociological versions of citizenship. One of the most influential normative and sociological versions of citizenship — helping to shape what I refer to as the "dominant paradigm of citizenship" (Roche, 1992a) — has been that of sociologist T.H. Marshall. His writings expressed the spirit of the early post-war British welfare State and the new form of social citizenship it embodied. We will briefly consider Marshall's analysis, and then the way it addresses the three key issues which are identified here.

T.H. Marshall's Sociology of Citizenship

Citizenship was not a strong theme in modern sociological analysis until British sociologist T.H. Marshall (1963) put it "on the map" in his classic discussion of "Citizenship and Social Class," contained in lectures given in 1949 and first published the following year. His relatively brief discussion provided one of the earliest, clearest, and most suggestive accounts of the historical and social reasons for the emergence of the postwar welfare State and of the moral and political justifications for it. What little sociology of citizenship there is derives to a considerable extent from Marshall's thinking on the subject (Barbalet, 1988; Roche, 1987; Roche, 1992a: ch.1; Dennis and Halsey, 1988).

For Marshall, our understanding of what citizenship is has changed and developed over time. In his 1949 lectures, he based himself on the British historical experience of it, but he also attempted to speak in general terms and thus implicitly for all modern Western societies and States. He argued that the modern concept of citizenship consists of a combination of three elements: civil, political, and social. These elements can be roughly observed to have emerged in a sequence of steps from simple to complex over the course of history. Thus, the simple form of exclusively civil citizenship came earliest, then the more complex formations consisting of civil and political citizenship, and finally, in the era of the welfare State, social citizenship emerges to more or less complete both the picture and the development.

Marshall's analysis of the three elements of citizenship was, he notes, "dictated by [British] history even more clearly than by logic" (1963:73). He suggests that "It is possible . . . to assign the formative period in the life of each to a different century — civil rights to the eighteenth, political to the nineteenth, and social to the twentieth" (1963:76). On this basis he then observed that each element of citizenship consists of a set of rights together with a set of institutions in respect of which those rights are exercised, or which exist to serve those rights. For Marshall, citizenship in general involves an equality of membership status and of ability to participate in a society, and it refers to what the society collectively acknowledges as legitimate and enforceable citizens' rights in respect of the various elements of the concept. Marshall drew this picture in the course of a discussion of the social inequalities, particularly those of class, generated during the course of the development of, and by the contemporary operation of, the modern capitalist economy. Against this background of capitalism's tendencies to general social inequalities and class divisions, Marshall saw the evolution of citizenship as representing something of a "war" between two opposing principles. With the establishment of the welfare State, he saw this war as slowly being won by citizenship and by its egalitarian and integrative effects and implications.

In terms of the three contexts and sets of questions identified earlier, Marshall's, and indeed more generally the dominant paradigm's, conception and assumptions can be summarized in the following way. First, there is citizenship's phenomenological context. In his lecture, Marshall proposed that citizenship consists of three types of rights, i.e., civil, political, and social. He implies that the citizen world or community is a sphere in which rights-claiming citizens have their claims serviced by State-based institutions of the law, parliamentary democracy, and the welfare State. Social rights are distinct from, but nonetheless continuous with and complementary to, civil and political rights. They enable people to participate in a civilized society, and in some sense they "complete" the achievement of civil and political rights.

Second, there is citizenship's structural context. In Marshall's view, social rights are necessary to counter the class-based inequalities deriving from the main context of citizenship, namely the industrial capitalist economy. Nonetheless, merit-based inequalities are essentially ineradicable from a free society, in which the State can only seek to ensure equality of opportunity rather than equality of outcome. Marshall held that there is an inevitable tension between the principles and institutions of welfare and social citizenship on the one hand and those of capitalism on the other. He formulated this tension in various ways in different studies, for example as "welfare-capitalism" (1963), and "the hyphenated society" (1981). Nevertheless, the image he conveys throughout is that of the manageability of this tension and of the reciprocity and functionality of the major sectors of the modern social system, particularly the State and capitalism. I will refer to this sort of dominant paradigm assumption about social citizenship as the assumption of "national functionalism."

Finally, there is citizenship's historical context. Overall, Marshall's, and the dominant paradigm's, conception of the history of citizenship in general is that of a fairly continuous long-term growth, formation, and coalescence between processes of nation-State democratization on the one hand and the development of industrial capitalism on the other. At the same time, its conception of the history of social citizenship is that of the long-term growth of a conflictual, but contained and ultimately functional, relationship between the welfare State and industrial capitalism. In Marshall's view, the growth of the welfare State tends to "civilize" capitalism (1963:284; Turner, 1986).

From this brief review, three main characteristics of the dominant paradigm need to be noted. First, its emphasis on rights-oriented and State-oriented versions of civil society. Second, its national functionalist assumption of the differentiation-but-integration of social rights and the welfare State, within the context of the wider modern political-economic system. Finally, its conception of citizenship's history in terms of a more or less unilinear and continuous social progress. These assumptions show up equally clearly in the writings of other significant social policy figures, such as Beveridge and Titmuss, working in Britain in the early postwar period, and generally in popular political discourse and understandings, particularly in Britain and Europe until the mid to late 1970s and the onset of such factors as the great oil price-induced inflation, the faltering of Keynesian economic management, the recognition of tax and welfare expenditure limits to economic growth, etc. (Roche, 1992a:ch.1-2).

Until the mid to late 1970s, the dominant paradigm of social citizenship was developed in the postwar West through various forms of what I refer to as national functionalism. This concept refers to the functional interdependence, or symbiosis, which was developed and maintained between the major societal sectors, namely the economy, polity, and culture, and their systems of institutions in modern society. Another way of referring to this type of societal arrangement is to see it as a de facto "national social contract." The contract was formed between democratic nation-States and the nationally based and organized industrial capitalist economies to which they played host. Welfare and social citizenship, both the welfare State and the welfare market, were central to this accommodation. Capitalism would undertake to deliver employment and income, and thus market-based welfare, in return for various State services. The State would undertake to produce and reproduce a relevantly skilled and healthy labour force via an educational and welfare State. It would also undertake to maintain the cultural, institutional, and physical infrastructure of the market and of social life in general at the local-urban and national levels.

T.H. Marshall had early on pointed to the inevitably dialectical character of the societal arrangements involved in the development of the welfare State and the institutionalization of the social rights of citizenship. He acknowledged the underlying tension of a "war", between capitalism on the one hand and democratic citizenship and social justice on the other, as many analysts have done since (Walzer, 1985; Bowles and Gintis, 1986). Nonetheless, he also implied that the accommodation between capitalism and democracy, via the State's development of a "welfare State" on behalf of the "nation" in the postwar period, represented an event of historic and lasting significance for modern Western society. The war could be controlled, the warriors pacified, and capitalism civilized.

However, evidently the war is not over. It has been renewed by the forces of ideological and social structural change. The dialectics of capitalism and citizenship have been renewed, and their relationship needs to be rethought. The problem of social citizenship, particularly the persistence of second-class citizenship or non-citizenship associated with poverty, remains an important and recurrently controversial focal point in contemporary politics. In this chapter, I suggest that the main structural contexts of social citizenship, the national functional system and the national social contract, are both breaking down under the pressure of social change. Thus, the dominant paradigm of citizenship, which is a vitally important integrative and identity-conferring myth in modern Western society (Roche, 1992a:ch.9), is in profound and probably irreversible crisis.

Social Change and Citizenship

Background
Social citizenship in modern Western society involves, at its very heart, rights and duties regarding work. Max Weber (1970) showed,

and many other social analysts have since argued on similar lines, that from the eras of preindustrial capitalism and early industrial capitalism, eras in which a new market in free labour was created, the West inherited a distinctive work ethic and a conception of the duty to work. This was taken for granted in the postwar period of the construction of modern welfare States and welfare capitalism. In the era of the dominant paradigm, these work/duty assumptions were overlaid and overshadowed by the apparent power of the new Keynesian techniques for managing national capitalist economies and their labour markets to deliver full employment and thus to deliver the de facto right to work, at least to male breadwinners. In the modern West, work in the form of labour market employment is important both for intrinsic moral and cultural reasons, including psychological (Roche, 1990a) ones, and also for the instrumental reason that it generates income for consumption and thus for survival and welfare. Thus, the duty and right to work are intimately connected, instrumentally as well as morally, with duties and rights regarding income, and through income, welfare.

Contemporary right-wing social thinking and social policy, particularly American Neo-Conservatism, is important to consider in this respect (Roche, 1992a:ch.4-6). From the neo-conservative point of view, cultural and political changes in modernity, particularly in family structure, but also involving capitalist consumerism and the development of income rights in the welfare State, have tended to undermine the work ethic. This, in turn, has tended to undermine the early capitalist duty of individuals to generate welfare for themselves and their dependents from income derived from the sale of their labour in the labour market. From this point of view, then, the dominant paradigm's provision of work and income rights, through national Keynesian and welfare State policies, has tended to undermine the work-generating and income-generating duties which the paradigm itself, and these policies, tacitly presuppose. The neo-conservative case may be badly flawed, but the dominant paradigm evidently remains in great difficulty in Western societies in the early 1990s, and it is not in these difficulties merely because it has been politically, administratively, and financially attacked by right-wing governments in the 1980s.

The radical laissez-faire New Right thrust of the Right's attack in the early 1980s has, in many respects, been seen to fail. In the late 1980s and early 1990s, it has begun to recede and to be increasingly complemented, even replaced, in Right politics by neo-conservative approaches. But the problems of the dominant paradigm remain, and they go deeper than the ebb and flow of politics and ideology. As one commentator notes: "By the mid 1980s there were two points on which there was widespread agreement across the political spectrum. The first was that the labour market was in a mess, the second that the social security system was in a mess. There was of course rather less consensus on what should be done about either" (Standing, 1986:134; Offe 1984; Offe, 1985). My argument is that the dominant paradigm's problems are not just ideological, but also structural, and connected with sea-changes in the political economy of late twentieth-century Western capitalism.

These are evidently very large and speculative themes; it would be misleading if I claimed to be attempting to do more here than merely introduce them to the contemporary sociology of, and policy debate about, social citizenship for some preliminary consideration. Nonetheless, in periods of major social change such as the present, whatever the inevitable limitations of the exercise, there is no alternative but to make some attempt to grasp the larger picture and to "see the wood rather than the trees." As indicated earlier, the main parts of the larger picture which impinge most on social citizenship relate to two changes in the nature of contemporary Western capitalism evident since the mid-1970s, namely post-industrialism and post-nationalism. Social citizenship is being, and needs to be, rethought in many ways in relation to these long-term and irreversible processes of structural change.

For the purposes of my discussion here, I will consider these two processes of change relatively independently, making some connections as necessary. But in reality, of course, they are intimately interconnected, and together they are beginning to change the social order on which the dominant paradigm rests. In general terms, they are tending to undermine its operational assumptions about the nature of the labour market and social security systems and thus about the nature of work and income rights. In more particular terms, they arguably tend to generate new and intractable forms of familiar and long-standing limits to modern social citizenship. That is, new forms of second-class citizenship and exclusion from full citizenship are emerging in the 1980s and 1990s (Lister, 1990; Brubaker, 1992) which involve the distinctive character of being "poor in the midst of mass affluence," or at least in the midst of the historically high standards of living of the majority populations in Western societies in this period. This particular kind of exclusionary poverty has been associated with a distinctive development in class structure in modern societies, namely the emergence of a significantly self-reproducing, anomic, and marginalized underclass formation (Roche, 1992a:ch.3). Arguably, these processes are particular effects of the general impact of post-industrial and post-national processes on unemployment, national labour markets, and national welfare systems.

Post-industrial Change and Social Citizenship

For my purpose, "post-industrial change" refers to a complex of changes in the modern capitalist economy, associated with the use of new technologies, the decline of manufacturing and the rise of service employment, the increasing emphasis on consumerism, and the increasing emphasis on the need for capital (financial and technological) and labour to be flexible and adaptable to changing market conditions and consumer preferences (Roche, 1992a:ch.7). Some of the most negative features of post-industrial change have been clearly visible in the massive increase in unemployment and physical deterioration in traditional rust-belt industrial cities and regions of the U.S.A., Britain, and western Europe in the late 1970s and 1980s (Bluestone and Harrison, 1982). The problems created in these heartland cities of the industrial era, by de-industrialization and also by the international economy, are broadly comparable in most Western societies. So too are the urban political strategies adopted to try both to react to them, and more pro-actively, to regenerate and restructure industrial cities' urban economies on more post-industrial lines, i.e., consumerist, high-technology, and service employment (Judd and Parkinson, 1990; Jacobs, 1992; Roche, 1992b).

Long-term analysis and projection are not exact sciences, to say the least, and they may or may not lend much support to the personal hopes and fears about the future which usually infuse futurologists' visions. But it seems to me to be indisputable that contemporary techno-economic change is indeed of this order of importance. By contrast, what the consequences and implications are, what they ought to be, and how they might be politically controlled or steered are of course eminently disputable. The advent of the new technologies, and the beginning of their permeation not only of economic production, but also of transport, architecture, city design, politics, and the home, undoubtedly give people in the advanced Western societies new powers, possibilities, and freedoms. But they also require them to make choices if traditional social and economic organization is not simply to fall in on itself. The fact of the continuous diffusion of technological change, mainly through markets and market forces, means that policy decisions about many profound political choices and decisions on strategic aspects of contemporary social and economic organization in Western societies ultimately cannot be avoided. This is not least the case for the organization of employment, with all of its consequences for income distribution, and thus for welfare (Pahl, 1988).

The post-industrial capitalist economy increasingly requires various forms of flexibility from its workers and its labour supply. In the productive process, employers require workers to be able and willing to be flexibly deployed between a variety of roles, while in the labour market employers ideally require a flexible supply of labour, able and willing to be taken into employment and put out of work as market conditions and the trade cycle demands (Piore and Sabel, 1984; Standing, 1986). The shift towards flexible labour uses and markets is structurally based and capable of being steered in various political directions. But the insecurity problems associated with it have been greatly accentuated by the social and economic policies of right-wing governments in the West in the 1980s. Trade union power, professional power, government regulation, and of course the welfare State were all regarded as "obstacles" to the efficient functioning of the national labour market and were more or less vigorously and effectively attacked as such.

The profound implications of these structural and political developments for the dominant Western paradigm of social citizenship can be seen, for instance, in Standing's analysis of British unemployment and labour market policy in the 1980s. Standing argues that the "post-1945 social consensus . . . (and) . . . the welfare State and mixed economy" accorded citizens a number of labour rights, formulable as rights to various types of security: in the labour market, in terms of income, and within employment. Thus, labour market security was provided "through insurance benefits and State-preserved 'full employment'," while income security was provided through "legitimized trade unionism, minimum wage legislation and tax-benefit systems that checked the growth of income inequality"; employment security was provided by controls on employers' powers to make workers redundant or dismiss them, by accepted middle-class and working-class job demarcations and other restrictive practices, and by health, safety, and hours of work regulation (Standing, 1986:113).

Post-industrialism, with its de-industrialization and its labour flexibilization dynamics, raises problems for each of these aspects of labour rights and their related forms of security. These problems are intensified by the transnational context in which States and capitalists are increasingly operating. Labour markets are becoming internationalized, and nation-States' powers to defend national labour rights, even where they wish to do so, are becoming increasingly curtailed. Citizens' social rights to work and income need to be considered in the context of post-industrial social and economic change. It is clear that such structural change poses major policy problems for Western nation-States in the spheres of employment, income, and welfare. Traditional dominant paradigm approaches, which rely on assumptions about the effectiveness of full employment policy and of welfare State policy, are likely to run into major problems in the emerging context of post-industrial capitalism. "Full employment," a "living wage," and/or "an income adequate to raise a family," together with a State-organized contribution-based welfare system, look set to become extremely difficult to achieve on the basis of the sort of segmented labour market that post-industrial capitalism is calling into existence.

Problems of employment and income are evidently closely interrelated, and policies to tackle them by developing new social rights will similarly need to be interrelated. Post-industrial forms of poverty and non-citizenship are likely to grow unless coordinated productionist and distributionist strategies can be developed. The post-industrial labour market needs to be regulated and supported in new ways, particularly through qualitatively enhanced equal opportunities and training policies. The connection between rights and responsibilities regarding employment and income, and thus welfare, in a context of post-industrialism will need to be rethought, and as many analysts have observed in recent years, new ways will need to be found to distribute both employment and income in terms of citizenship principles (Van Parijs, 1992; Coenen and Leisink, 1993; Pixley, 1993; Roche, 1992a:ch.7). The problems of post-industrialism are intractable enough and set a difficult agenda for the politics of contemporary social citizenship. However, the new work, income, and welfare policies which post-industrialism demands will have to be developed against the background of, and in response to, the other major set of structural changes in contemporary Western capitalist society, namely those of post-nationalism.

Post-National Change and Citizenship

Background
Contemporary social structural change is occurring along a distinctively post-national political and political-economic vector, as well

as along the techno-economic vector of post-industrialism. Post-national change is associated with various processes of globalization in contemporary economies and culture (Featherstone, 1990; Hall and Jacques, 1989; Sklair, 1990). Post- national change is as challenging to the dominant paradigm of citizenship in general, and to social citizenship in particular, as we have seen post-industrial change to be. In this section, I will focus on the historically most important example of post-national change in the late twentieth century, namely the development of the European Community (E.C.), or, since the ratification of the Maastricht Treaty in 1993, the European Union (E.U.).

The forces of globalization in the contemporary capitalist economic order are very powerful. In the late twentieth century these forces are continuously eroding the economic power and sovereignty of nation-States, just as in the late nineteenth and early twentieth century they had built them up, together with their grandiose supra-national incarnations, as competitive and militaristic empires. Many social and political analysts have recently acknowledged these trends. For instance, Mann observes that in the postwar period, "The global capitalist economy has produced more genuine internationalism, weakening nation-State divisions, than at any period in the historical development of nation States" (1990:11). Gamble reviews the Thatcher experiment of opening the British economy to global capitalist economic forces in the 1980s, and concludes: "As internationalization proceeds, one of the key questions becomes how far national models of economic development are still relevant" (1990:90). At the same time, Held argues that given the decline of the nation-State, there is a need to create "a politics beyond the sovereign nation-State" (1989:204).

The case of the European Union nations illustrates the degree to which international models of political, social, and economic development are more relevant than national models in the contemporary period. For instance, as its current leadership emphasizes, the future of a reunited Germany is more likely to lie inside the E.U., albeit as the dominant political-economic force within it, than it is in attempts at national self-sufficiency or aggrandizement. The eastern European nations and the ex-Soviet Union nations are economically so weak that the logic of their situation will force them, probably sooner rather than later, to create new post-Stalinist political-economic alliances and organizations both among themselves, such as the Commonwealth of Independent States (C.I.S.) project of 1992, and with the West. Indeed, Poland, Czechoslovakia, and Hungary could well gain some kind of E.U. membership in the late 1990s. Post-nationalism is as much of an historical reality and predicament for the eastern European and ex-Soviet Union countries as it is for the West.

The pre-eminent historical importance of the western European example of post-national political and economic change should not be mistaken for uniqueness. The world capitalist economic order is world-regional and multipolar. World-regional economic, and thus potentially political, groupings of nations exist on every continent and on the borders of every ocean, not least in the Far East. Japan's rise to economic superpower status has been engineered on a nationalistic basis throughout the postwar period, but it is unlikely to be sustained on this basis in the long term as Japan becomes vulnerable to competition from the "little Japans" such as Taiwan and South Korea. Greater regional economic organization looks to be as much in Japan's interest as the development of the E.C. is in Germany's.

With the continuous development of the world economy, existing world-regional economic groupings in the Far East, South America, and Africa and also between the U.S.A. and its immediate neighbours in the North American Free Trade Agreement, together with relations between these blocs, look set to take on a greater political-economic importance. Each of the major blocs is likely to remain as relatively open to the influence of global financial markets, and of multinational companies based elsewhere but operating in their economic space, as the U.S.A., Japan and the E.U. currently are (Grahl and Teague, 1990:ch.4). World-regional groupings are likely to be principally concerned with the facilitation of global economic processes and with the organization of world-regional markets and their infrastructures. They are also likely to be capable of forms of protectionism and other interventions in the global economy. Such economic power, and the need to control it politically, may provoke some significant political restructuring beyond the nation-State level in the medium to long term. But this is unlikely to compare with the political-economic integration likely to be achieved by the E.U. by the early twenty-first century.

Post-National Social Citizenship: The E.C. Charter of Social Rights
Speaking about the Single Europe Act of 1986, which provided the legal basis for the single market project of 1992, European Community Commission President Delors observed: "All of these objectives are inextricably linked: the large market; technological

cooperation, strengthening the European monetary system, economic and social cohesion, and the social aspects of collective action" (Betten et al., 1989:103). The idea of making such major changes in such a short period of time has called for innumerable intensive planning exercises by the Commission and intense political negotiations between the member States on both the economic and social fronts. Delors had hoped that the social dialogue between the E.C. trades unions (ETUC) and employers (UNICE) might generate the substance of the post-1992 social dimension policies. But his hopes have not been fulfilled because of the lack of interest shown by UNICE in social regulation in the new market (Teague, 1989:ch.4-5; Grahl and Teague, 1990:ch.5). In addition, the inter-State politics over 1992 have often been acrimonious. Margaret Thatcher and the British government time and again turned their faces against more than minimum integration on the economic front. Throughout the 1980s they opposed, on the grounds of costs and also, allegedly, of principle, any and all movements towards the creation of common E.C. social rights.

However, by 1989 the E.C. heads of State, with the exception of the British, were in a position to commit themselves formally to a Community Charter of Fundamental Social Rights at the Strasbourg Conference (IGC) (E.C., 1990a; Teague, 1989; Teague and Brewster, 1989). This position was reaffirmed, again with the exception of the British, at the Maastricht IGC in 1991, although not in the Union Treaty agreed there. The social rights in question are mainly rights relating to workers; they are rights in work and represent the social dimensions of an economic labour market. They do not, at this stage, include a basic right to work, as the Council of Europe's Social Charter does and as Delors implied they would in his original 1985 speech to the European Parliament (E.C., 1985; Betten et al., 1989:103). They thus represent rights of workers, or citizens-as-workers, rather than rights of citizens per se. This has led the Commission to ask: Is the citizenship [that the Community] proclaims only for workers? Will it extend it resolutely to all? (E.C., 1990b:50). The British response to this question in recent years has indeed been resolute; they have opposed any such extension. For instance, in part in deference to British objections, proposals to fix a minimum E.C. wage and to integrate social security systems and payments were deleted from the E.C.'s 1989 commitment to the social charter and to the construction of new European social rights.

Except for Britain, the E.C.'s social charter enshrines various social rights of employees on a Community-wide basis, for part-time and temporary workers in addition to full-time permanent workers. These include the right to a decent wage; maximum working hours; joining trade unions and striking; vocational training; health and safety at work; information, consultation, and participation by employees in their companies; equal treatment for male and female employees; and social security. When fully implemented, these rights are intended to remove national barriers to labour mobility within the E.C. and to discourage "social dumping."

The charter itself is not legally binding, and attempts to make it so in the Maastricht Treaty negotiations in 1991 foundered on British objections. However, the Commission's action programme to implement it by 1993-94 periodically brought forward elements of the charter in the form of directives, which are legally binding on E.U. governments, or recommendations, which are implemented on a voluntary basis, for scrutiny by the European Parliament and for agreement by the Council. The charter's principles would thus be implemented over a period in the early to mid 1990s by a mixture of binding and voluntary regulation. The European Court of Justice's interpretations of both the directives and the basic E.C.-E.U. treaties of 1957 and 1986, together with their references to social rights, are likely to play an important role in determining the nature of European citizens' social rights in the 1990s.

The first draft directive brought forward in 1990 concerned social rights, including the right to join a union and to strike, for part-time and temporary workers. These workers form a substantial sector of the labour force, 25 percent to 33 percent, and a growing one in all post-industrial economies. In addition, this sector provides most of the new job opportunities, not to mention most of the social problems of low pay and insecurity, for groups such as women, young people, and ethnic minorities. So, both in economic and social terms, part-time and temporary workers are a new, strategically important sector to incorporate into modern social-rights provisions such as health and safety, night work, shift work restrictions, etc.

The draft directive was criticized and resisted by both the Thatcher and Major governments. Given their ideological posture this was, of course, not at all surprising. In any case, it is worth noting that the unwritten and in many respects outdated British constitution does not actually recognize a right to strike in law. However, the inclusion of this right in the E.C. Charter merely "Europeanizes" a right which has long been established in many of the national constitutions of E.C. member States. Whether British exceptionalism in social policy and in many other spheres can indefinitely survive the processes of legal harmonization, of economic interdependence and market integration, and of institution-building and constitution-building currently under way in the E.U. in the 1990s, remains to be seen. Given a reasonable degree of economic convergence between E.U. nations in the medium term, the efforts of particular national governments to maintain idiosyncratic welfare State and labour market policies look likely to be ultimately unsuccessful.

Post-Nationalism, Europe, and Citizenship

Western concepts of politics and of citizenship have their historical origins in the European political experience. That experience has involved the construction of political communities, States, and citizenship at every level; from the level of the city in ancient Greece and Renaissance Italy to that of the nation in post-medieval Europe, particularly Spain and Britain. So the contemporary structural complexity which began to emerge in the 1980s, while it represented a great change from the oversimplifications of political and cultural identity of the nation-State era, is nothing essentially new from a deeper historical perspective. Europeans in the 1990s will continue to be simultaneously both united and divided in their political loyalties and identities, much as they always have been in spite of the veneer of nationalism. The three factors of locality (the ethnicity and "nationhood" of city and region), nationality, and Europeanness will continue to be the determining ones.

In creating the European Union, the Maastricht Treaty has thereby created a new level of organizational integration between the member States, prefiguring the creation of a formal federation. Historically, it is also notable in that it legally created a new form of citizenship, namely "citizen of the European Union." In spite of relatively short-term difficulties around the ratification of the Maastricht Treaty in 1992-93, there is every reason to expect that in the medium term, economic, social, and possibly political integration and federalism in a United States of Europe are likely to develop. This will give historically unprecedented form to the traditional complexity of the European political experience, and it will allow it to be expressed and reinvented in new and unpredictable ways.

A feature of the post-industrial and post-national world emerging in the late twentieth century has been the simultaneously increasing importance of both transnational-level and subnational-level (global-local) political-economic systems and processes. In the E.C. context, this has been illustrated by the simultaneous growth in size and importance of the transnational E.C. level itself and of E.C. regions at the subnational level. Both levels offer people forms of general citizenship and of social citizenship in addition to their national citizenship. Circuits of citizenship capable of bypassing the nation-State level were created with the Treaty of Rome; circuits on the one hand between E.C. citizens and interest groups and E.C. political and legal institutions, and on the other hand between the latter and local (urban and regional) governments. These circuits and relationships have often filtered and detoured through the national government level, but there is every probability that in the post-1992 era they will increasingly become relatively independent of the national level and will grow in scale, complexity, and importance.

These political and social changes will require a rethinking, not only of traditional national citizenship, but also of the nature and balance of rights and duties of individuals and collectivities within and between all three of the political levels: local, national, and European (Bryant, 1991). This new complexity in the circuits of citizenship evidently has profound, if currently unclear, implications for the nature and future of social citizenship in Europe. The construction of the E.C. arguably provides a forerunner and a model of post-national world-regional political arrangements, which could well develop elsewhere in the world order over the course of the next century. To a large extent, it is in these world regions and in the world order itself, rather than in the nation-State, that the future of citizenship lies.

Conclusion

Capitalism, Change, and Social Citizenship
Given the continuing if eroding strength of nation-States in a post-national era, it is likely that a large part of the future politics of social citizenship will be concerned with attempts to repair and reconstruct the sorts of national functionalist arrangements between capitalism and its host societal context at the nation-State level, as discussed earlier and traditionally associated with what I have termed the dominant paradigm of Western social citizenship (Roche, 1992a:ch.9; Jordan, 1987; Walzer, 1985). In addition, however, it seems highly probable that the circuits and networks of post-

national power, political economy, and communication will continue to proliferate within Western and global society. With the example of the European Community in mind, it is reasonable to speculate that new projects of real and symbolic community formation will continue to emerge, together with possibilities for the renewal of citizenship politics. New sorts of functional and social contract arrangements, between capitalism and its societal context both at local and urban-regional levels and also at world-regional and global levels (Galtung, 1980; Dilloway, 1986), will be sought for and will develop, providing new spheres of struggle for identity and membership, for rights and obligations, in a word for the politics of citizenship.

Capitalism and the market system, relative to any other system, generate high standards of welfare for the mass of the population in Western countries. But, particularly in the recently fashionable unregulated form, they also generate severe diswelfare for marginalized groups, and social inequalities and ecological costs for all. Markets certainly embody some important principles of civil society, such as rights of privacy and private property and contractualism. They may also be managed so as to remain compatible with democratic and social citizenship principles. But this requires close monitoring, regulation, and where necessary, "fixing" by democratic political power; this is necessary to prevent the emergence and abuse of monopoly economic power, to provide equality of opportunity, and so on. In addition, as Walzer (1985) argues, for capitalism and market organization to remain compatible with social and political citizenship, clear and principled limits need to be developed and enforced, banning commodification and market-making in many spheres, building on such obvious spheres as the governmental process itself, human life itself, and so forth.

It is possible, but by no means certain, that out of the disorganization (Offe, 1985; Lash and Urry, 1987) of relations between capitalism and society in the late twentieth century, a new modus vivendi might be achieved. Arrangements roughly comparable to the national social contracts of the dominant paradigm could possibly emerge sooner or later; if they do, then they will necessarily be much more structurally complex in terms of subnational and transnational levels than before. Importantly, they will also in addition be more structurally complex in terms of providing a much larger, clearer, and more legitimate role for markets, along with the other elements of the mixed welfare economy, such as those embedded in the informal economy, the family system, voluntary associations, etc., elements which for too long have been hidden in the shadow of the welfare State.

They will also be more explicitly morally complex than dominant paradigm arrangements. These latter arrangements at least appeared to encourage one-dimensional, demoralized, and depoliticized conceptions of social citizenship in terms of social rights claims and the status of welfare clienthood. At the same time, by casting social citizenship as a mainly citizen-State process, they also tended to downplay citizen-citizen and citizen-capitalist corporation relations. In the modern period, social rights claims have been made as much against other citizens, usually relatives and usually female, and capitalist corporations, albeit with varying degrees of success, as they have been made against the State, also with varying degrees of success.

Public attention, given mainly to political struggles concerning the latter in much of the twentieth century, misrepresents the importance of the underlying civil society process of rights-duties exchanges in the familial and voluntary sectors, and of duties enforcement on capitalists in markets, the productive process, and the economic sphere in general. Expressed in terms of the metaphor of "figure and ground," in contemporary and future versions of any new social contract we are likely to see much more of social citizenship's civil society "ground", and by comparison, relatively less of the "figure", or now, given subnationalism and transnationalism, the figures of the State's servicing of welfare rights.

Future Citizenship: The Complexity Problem

The period in which it was possible to conceive of citizenship in general, and social citizenship in particular, in national and welfare State terms is clearly coming to an end. New positive myths and ideals of citizenship rights are developing, such as those involving notions of "the Earth's rights," the "rights of the unborn," and "world citizenship." They both enrich and complicate the more conventional modern myths and ideals relating to citizenship, such as those involving notions of human equality, of place and territorial identity, of nation, and of heritage. The new agendas for politics, and also for social theory and research, regarding social citizenship in the 1990s and beyond must, of course, continue to be concerned with nationally defined social citizenship and with the future of the welfare State. But they also need to be sensitive to these new developments. With this in mind, I have suggested that both contemporary politics and the social analysis of social citizenship need to be rethought by confronting citizenship's essential moral and structural complexity.

The development of social citizenship has always involved political mobilization and conflict, and the future doubtless will be no different in this respect. But the new lines of conflict are unlikely to be as clearly drawn as in the past, since they are likely to reflect these forms of complexity. To address the challenges of the 1990s and the early twenty-first century, both the politics and the study of social citizenship will need to go beyond the nation-State and the welfare State. They will need to grasp the emerging structural complexity and the new post-industrial and post-national dynamics influencing social citizenship, from familial and local levels to the transnational level and the inter-generational sphere. The far-reaching implications of these dynamics for the generation and transmission of poverty and social inequality, i.e., for the institutionalization of non-citizenship and second-class citizenship in modern and postmodern society, will need to be much better understood than they currently are in social policy and social research.

The political and moral complexity of social citizenship will also need to be much better understood than it currently is, both in theory and in practice. This form of complexity arises in part from the fact that, in all sorts of ways in our political and moral experience, rights and duties both conflict with and also imply each other. My discussion suggests that in the period of history that Western societies are now entering, the dominant paradigm's institutionalization of social rights claims is in crisis and will need to be fundamentally reconsidered. The various claims that social duties, both old (e.g., parental) and new (e.g., ecological), make on us all, both individually and collectively, will now need to be fully recognized. A new generation of social rights appropriate to changing structural conditions will need to be fought for and developed.

Given the West's long-standing experience of the development of what appear to be relatively "duty-free" rights, and given also the new structural and historical context and its associated problems and opportunities, a new and principled approach to social rights must now be on the agenda for any citizenship-oriented politics and social policy. This approach should, for instance, be one connecting them with human needs, including autonomy needs (Doyal and Gough, 1991; Roche, 1987; Roche, 1990b; Roche, 1994) as well as with human responsibilities.

The contemporary West has inherited a moral and political dialectic from the Enlightenment, between human rights in general and human social rights in particular on one side and human obligations and responsibilities on the other. On the one hand, as Kant argued, obligation and responsibility form the moral ground of human rights. On the other hand, as democrats and socialists have argued since the nineteenth century, the possession of need-satisfying rights is a necessary material ground, an empowering existential precondition, for the human ability to recognize and exercise responsibilities. This dialectic ought to be recognized as a necessary part of any post-national world and of any world-view which aims to be relevant to it.

References

Barbalet, J., (1988), *Citizenship* (Milton Keynes: Open University Press).

Betten, L. et al., eds., (1989), *The Future of European Social Policy* (Deventer and Boston: Kluver).

Bluestone, B., and B. Harrison, (1982), *The Deindustrialization of America* (New York: Basic Books).

Bowles, S., and H. Gintis, (1986), *Democracy and Capitalism* (London: Routledge).

Brubaker, R., (1992), *Citizenship and Nationhood in France and Germany* (Cambridge: Harvard University Press).

Bryant, C., (1991), "Europe and the European Community 1992," *Sociology,* 25, 2, pp.189-207.

E.C., (1985), "The Thrust of Commission Policy," *Bulletin of the European Communities,* Supplement 1/85 (Luxembourg: European Community Documentation).

E.C., (1990a), *1992 - The Social Dimension,* 4th edition (Luxembourg: European Community Documentation).

E.C., (1990b), *A Human Face for Europe* (Luxembourg: European Community Documentation).

Coenen, H., and P. Leisink, eds., (1993), *Work and Citizenship in the New Europe* (Aldershot: Edward Elgar).

Dilloway, J., (1986), *Is World Order Evolving?* (Oxford: Pergamon Press).

Doyal, L., and I. Gough, (1991), *A Theory of Human Need* (Basingstoke: Macmillan).

Galtung, J., (1980), *The True Worlds: A Transactional Perspective* (New York: Free Press/Macmillan).

Grahl, J., and P. Teague, (1990), *The Big Market: The Future of the European Community* (London: Lawrence and Wishart).

Hall, S., and M. Jacques, eds., (1989), *New Times* (London: Lawrence and Wishart).

Dennis, N., and A. H. Halsey, (1988), *English Ethical Socialism* (Oxford: Clarendon Press).

Held, D., (1989), "The Decline of the Nation State," in *New Times,* edited by S. Hall and M. Jacques (London: Lawrence and Wishart).

Featherstone, M., ed., (1990), *Global Culture: Nationalism, Globalization and Modernity* (London: Sage).

Gamble, A., (1990), "Britain's Decline: Some Theoretical Issues," in *The Rise and Decline of the Nation State,* edited by M. Mann (Oxford: Blackwell).

Jacobs, B., (1992), *Fractured Cities: Capitalism, Community and Empowerment in Britain and America* (London: Routledge).

Jordan, B., (1987), *Rethinking Welfare* (Oxford: Blackwell).

Judd, D., and M. Parkinson, eds., (1990), *Leadership and Urban Regeneration* (London: Sage).

Keane, J., and J. Owen, (1986), *After Full Employment* (London: Hutchinson).

Lash, S., and J. Urry, (1987), *The End of Organized Capitalism* (Cambridge: Polity Press).

Lister, R., (1990), *The Exclusive Society: Citizenship and the Poor* (London: Child Poverty Action Group).

Mann, M., (1990), "Empires without Ends," in *The Rise and Decline of the Nation State*, edited by M. Mann (Oxford: Blackwell).

Mann, M., ed., (1990), *The Rise and Decline of the Nation State* (Oxford: Blackwell).

Marshall, T. H., (1963), *Sociology at the Cross Roads* (London: Heinemann).

Marshall, T. H., (1972), "Value Problems of Welfare-capitalism," *Journal of Social Policy*, 1, 1 (January), pp.18-32.

Marshall, T. H., (1981), *The Right to Welfare* (London: Heinemann).

Offe, C., (1984), *Contradictions of the Welfare State* (London: Hutchinson).

Offe, C., (1985), *Disorganized Capitalism* (Cambridge: Polity Press).

Pahl, R., ed., (1988), *On Work* (Oxford: Blackwell).

Pierson, C., (1991), *Beyond the Welfare State? The New Political Economy of Welfare* (Cambridge: Polity Press).

Piore, M., and C. Sabel, (1984), *The Second Industrial Divide* (New York: Basic Books).

Pixley, J., (1993), *Citizenship and Employment: Investigating Post-industrial Options* (Cambridge: Cambridge University Press).

Roche, M., (1987), "Citizenship, Social Theory, and Social Change," *Theory and Society*, 16, pp.363-99.

Roche, M., (1990a), "Time and Unemployment," *Human Studies*, 13, 1, pp.1-25.

Roche, M., (1990b), "Rethinking Social Citizenship," World Congress of Sociology, ISA, Madrid, (mimeo), revised as "Rethinking Social Citizenship and Social Movements," in *Social Movements and Social Classes Today*, edited by L. Maheu (London: Sage, 1994).

Roche, M., (1992a), *Rethinking Citizenship: Welfare Ideology and Change in Modern Society* (Cambridge: Polity Press).

Roche, M., (1992b), "Mega-events and Micro-modernization: On the Sociology of the New Urban Tourism," *British Journal of Sociology*, 43, 4, pp.563-600.

Roche, M., (1994), "Citizenship and Anomie," in *Debating the Future of the Public Sphere*, edited by S. Edgell et al. (London: Avebury).

Sklair, L., (1990), *The Sociology of the Global System* (Brighton: Harvester-Wheatsheaf).

Standing, G., (1986), *Unemployment and Labour Market Flexibility: The U.K.* (Geneva: International Labour Organization).

Teague, P., (1989), *The European Community: The Social Dimension* (London: Kogan Page).

Teague, P., and C. Brewster, (1989), *European Community Social Policy* (Wimbledon: IPM).

Turner, B., (1986), *Citizenship and Capitalism* (London: Allen and Unwin).

Van Parijs, P., ed., (1992), *Arguing for Basic Income* (London: Verso).

Walzer, M., (1985), *Spheres of Justice* (Oxford: Blackwell).

Weber, M., (1970), *The Protestant Ethic and the Spirit of Capitalism* (London: Unwin).

Chapter Eight

A New/Old Frontier of Inequalities: Respect and Self-Respect As Policy Issues[1]

S. Michael Miller

The nation's problems come from the way people treat each other.

— Lorraine Smorol, art critic and musician

Respect and self-respect are no longer mainly issues of personal relations. They are now burning questions of inequality, policy, and politics; they share the public spotlight, with the distribution of income and wealth, as central stratificational worries.[2] At a time of widespread unemployment, declining wages and incomes, welfare State tightening, and profound fears about the economic future, it may appear strange to point to these terms of social appraisal and personal feelings as the cutting edge of policy and as key wedge political issues. But economic difficulties have fed, rather than undermined, the significance of respect and self-respect. This is evident in the heightened sensitivities in public and personal life about harassment, racism, sexism, ageism, homophobia, and multiculturalism-as-remedy. Slurs, neglect, and discrimination are not taken lightly today. This situation discomforts the many who do not understand, or who oppose, the new demands for respect.

In bad times the growing stress on respect and self-respect is a result of the fact that they are more than issues of civility and politeness. They count economically, socially, and politically, as well as emotionally. *How a society regards particular groups affects how it treats them.* In many countries, the negative treatment of women, minorities, immigrants, would-be immigrants, and many other social categories (e.g., those in means-tested programmes), is fostered by disrespect (Bourdieu, 1984:413-414).

Emphasizing respect and self-respect as questions of inequality does not downgrade the importance of poverty and economic inequalities or concerns with the level and distribution of income and wealth, because many of the adverse consequences of those pressing issues are most manifest among those who are disrespected. Low respect leads to low income, as evidenced in many employers' reluctance to hire African-Americans; low incomes reinforce the lack of respect for particular groups, for they can then be characterized as reluctant to work.

As we continually relearn, economics is not everything if we seek to redress the manifold injustices of society. Today, therefore, respect and self-respect are central components of an enlarged concept of citizenship. The concern here is with the way that social categories, not individuals, are regarded and treated. As Ervin Goffman pointed out, "... the nature of an individual, as he himself and we impute it to him, is generated by the nature of his group affiliation" (1963:2). Currently, social categories are fitted into two divisions. One is the long-term concern with classes, largely defined by their economic characteristics; class is termed an "achieved status," something that is changeable. The second consists of so-called "ascribed" characteristics, those which we can do little or nothing to change. Ascribed characteristics mark off social identities around gender, race, age, ethnicity, and religion. Other politically important social identities are sexual preference and disabilities.

The notion of "pillars," taken and extended from the governmentally recognized religious divisions in the Netherlands, is used to distinguish social identity groups, which theoretically at least could be from all classes, or from class or economically-based groups. All of us are in several pillars. Members of pillars are respected or disrespected because of the ascriptive characteristics of the group to which they are unavoidably connected. By contrast, those in high or low "achieved" statuses are respected or disdained because of where they are, their class position. The term "segment" will be used to refer to both pillars and classes.

The emphasis on group respect, whether pillar or class, does not mean that the characteristics of a given individual are unimportant in shaping the respect or disrespect that he or she receives. Respect refers to the way that a group or category is viewed; esteem is the rating given to an individual. It is not uncommon to hear that "if only all [blank] were like you." That blank could be filled by "academics," or "activists," as well as by many other categorical designations.

Most members of a disrespected segment must cope in some ways in their daily life and long-term prospects with how they are regarded and treated by those who exercise the privilege of judgement. Not infrequently, those disrespected by the mainstream may cope by not respecting those who feel that they have the sole right to judge others. Of more importance is the fact that low respect from others may induce low self-respect, which can be very disabling for group, as well as for individual, action, if it affects many in a class or pillar.

This chapter is *not* about the personal self-esteem that is promoted in individualizing self-improvement books. The focus is *not* on individual self-improvement, but on the impact of economic, political, and social structures on classes and pillars. Disrespected segments encounter distorting opportunities and obstacles in their everyday lives. Their life chances are shaped by degrees and types of disrespect. They must deal with disrespect in some way given that it has deep effects on their daily life as well as long-term prospects. Both disrespect and consequent adverse economic experiences influence the self-respect of a class or pillar and shape their actions and inactions. Respect is not a minor issue of stratification, nor of economic and political life.

The Functions of Respect

The ultimate test of a society is not only how well its citizens live but how they feel about themselves and others. The basic, though not exclusive, standard of a society is that people feel good about themselves, that they are respected, respect others, and have self-respect. Respect and self-respect shape what happens to people, politically and economically as well as socially; respect and self-respect are not relegated only to self-seeking prestige struggles.

The respect accorded to particular pillars and classes affects their participation in the economy and the extent and the way that a society responds to their needs and interests. Respect affects economic interactions and national attention and help. In short, *respect is an economic resource*; it is part of the competitive game. It provides access, information, and responsiveness. True, disrespect has psychological benefits for those who seize for themselves the right to be judges; it gives them a feeling of superiority and it enhances their chances of capturing rewards in economic and political markets.

Those who control the distribution of respect use it as a way of isolating competitors, of giving themselves an edge. The self-

assured qualities of those "to the manner born" enhance their bargaining power (Bourdieu, 1984). Payoffs of respect that groups
receive affect their ability to make deals, attract financial support,
and make their actions acceptable. C. Wright Mills pointed this out,
although his term was "prestige" (1956:83,88-90); respect yields an
economic return. This is true not only at the top end of the economic
ladder but at lower levels as well.

Disrespect from the larger society is a barrier to many opportunities; respect opens gates and doors. Disrespect disables some
while respect enables others; there is a *political economy of respect.*
Many employers are reluctant to hire workers from particular pillars
which are stigmatized as low-productivity, unskilled, or trouble
makers; job applications from those who live in certain residential
areas or who receive governmental aid may be ignored. Such splits
in respect divide or segment the labour market, so that those in pillars with low respect can only fill low-level or high-turnover jobs.
Some pillars have been restricted to occupational ghettos; the concentration of women in clerical jobs has led to low wages in these occupations. When wages begin to rise in low-skill jobs, immigrants
and rural people are recruited in order to depress wage levels. The
low respect for these people boxes them into these jobs. By contrast,
those with the markers of respect gain access to the better positions.
With the demographic projections that women and minorities will
become the majority of entrants into the labour force in the coming
decades, there is growing interest in promoting the productivity of
this future labour force. Building respect for, and self-respect
among, the entrants will be an important part of improving their
condition.

Disrespect has consequences in many realms. The disrespected
are treated discourteously in public exchanges and in public services; their political objectives get short shrift. Respect, on the other
hand, has political payoffs which may also contribute to economic
gain. Those classes and pillars which have high respect, such as
WASP or Anglo business figures, have access to political leaders and
the media, are consulted on issues important to them, are treated
seriously, and are often considered to be disinterested voices for "the
national interest." Those classes and pillars that are not respected
are often regarded as self-seeking and to represent "special interests." Disrespected pillars may be regarded as "strident," "unruly,"
or "loud," making it easy to discount their views.

As U.S. President John Adams noted as long ago as 1805, respect
is an "instrument of order and subordination in society, and alone

commands effectual obedience to laws" (quoted in Mills, 1956:90). Although Adams wrote in terms of individual esteem, its withholding or bestowal shaped the behaviour of classes and pillars. At the social interaction level, disrespect means the loss of "the right to expect civility from others" (Williams, 1991:165). "Being victimized by virtue of one's race, gender, or other immutable and morally neutral personal characteristic is universally acknowledged to represent an affront to one's humanity and dignity. . . ." (Tribe, 1992:4). Unfortunately, this acknowledgement is too often breached in practice.

Those whom we would exploit or dominate, we first disrespect, and then we attribute the subordination to the presumed disreputable condition or attributes of the dominated. Viewing a group as being deficient in some human qualities or desirable social practice makes it easier to mistreat them; guilt is banished. Slavery seemed acceptable when those enslaved were not regarded as fully human; holocausts do not appear reprehensible when victims are seen as threatening or lacking the positive qualities that the perpetrators believe that they themselves possess. It eases one's conscience to believe that exploited workers are dumb, depraved, and undeserving of respect. Those who are deemed different or less worthy, whether it is because they are believed to be incompetent, improvident, work-shy, or to engage in disapproved cultural styles, are regarded as undeserving and available for social and economic denigration. Those who are competing with us for resources of whatever kind can be subjected to chicanery and harshness because they are deemed unworthy of the prizes. In conditions of disrespect, it is possible to treat other groups as means, not ends. The Golden Rule is thus reversed: treat "the others" as you would not have your group treated.

The very disturbing rise of ethnic nationalism, of scapegoating, and of brutality, which dehumanize and demonize a people, should make us aware that disrespect for pillars, and less often, classes, is both powerful and dangerous — and functional for some. The call for "ethnic cleansing," that chilling reminder of the Nazis, is the other side of political solidarity and military power. The slogan not only intensifies support among the dominant ethnic or national group in a region, but it also removes those who might disagree with the ruling force. Recent events underline that demonizing a group has not been erased once and for all. While frightening manifestations are weaker in North America, nonetheless we too suffer from treating many groups as "the others."

Negative feelings about "the others," those identified as different from the supposed mainstream or dominant group or outlook, develop or intensify during difficult, strained times. Economic difficulties have fuelled people's fear of immigrants. Concern about "die Anderen" or "les étrangers" have resulted not only in barriers to immigration but to onslaughts against immigrants, with frightening results in Germany and disturbing prospects in the United States. Societal pressures and strains promote scapegoating and disrespect. One group can be played off against another, as in the long-time setting of poor whites against poor blacks in the American South. Right-wing hate groups, such as the Aryan Nation, are current threats. Calls for "English Only" reflect fears about demographic and social changes occurring in the United States. Although attacks and perceptions of attacks can build solidarity among pillars, it is inadequate recompense for the damage that is done.

The power to distribute or withhold respect is an important economic, political, and social commodity. Those who treat others or even only limit themselves to think of others with disrespect are according themselves the right to think and act as superior. Such outlooks and behaviours distort the self-assigned superiors as well as damaging those disrespected. Respect legitimizes economic gains; it strengthens the political position of particular groups. It divides society, improving the position of the favoured sectors. Disrespect toward some "others" has many benefits for those privileged to feel that they should, and do, control respect.

Respect is important in its own right, as well as because of its effect on self-respect, on a sense of personhood. To be treated only in terms of one's group label is to undermine one's personhood. As Martin Luther King Jr. stated in his stirring speech at the 1963 March on Washington: to be judged by one's colour, not by one's character, is distorting. Patricia Williams elegantly sums up the concern: "the trauma of gratuitous generalization" (Williams, 1991:82). One is treated as a category, not as a person. This is true for those who are accorded high respect for their group affiliation as well as for those who receive low marks because of their categorization. Of course, low marks have a more severe impact.

Class and Respect

The emphasis on pillars should not obscure the enduring impact of class. It is not only pillars that are negatively stereotyped; disrespect has a class bias. Grave economic disparities divide American society into a self-anointed deserving population and a growing, stigmatized, undeserving population, leading to what Robert Reich has termed "the secession" of the former from those who are suffering from the economic changes that are underway (Reich, 1991). As economic gaps widen, disrespect and revulsion towards the losers grow. Income differences count: "If you're poor you can't be happy because you're the object of revulsion and ridicule; if you're poor, you can't be satisfied because that's equated with laziness; if you're poor, you can't accept it as fate because poverty is your fault. . . ." (Williams, 1991:23-24).

In the contemporary United States, attitudes about poverty, especially that of African-Americans, often condemn the sufferers rather than criticize the conditions which produce low incomes and marginalization. The pejorative term "underclass" indicts the inner-city poor, largely but not exclusively defined as African-Americans, who are considered the authors of their own poverty because of their cultural practices. As we shall see, even money may not be enough to overcome the vilification of some pillars.

People in lower-level jobs and those with limited education are also cast in negative lights: "If you haven't been to college, you're dumb." Or at least limited in what you are capable of doing; many extraordinarily competent persons in high positions feel somehow intellectually limited because they lack a college degree. In 1991, less than a quarter (23.7 percent) of those aged 25-34 had completed college (U.S.A., 1992:Table 220); the percentage is considerably less for older groups. The vast majority of Americans, then, are likely to see themselves as intellectually and perhaps socially deficient or backward. This feeling may be particularly acute for those younger people who have not graduated from high school.

Often, respect issues are implicated in class actions. Many labour struggles are not about wages but about what workers see as disrespect by their employers. Workers feel belittled and unappreciated when employers are unwilling to discuss crucial changes in the conditions of work with them. Many labour historians believe that unions were formed more often because of employers' callousness than as a result of low wages. Despite historian E.P. Thompson's argument that class is about relationships, class respect and self-respect gain little attention even from social scientists.

Perhaps the classic statement on class disrespect (though it has many competitors) is that of Frederick Winslow Taylor, the "father of scientific management." Taylor saw "Schultz," his example of a strong-backed, weak-minded steel worker, as incapable of making judgements about the best way of carrying loads. Such tasks should be assigned to engineers who could calculate the one best way of carrying a load. The Schultzes of the world could only do the work of a beast; they could not do the job of figuring out how a beast of a job should best be done. The "strong back, weak mind" label has been attached to blue-collar workers and to others who do not do white-collar work. In general, it tends to be attached to those who do not speak formal English and who have a limited fund of school-based knowledge.

The disrespect experienced in daily life by blue-collar workers is also found in their portrayal on television. Bus driver Ralph Kramden, Jackie Gleason's classic character in the popular 1950s "Honeymooners" TV comedy, was represented as dumb, pretentious, duplicitous, and loud-mouthed. The prejudiced, narrow-minded, and ignorant TV character of the 1970s, Archie Bunker, could easily be accepted as only a slightly exaggerated depiction of a worker with limited education and understanding. In the 1990s, Lowell, the mechanic on the sitcom "Wings," is that of a dumb, slow, hapless worker in overalls. Indeed, the paucity of working-class shows and characters is striking in U.S. television. This is not a new phenomenon; we found a similar pattern in a study of class in television presentations in the late 1950s (Miller et al., 1961). Currently, TV's daytime soaps uniformly picture rich and near-rich characters ferociously competing for love, control, and money. The underlying message is that without money your life is uninteresting, deadened by quiet rather than loud desperation. The scarcity of blue-collar characters as a form of disrespect for the latter can be manifested by a lack of attention as well as by a negative portrayal.

Today, class disrespect receives less attention than pillar disrespect. What contributes to the underplaying of class disrespect is that weak political action around class issues often contrasts with the surging of identity politics. Obviously that oversimplifies the situation, since identity or pillar politics are also importantly about economic questions. Nonetheless, the weakening of labour unions has resulted in the downplaying of class politics. The rhetorical absorption of the "working class" into an enormous loose-bounded middle class has not highlighted the plight of those at the lower end of this omnibus category.

Class may converge with social identities or cut through them, producing tensions within a social identity category, as in the contention that U.S. women's groups are primarily dominated by white

middle-class women and their concerns, paying inadequate attention to the issues confronting low-income African-American
women. Identity politics now threads through class politics. Certainly identity politics is not as powerful in economic politics as it
should be, but it is recognized, increasingly, as vital in a politics of
class and economics. No longer can the pillar characteristics of members of a class be ignored. *Class members are not social ciphers.* The
social identity of those who would benefit from a class action is part
of the politics of class. The question of who leads class formations
has become significant, as seen in the demands for more leadership
representation by women, African-Americans, and Latinos. Both pillars and classes and their interaction are now important, both in the
issue of respect as well as in political and economic action.

Producing Disrespect

Disrespect takes many forms: discrimination, physical action,
prejudice, mocking, segregation, looking down upon, marginaliz-
ing, scapegoating, physical action against, automatic relegating to
subordinate positions, oral or written putdowns, harassing,
demonizing, stereotyping, over-generalizing, and one-sided interpretations of attitudes and behaviour. Many social categories suffer
from one or another of these manifestations of disrespect. Both
stereotypes and institutional practices are essential processes of disrespect. The respect/disrespect view is likely to be largely shaped by
stereotypes, which are based on limited and misleading information; in short, an unsound basis for judgement. Nonetheless, or perhaps because of the weakness of the knowledge base, the respect
outlook is important in terms of what happens to people and how
the group thinks of itself.

The impact of respect is felt economically, socially, and politically
as well as psychologically. Disrespect results from institutional practices as well as from ad hoc, personal, and circumstantial actions.
Patriarchy and racism are powerful influences on respect and self-
respect. They become enshrined and encoded in the practices of
many organizations, so that the outcomes burden particular pillars
and classes. Disrespect is produced in a variety of ways. In general,
enforced segregation in housing, schools, or daily life not only
evidences disrespect, but produces it by facilitating its expression:
"People who live in public housing are shiftless." Social distance

leads to rumours, stereotypes, and fears about those who are isolated.

All too frequently, schools are prominent agencies for disrespect. They have labelled some pillars and classes as having low educability and have made them feel that they are stupid in one way or another. They convinced girls that they were not good in science and mathematics, although that disabling is now less frequent. African-Americans, especially if they come from one-parent families, are sometimes characterized as having "educational deficits" when they enter school and therefore as unable to learn. Many African-American school and college students have teachers and peers who display open disdain for their competence and potential. Ethnic groups have also been regarded as "uneducable." This was the label attached to East European Jews in New York City in the 1890s, who lived in deplorable housing conditions and were regarded as an unclean rabble (Greer, 1972); their progeny went on to considerable educational achievement. For some, schools educate; for "the educational others," they often make them feel and act dumb. Disrespect and low self-respect feed each other.

Media accounts mainly report on African-Americans when welfare, poverty, crime, or violence are involved. Latinos gain attention mainly when illegal immigration is the focus. The activities of those who are not poor, or who are attempting to improve communities, get much less attention unless they are celebrities. The public's false impression is that most African-Americans are poor and on welfare, and that underclass conditions are their usual way of life. Hollywood has contributed to the stereotyping of African-Americans, especially the young, as mainly poor, hostile, and violent. Disrespect and fear join to create a disturbing situation for young black men. They are bitter about the disrespect shown by those white people and police who assume that their presence means crime or violence will occur. Getting "respec'" becomes a prime motive; such a concern may lead to a swaggering, tough demeanour. In turn, this may make some whites and police feel more threatened, and they may then respond with more disrespect or with force.

The Production of Self-Respect

To a major extent, self-respect depends on respect from others, the way one's group is regarded and treated, the experiences encountered in interactions, the standards that are deemed acceptable in society, and the economic and social prospects that are likely. In this perspective, *self-respect is a social product,* not an individual, independent, completely autonomous judgement. How people feel about themselves, their sense of their capacity to do things, their experience of well-being, all these affect the ability to manage their economic and personal lives. Those low in self-respect find it difficult to get, or to advance in, a job; their daily challenges can become overwhelming; the capacity to avoid unproductive ways of responding to pressures and to difficulties is weakened. Social processes push people into self-disrespect.

The parent of self-respect is respect or disrespect. Acts, and even intimations, of disrespect not only cause discomfort and pain, they lower feelings of competence ("People like us can't learn from books"), and they weaken the self-power of classes and pillars. Public opinion analyst Ethel Klein contends, for example, that pregnancy among female African-American teenagers is related to their unsureness about their right to make demands of their sexual partners. Disrespect may produce responses that are unproductive, counter-productive, or even destructive: ". . . if individuals are members of a group in society, usually a minority group, that is routinely abased, thought to be inferior, and denied access to chances for advancement and a share of the good things in life, those individuals may pick up and wear the image that they do not count for much or deserve much" (Mecca et al., 1989:2). They may instead ". . . take refuge in behaviours that are unproductive, costly, deviant, and dangerous" (Mecca et al., 1989:1).[3]

Respect affects what people are encouraged or discouraged from doing; self-respect affects the ability of people to undertake worthy tasks or to avoid detrimental actions or to be taken seriously and positively. Patricia Williams has been particularly eloquent in expressing the experience and demands of African-Americans. She decries the "incomplete social relations" that they encounter (1991:154), because fear, hatred, and taboo are widespread (1991:159). For the poor, especially, ". . . if being is seeing for the subject, then being seen is the precise means of existence for the object" (1991:25). "The right to expect civility from others" (1991:165) is breached. "For blacks, then, the attainment of rights signifies the respectful behaviour, the responsibility, properly owed by a society to one of its own" (1991:153).

George Herbert Mead and Charles H. Cooley each contributed a widely quoted phrase to describe the process of child development: from Mead, "the generalized other"; from Cooley, "the looking glass self." The former term refers to the outside world that the infant begins to recognize as expecting certain kinds of response from it. "The looking glass self" conveys the understanding of self that the infant learns from the way that others respond to and deal with it (Mead, 1934; Cooley, 1922). Both terms convey how the outside world was brought to the child, so that the child learned how it was viewed and what was expected of it. Since so many adults in the U.S. ask "Who am I?" or are confused about how others feel about them, Cooley's mirror is cracked and Mead's normative structure shaky. People are not getting a firm, positive picture of who they are. This uncertainty is particularly powerful, negative, and harmful to those from social categories which are generally viewed disrespectfully. From an early age, the American looking glass is not presenting a clear, positive image to many pillars.

The response of a pillar or class segment to the respect or disrespect that it experiences can be very varied. Respect breeds self-respect; certainly the respect of others makes it easier to have respect for one's group. Nonetheless, a group can have self-respect even if it is looked down upon by many. Indeed, fighting against disrespect, as in the consciousness-raising groups prominent in the women's movement in the United States, can strengthen self-respect. Identity politics is based on, and contributes to, the production of self-respect. A demeaned group needs ideology, a positive self-portrait, if it is to resist negative views of it: "Black is beautiful" is a way of armouring against the arrows of the fault-finders. But disrespect is powerful: it can produce self-disrespect. Even fighting negative societal evaluations can be debilitating, wearisome and distorting.

Doesn't Money Do the Job?

Certainly, increasing incomes is a way of increasing respect. But it does not assure that result. The use of terms like *parvenu* or *arriviste* to apply to those who have made it into the higher reaches of society indicates that R.H. Tawney overstated the speed of change when he said that money is the catalytic agent that turns red blood into blue. The withholding of respect is a form of social control that money can only partially dent. That money and/or position do not buy automatic respect is not restricted to the upper reaches of society. Upper middle-class African-Americans complain they are treated disrespectfully by police, shop clerks, co-workers, and others in daily interactions. "Successful" women report widespread incidents of disrespect. The disgraceful Tailhawk episode, where U.S. Navy women officers were forced to run a gauntlet of male officers who sexually harassed them, indicates that liberties can be taken with women regardless of their official position. The initial attempts to cover up the incident revealed the acceptability, and probably the widespread occurrence, of such behaviour. The "glass ceiling," thus far in the executive suite and no further, hit by effective and aspiring women and African-Americans, is again an indication of the barrier of disrespect. The attack on affirmative action by some successful African-Americans and Latinos is based on the undermining of others', and perhaps their own, confidence that they merit their success. Disrespect of a pillar can undermine the rise of members of that pillar.

Politicizing Respect

Categorizations by race, gender, and class structure the respect and self-respect available to people. This situation has led to, and has been accentuated by, the emergence or strengthening of identity politics, the concentrating of affiliation, ideology, and political outlook around social identities as women, African-Americans, Latinos or Asians, gays and lesbians, ethnics, seniors, and people with disabilities, or around universal issues, such as peace or the environment. The "new social movements" emerged from and stimulated identity or pillar politics. They stand in contrast to more sharply focused class-oriented or class-based social movements or institutions, like labour unions or tenants' movements; not that gender and race are uninvolved in these movements, but they have not been the main basis, at least so far, of the organizing call. Class, though less accentuated today, still influences identity, for respect and self-respect for people in lower economic positions are thwarted in many ways, while approbation for those economically or educationally successful is exaggerated.

In recent years, at least in the United States, respect has become politicized. Both in the broad sense of public discussion, and in the more narrow realm of political action, respect has gained attention. Expressions like "the personal is political" capture the broadening of the political world and point to the conflicts around respect. Public consciousness has certainly grown about language: "nigger" is assigned to the scrap heap, no longer the widely used term it once was. The term "girl" is disappearing more slowly as a reference to adult women. Some colleges and universities have instituted speech codes to restrict the use of terms that are offensive to African-Americans, Latinos, women, or gays and lesbians. Breaches of acceptable language can lead to penalties. For example, sports broadcasters who expressed doubts about the capacities of African-Americans to perform as coaches have lost their jobs. Ethnic epithets and negative portraits are on the wane or, at least, denounced when made public. The attention to language, such as the way people are addressed, is not an affectation; it is about the maintenance of hierarchies by belittling some pillars. The confronting of the implicit or explicit assumption, expressed in the title of an English literature course, that "dead, white, male heterosexuals" alone have made history, or the contrasting call for multicultural education, indicate the increasingly recognized importance of respect and self-respect.

The furor about these excursions into once-settled issues is in considerable part a struggle about the power to anoint and to denigrate. As Jacqueline Ortiz has noted, "clashing epistemologies and historical versions" imply a bid for the transfer of power from once firmly perched elite groups, defined by their pillar characteristics (e.g., male, white), presumably as well as by their intellectual achievement. Traditionally accepted interpretations of social realities are now challenged and undermined, raising questions of who and what is to be respected. Pillar groups are speaking up and sometimes acting out to combat disrespectful language and action. They have developed the expectation and largely won the right to defend themselves against negative accounts. They do not turn the other cheek or ignore insults; they combat attacks on their social space and social identities. Pillar groups have become actors in promoting respect and self-respect.

The obvious need is to connect identity politics with class politics. Respect and self-respect can be major linkages because those in dominated classes also endure low respect and frequently suffer from the pressures of low self-respect. Respect/self-respect issues are common to both classes and pillars. Indeed, some contend that class politics will not succeed today without pillar connections. To join the two requires transcending the zero-sum rhetoric that is used to keep them apart: that the gain of one pillar is at the expense of the economic and social situation of a dominated class, or of other pillars. The task is to improve wages and expand jobs for all rather than squabbling over a dwindling pie. The important understanding is that respect and self-respect are now issues of both civility and inequality; in short, they are stratificational, political, and policy concerns.

The Public Policy of Respect

Respect is no longer regarded as only an individual act. It is seen as having deep long-term effects on society and the economy. Governments and institutions such as universities are expected — it may not be too strong to say charged — with the responsibility to do something about blocking disrespectful actions. Or to emphasize the pro-active rather than reactive side, to actively promote pillar self-respect. To recognize this new responsibility of government and institutions is not to assert that they always accept that burden or pursue it well. For example, the treatment of those receiving welfare assistance and other means-tested programmes can be punishing and demeaning. A suspicious observer might conclude that stringent and distasteful welfare procedures in the United States not only are a deliberate effort to reduce the rolls, by making it difficult to gain and maintain eligibility, but also are politically acceptable because they are incorrectly thought of as almost exclusively affecting African-American and Latina mothers. Consequently, there is a broad public interest in promoting respect.

Policies and pressures to contain disrespect have several objectives. One is that they are aimed at reducing prejudice, by leading people to think about pillar and class groups in less stereotyped ways. Addressing them in more positive terms begins to change the way that they are viewed; it is an educational step. The second hope is that opportunities will expand. For example, viewing manual workers as having a special knowledge of how their tasks are best done can lead to an expansion of their autonomy on the job. The third expectation is that a change in terminology makes life easier, or more comfortable, for groups that have been disrespected. The fourth aim is that respect will engender more effective economic and social activity by those in once-disrespected social categories.

Policies extend much beyond language to affect the circumstances of demeaned social categories. The current debate about the merits of affirmative action should not obscure the public, political, and judicial consensus that discrimination against pillars is now deemed unacceptable. While this principle is breached in practice, it is done covertly rather than openly pursued as in the past, when "no Irish need apply," "whites only," "men only," or "Christians only," were listed in want-ads and were well-known personnel practices of many companies. It is now unlawful in the U.S. to practice such policies. In the sphere of employment, and to a lesser extent in the housing field, there is general agreement that discrimination should end. How to do that produces strong controversy; the objective engenders much less.

Involving pillars and classes in roles and activities that have been unavailable or denied to them is an important way of enhancing self-respect. For example, the international poverty organization, *Aide à Toute Détresse-Fourth World*, which works in many countries with the poorest of the poor, the most excluded, strives to have spokespersons from the poor speak on their own behalf and in their own name. In general, increasing the participation and widening the role of once-marginalized people can result in heightened self-respect. The "maximum feasible participation" requirement of the legislation which established the American war on poverty was not only a political step in that it gave the poor in their localities some say in what policies were adopted; nor was it only an economic step in its encouragement of the employment of neighbourhood people in publicly funded projects. It was also a step toward self-respect, enlarging not only what people thought that they could demand of government but also what they and their neighbours were capable of doing. It was not completely successful in achieving these objectives, but it made some progress.

Building self-respect, then, is not only a matter of some in a disadvantaged group having a strengthened self-image, advancing into mainstream sectors, and thereby presumably providing role models for those left behind. All too often, unfortunately, so-called role models have not carved out a path which makes it easier for the next individual or individuals to cross over into the mainstream. A major reason is that the role model has not changed the difficult rules of the game but has only learned how to play them. More important than role modelling is encouraging members of a pillar or class to join together in collective activities that give them feelings of competence and achievement. The very act of joining together, working effectively together, can be a powerful move in promoting both respect and self-respect. Those who are disparaged frequently do not see how they can work together, and of course others who benefit from the absence of protest encourage dulled acquiescence or the divide-and-conquer tactic of encouraging bickering among the exploited. If the joint action also produces positive results, then self-respect is enhanced and perhaps respect as well. For example, a strong neighbourhood movement that started in low-income Latino areas of San Antonio has not only changed the politics of that city but has also strengthened feelings of self-respect and empowerment and forced Anglos to change their unwillingness to treat Latinos with respect (Boyte, 1989:86ff).

A pillar or class with self-respect is more likely to be politically active than one that lacks this quality. Self-respect, then, is a political act in gaining it and a political action in using it. Political activity affects two components of citizenship: widening and deepening the rights and everyday expectations of those who are usually neglected or suppressed, and promoting the participation by the marginalized in decision-making.

As sociologists and political scientists have taken up T.H. Marshall's analysis of the evolution of citizenship (Marshall, 1950) after a lapse of almost forty years, some sense not only that Marshall may have been too optimistic about the sturdy and secure future of citizenship but also that his approach is too narrow. Marshall saw, at least in Britain, the evolution of citizenship from the institutionalization of judicial equality (equal justice for all), to political justice (universal suffrage and one person, one vote), and finally to social or economic justice (full employment and an extensive welfare State). Marshall's analysis does not pay attention to respect and self-respect as important components of the new citizenship, a citizenship that touches social relations as well as juridical and political standing, nor does it face the added responsibility of government to strongly promote them. Economic, political, and social rights are now qualitatively different from what they once were.

The difference can be seen in the questions that are raised about the conceptualizing, framing, and administering of economic and social programmes, so that they demonstrate respect and enhance self-respect. How are once-marginalized groups treated; how to build genuine participation of recipients/customers in programmes that have long been dominated by socially distant administrators and professionals; how to demonstrate respect in the facilities and everyday transactions of an agency? Such issues, built on the American efforts in the 1960s to increase the participation of the poor, are now broadened to pillars and other classes.

The attraction of self-help/mutual aid activities point to the enhancement of self-respect when people feel that they are helping themselves and each other in coping with their problems. Could self-help/mutual aid processes play a prominent role in social programmes, not as a way of saving money, but as a means of building self-respect, improving outcomes, and contributing to respect? Threading self-help and mutual aid into public programmes probably would mean changing some of their important components, like prohibiting responsibility to an outside party.

Conclusion

The problem of respect is not new, for struggles about it have been occurring for a long time. What is new is the variety of the groups seeking respect and the intense politicization of so many issues of respect. The argument here is *not* for a downgrading of the importance of the level and distribution of the economic resources of income, wealth, and services. They are crucial in making societies better and less stratified. Mickey Kaus (1992) has made a strong case for the importance of social or civic equality which, in effect, means mutual respect and acceptance. Where he is misleading is that he contends that this important form of equality can be achieved without reducing economic inequalities. In my view, reducing economic inequalities is basic. For if inequalities remain as great as they now are, it will be very difficult to build the common institutions of schools and communities that Kaus advocates. But reducing economic inequalities is not all that we must seek. The contention here is that they do not, in themselves, guarantee everything that is important in the struggle to lessen inequalities; in that respect, Kaus is certainly right. Exclusively concentrating on income issues downplays the importance of pillar concerns today. Who benefits and how are significant questions.

Respect and self-respect affect not only the command over resources but also the character of our daily lives.

Which brings us to Polanyi, who always understood that social relations formed the underpinning of society (Polanyi, 1944). But we cannot be confident any longer that "societal" control of the economy assures respect for all. That is why the objective of greater economic equality has to be joined to the promotion of respect and self-respect. It is not better incomes and a better distribution versus lessened disrespect, but the pursuit of both, that is important. To some extent, reducing disrespect and promoting self-respect will contribute to the political process of reducing economic inequalities. The other side of the coin is that lessened economic inequalities will blanket more segments with respect. Today, both money and respect are critical policy and political objectives.

Notes

1. I want to acknowledge Jacqueline Ortiz's useful assistance. Harold Beneson offered useful comments.
2. Respect and disrespect, as used here, refer to the generalized approval or disapproval of a group by those not in other groups. Respect and disrespect are most important when the verdict is made by a large majority of a group which is regarded, and regards itself, as in an authoritative position to make and carry out judgements. Self-respect is the outlook of the majority of members of an appraised group.
3. These quotations are from a book which was a project of a commission that was established by the California legislature to study the impact of low self-esteem. Unfortunately, the outlook focused on individual rather than group bases of esteem, but some beginning was made to see issues of respect as a public issue.

References

Bourdieu, Pierre, (1984), *Distinction* (Cambridge: Harvard University Press).

Boyte, Harry, (1989), *Common Wealth: A Return to Citizen Politics* (New York: Free Press).

Cooley, Charles H., (1922), *Human Nature and the Social Order* (New York: Charles Scribner's Sons).

Greer, Colin, (1972), *The Great School Legend* (New York: Basic Books).

Goffman, Ervin, (1963), *Stigma: Notes on the Management of Spoiled Identity* (New York: Prentice Hall).

Kaus, Mickey, (1992), *The End of Equality* (New York: Basic Books).

Marshall, T. H., (1950), *Class, Citizenship, and Social Development* (Garden City, N.Y.: Doubleday).

Mead, George H., (1934), *Mind, Self, and Society* (Chicago: University of Chicago Press).

Mecca, Andrew M., Neil Smelser, and John Vasconcellos, (1989), *The Social Importance of Self-Esteem* (Los Angeles: University of California Press).

Miller, S.M., et al., (1961), "Television and Social Class," *Sociology and Social Research*, (April).

Mills, C. Wright, (1956), *The Power Elite* (New York: Oxford University Press).

NYT, (1992), *The New York Times*, (11 May).

Polanyi, Karl, (1944), *The Great Transformation* (Boston: Beacon Press).

Reich, Robert B., (1991), *The Work of Nations* (New York: Knopf).

Tribe, Lawrence, (1992), "Correspondence: Proper Punishment," *The New Republic*, (9 November).

U.S.A., (1992), *Statistical Abstract of the United States* (Washington: Bureau of the Census).

Williams, Patricia, (1991), *The Alchemy of Race and Rights* (Cambridge: Harvard University Press).

Chapter Nine

Dissidence and Insurgency: Municipal Foreign Policy in the 1980s[1]

Warren Magnusson

Municipalities occupy ambivalent spaces between the State, the market, and everyday life. They are constituted as expressions of local community, and as such are designed for local self-government, and yet they also operate as police agencies of the State and as businesses seeking profits for their shareholders. This ambivalence is expressed in the legal status of the municipality as a corporation, at one and the same time a political *association* of the inhabitants of a place, a *public agency* that derives its powers from the central authorities, and a *business* whose shareholders are the owners and occupiers of land in the community (Frug, 1980; Isin, 1992; Magnusson, 1986). In the rhetoric of statism, each of these guises is a sign of subordination: the State itself is the supreme political association; it claims authority over every business within its territory and it governs public agencies under its constitution. Nevertheless, the subordination of municipalities is never complete. The people who enter these ambivalent spaces can tap into demands for local autonomy, wring concessions as agents for the centre, and connect with processes beyond the control of any State. As such, they can, by artful practices, begin to disrupt the oppressive enclosures and relations of domination that characterize the contemporary world.

There is no guarantee that the political spaces afforded by municipal government will be used in such an innovative way, and indeed there is strong pressure to fix the municipality as an executive committee for the local bourgeoisie. In this respect, Singapore and Hong Kong appear as post-modern exemplars of the civic republics of an earlier era, prospering in the gaps between States and empires and organizing themselves as nodes in the global economy. In an era of diminishing nation-States, the free marketeers imply that aggressive municipalities, which put business first, can aspire to "world-city" status. (There is even a social democratic variant of this theory that points to the possibility of binding labour to capital by appropriate social contracts). It is thus that we see cities opening offices of international affairs, developing sister-city linkages, sending trade missions abroad, fostering cultural exchanges, competing for international games and expositions, and generally promoting themselves independently of their national governments (Fry et al., 1989). For the most part, the States concerned have treated such municipal activities with benign neglect if not active encouragement, since there is nothing at stake that threatens the existing order. On the other hand, a surprising number of dissident or insurgent municipalities have begun, since about 1980, to challenge the policies of their national governments and to open up their own international relations, focused on matters like global peace and security, universal human rights, environmental protection, and conditions of life for the poor. These activities have been facilitated by the globalization of international communications, but they have not been geared to the market purposes implicit in the drive toward world-city status.

In the U.S.A. and Britain, the development of dissident foreign policies at the local level can be attributed in part to the triumph of neo-conservatism in national politics. Whatever the ideological inclinations of the Left, dissidents in the 1980s were forced to operate within the political spaces that remained to them. On the one hand, there were social movements like environmentalism and peace activism, which increasingly defied the boundaries between States, and on the other hand, there were enclaves of provincial or municipal authority that the Left could take by electoral means. Without much sense of an overarching strategy, "Left" municipal councils began to use their own authority to challenge national policies on nuclear armaments, civil defence, relations with revolutionary regimes, the reception and treatment of refugees, the control of pollutants, and the character of assistance to the poor. By connecting with one another in national and international unions of local authorities, tapping into the programmes of the United Nations and its agencies, and concerting their activities with wider social movements, progressive municipalities were able to articulate alternatives on a global scale. This activity has not received much attention from political scientists,[2] and it is often discounted, even by participants, as purely gestural. Nonetheless, in a world of weakening States and strengthening cultural and economic connections, the political possibilities foreshadowed by these practices deserve closer attention.

Free Zones, Sanctuaries, and State Sovereignty

Many of the dissident municipalities have declared themselves "free zones" or "sanctuaries," the former in relation to nuclear weaponry and the latter in relation to refugees or military deserters. The language of the declarations is redolent of the medieval German idea that "city air makes free": that a serf could win his freedom by living peaceably in a city for a year and a day. Civic authority originally was rooted in popular freedoms and had to be won from both the nobility and the clergy. The post-modern notion of the free zone or sanctuary is an expression of a similar claim that people in particular communities have the right to opt out of practices that, while they may have the sanction of regal or national authorities, are at odds with more fundamental principles. The question is whether such opting out can be made effective in face of the apparently overwhelming power of the nation-State. The history of the free zones and sanctuaries is surprisingly positive in this respect.

The sanctuary movement in the United States began within religious congregations, which invoked the ancient principle that churches and temples were spiritual sanctuaries that should be respected by the secular authorities.[3] Since the ministers and priests within these sanctuaries were to provide help and succour to any who sought it, they could not be expected to reject or expel anyone who looked to them for protection. By extension, this principle could apply to the whole of a congregation and their property. Moreover, people who wanted to live out their religious convictions could well claim the right to extend help to those who were seeking refuge but had not yet arrived in places of sanctuary. In the case of Central Americans fleeing oppressive regimes, this pointed towards helping the refugees across the border with Mexico, transporting them to more northerly cities, getting them food, shelter, and medical care, finding them work — and shielding them from the federal Immigration and Naturalization Service (INS).

Municipal declarations of sanctuary originally were intended to provide local political support for sanctuaries established independently by religious congregations or similarly minded secular groups. Berkeley had actually declared itself a sanctuary for draft resisters and deserters from the U.S.A. armed forces in 1971, in the context of protests against the Vietnam War. At a conference in Tucson in January 1985, the old Berkeley resolution was brought forward as a model response to recent arrests of activists accused of aiding illegal immigrants. Delegates went home and quickly secured council resolutions in a number of cities, beginning with Berkeley and Madison. As the municipal sanctuary movement spread, the religious and secular activists intensified their efforts. A version of the Underground Railroad was established to get people from the Mexican border areas to northerly sanctuaries, and it was in this context that a number of sanctuary workers were arrested for transporting illegal aliens. A National Sanctuary Defence Fund was established, partly with money raised by sympathetic European churches, themselves involved in their own refugee work. The sanctuary workers were connected informally with various other organizations doing Central American support work. Thus they became involved not only in providing refuge but in accompanying people back to the areas from which they had fled and to which the U.S. government thought they should return.

When municipalities got involved, they appealed not only to principles of morality but also to their rights and duties under international law. For instance, the city of Madison, Wisconsin adopted the following resolution on March 5th, 1985:[4]

> WHEREAS, the United Nations Convention relating to the Status of Refugees has defined the conditions of political refugee as "any person who owing to a well-grounded fear of being persecuted for reasons of race, religion, nationality, membership in a particular social group or of a political opinion, is outside the country of his(her) nationality and is unable, or, owing to such fear, is unwilling to avail himself of the protection of that country"; and

> WHEREAS, the United States Congress has adopted this convention in the Refugee Act of 1980; and

> WHEREAS, the United Nations High Commission on Refugees has recognized that persons fleeing El Salvador and Guatemala are bona fide political refugees, yet fewer than two percent are being granted that status by the U.S. Immigration Service; and

> WHEREAS, deportation of those seeking asylum has often meant disappearance or death upon their return home; and

> WHEREAS, members of those religious communities offering sanctuary to the refugees believe themselves

to be acting not in civil disobedience but under the law of the land; and

WHEREAS, both refugees and sanctuary workers in Texas, Arizona, Washington, New York, California, and Pennsylvania have been detained or indicted in recent days; and

WHEREAS, within the City of Madison, we have both refugees and sanctuary providers for whom fear of deportation and the threat of arrest have an increasing immediacy; and

WHEREAS, the Common Council passed a resolution on June 3, 1983 in support of those sanctuaries when first refugees came to our City;

NOW THEREFORE, BE IT RESOLVED, that the Common Council of the City of Madison reaffirms that resolution, declares Madison a City of Refuge, and supports the religious communities of the City of Madison in their efforts to provide sanctuary; and

BE IT FURTHER RESOLVED, that the people of Madison will not condone for its own citizens who are providing sanctuary the harassment, indictments or arrests which have been experienced by sanctuary workers in other cities at the instigation of the U.S. Immigration Service; and

BE IT FURTHER RESOLVED, that no employee of the City of Madison will violate the established sanctuaries by assisting in investigations, public or clandestine, by engaging in or assisting with arrests for alleged violation of immigration laws by the refugees in the sanctuaries or by those offering sanctuary, or by refusing established public services to the established sanctuaries; and

BE IT FURTHER RESOLVED, that the Madison Common Council urges the Immigration Service to provide the refugees with the status of "extended voluntary departure," so that they may live among us free of the

threat of deportation until conditions allow their
return home.

The Madison city council was by no means isolated. By mid-1989
there were 29 declared sanctuary cities in the U.S.A. (BMFP,
1989a:18), including Detroit, Los Angeles (Merina, 1985),[5] and San
Francisco (NYT, 1985:7).[6] In some but not all of these cities, the police
and other local officials were ordered, as in Madison, not to
cooperate with the INS in its investigations. Where there were large
numbers of undocumented migrants, as in California, local
authorities could invoke legitimate concerns about public health
and welfare to resist demands that they should police immigration.
Since illegal immigrants would be afraid to present themselves for
medical treatment, send their children to school, or complain about
unsafe working conditions if they thought that they would be
deported as a result, there were credible local policy reasons for not
inquiring about people's citizenship status.

This resistance activity of the sanctuary movement in many
ways paralleled the activities of the anti-nuclear and disarmament
movements, not only in the moral fervor it generated but also in the
use it made of municipal powers. In December 1979, NATO decided
to modernize its nuclear weaponry and prepare itself to fight a
"limited" nuclear war with the Soviet Union (Thompson and Smith,
1980; Thompson, 1980). In response, the British CND (Campaign for
Nuclear Disarmament) began to mobilize its supporters in a major
struggle for European Nuclear Disarmament. This effort was soon
matched throughout western Europe and was echoed in a "Call to
Halt the Arms Race" issued by American peace groups in April 1980
(Solo, 1988). In Santa Cruz, California, local activists picked up on
the idea of a municipal "nuclear-free zone," pioneered in Japan in
the late 1950s and imitated in Australia and New Zealand in the
1970s but never before attempted on the home territory of one of the
nuclear powers, and tried unsuccessfully to get local ballot approval
to zone out a proposed weapons factory (Bennett, 1987:80-83). There
was a much deeper well of support for disarmament initiatives
among the Labour-controlled local authorities in Britain, and the
Manchester city council took the lead on November 5th, 1980, by
declaring the city a nuclear-free zone. The Council appealed to the
British Government "to refrain from the manufacture or positioning
of nuclear weapons of any kind in the boundaries of our city" and
called upon other local authorities "to make similar statements on
behalf of the citizens they represent" (Manchester, 1987). Within a

year, 119 councils in Britain had followed suit. The movement spread to other European countries, especially Italy, Holland, and West Germany, and by 1984 there was enough interest to hold the First International Nuclear Free Zone (NFZ) Local Authority Conference. Two years later, an international secretariat was created in Perugia, Italy, by which time there were 3,000 nuclear-free-zone authorities in 17 countries worldwide.

The movement spread slowly in the United States, partly because of the need for grassroots initiatives to get popular support for ballot measures or town meeting resolutions. The "nuclear freeze" campaign, in which resolutions were presented to "initiate an immediate, verifiable, mutual halt to the production, testing, and deployment of new nuclear weapons and their delivery systems," dominated peace politics at the local level in 1980-82.[7] The first American anti-nuclear ordinance, banning the transport or storage of nuclear materials, was adopted in Hawaii County in February, 1981. By the end of 1982, there still were only half a dozen American NFZs, but the number had climbed to 50 by the spring of 1984 and 100 by the fall of 1986. Many of the communities concerned were very small, but they included cities as large as Chicago and New York.[8] The exact wording of a NFZ declaration varies from one community to another, but it generally takes this form:

- The territory is declared off-limits to the design, testing, manufacture, and deployment of nuclear weapons. The declaration (ordinance) may also ban the transportation of such weapons through a community; or ban radioactive materials, whether related to weapons or nuclear waste from power plants. Signs may be erected on property declaring its nuclear-free status.
- Any activity which, in a local government's view, promotes nuclear weapons or nuclear war can be condemned or prohibited. Often this means that a community decides not to invest in or do business with industries that make nuclear weapons components.
- The community or school, church, office, or other organization, renounces its right to be defended with nuclear weapons held by any government, including its own.
- The NFZ community or entity asks the nuclear powers to take it off their target lists. Letters are sent to the proper authorities in Paris, London, and Peking as well as to Washington and Mos-

cow; and possibly to officials in India and Israel, whose nations may also be producing nuclear weapons (Bennett, 1987:7).

Thus, particular American municipalities tried to zone out nuclear industries,[9] divest from companies involved in nuclear weapons production (NFA, n.d.b:33-34),[10] re-direct contracts to nuclear-free businesses (NFA, n.d.b:33-34),[11] block (or at least regulate) the transport of nuclear materials,[12] turn civil defence into peace education,[13] facilitate the conversion of industries to peaceful production (Chicago, 1986:ch.202),[14] and encourage the development of non-nuclear energy sources (Skinner, 1991:14-15).

Particularly on matters of contracting and investment, the NFZ municipalities in the U.S. followed practices pioneered by the anti-apartheid movement, which had begun in the 1970s to pressure local authorities to break their economic links with South Africa (Love, 1985). Measures of this sort involved a more indirect challenge to the national government than attempts to zone out armaments factories, block convoys, or ban nuclear research. To protect themselves, local authorities usually tried to claim that they were acting within the limits of their traditional responsibilities for health, safety, and economic well-being. Thus, the city attorney in Portland, Oregon, advised the council there to avoid reference to matters of national defence or foreign affairs in developing its NFZ policy:

> ... the present revised ordinance should be redrafted to restrict its purposes to (a) enhancing economic stability in the City; (b) improving the psychological health of City residents; (c) protecting the civil liberties of City residents; and (d) accomplishing other traditional local police power purposes. There also should be a full record made before City Council containing evidence that the ordinance in fact will contribute to the achievement of these purposes (NFA, n.d.c:40).

This was the strategy followed in Chicago in 1986 (Sachnoff et al., 1986):[15]

> The Ordinance seeks to ban the manufacture of nuclear weapons and nuclear weapons components by private parties in the City of Chicago for the following reasons:

Economic instability: the nuclear weapons industry is unstable "because the demand for nuclear weapons may decline drastically in the event of an arms control agreement or a freeze or reduction in the United States Government nuclear weapons arsenal."

Depletion of the community's limited resources: nuclear weapon-related activities divert the City's limited public and private resources to non-productive uses.

Excessive security: "security requirements accompanying the nuclear weapons industry unduly restrict the dissemination of information" and require "the reallocation of scarce police and fire department resources."

Public health: the presence in the City "of an industry which could make the City a target of terrorism or nuclear attack" threatens the public health.

Morality: "the public morality is affronted by the presence of an industry profiting from activities which may ultimately lead to unprecedented death and destruction."

As the lawyers for the NFZ proponents noted, all of these reasons related to "the traditional police powers of the State to regulate the community's public health, safety, morals, economic well-being, and general welfare."

On the other hand, a case can be made, as with respect to refugee sanctuaries, that international law *requires* a municipality to act on these matters, even in defiance of the federal authorities.

All of these affirmative actions are supported by the body of law that has come to be designated peace law. The fundamental source of law supporting such action is the UN Charter, a treaty ratified by the United States in 1945 (89-2) and signed by the President as one of the treaties of the United States and therefore part of the supreme law of the land under the U.S. Constitution, Article 6, Sec. 2. The UN Charter provisions most frequently used are Articles 2.3, 2.4, 55 and 56. These establish standards of conduct for the United States, individually and collectively as a member of the United Nations. Another basic source of peace law

is the Nuremberg Principles, which are also part of
U.S. law as an executive agreement between the
United States, England, France, and the Soviet Union,
signed on August 8, 1945, and made part of international law at the request of President Harry Truman in
1946, in order to make permanent these rules originally
used to try Nazi war criminals. They are now found in
the U.S. Army Field Manual (FM 27-10, 18 July 1956)
and 59 Stats. at Large 1544, et seq. (1945), and clearly
govern the conduct of all U.S. military personnel and
all U.S. civilians (Meiklejohn, Civil Liberties Institute,
1986:4).[16]

The key claims that arise from this analysis are that Americans,
including American officials at all levels, have a legal obligation to
assist refugees, abstain from the use of nuclear, biological, and
chemical weapons, and abide by the decisions of the International
Court of Justice. On this view, then, Americans (and, indeed, citizens
of all the United Nations) have a legal obligation to create refugee
sanctuaries and nuclear-free zones. This is one of the grounds
offered for the NFZ ordinance in Berkeley, California.[17]

Such claims about the positive duties of municipalities complement the arguments advanced by Michael Shuman and Larry Agran
of the Centre for Innovative Diplomacy to the effect that the
paramountcy of the American federal government with respect to
foreign affairs does not preclude local action. Shuman notes:

Legal scholars have pointed out that the Constitution
forbids local governments from assembling their own
army or navy, declaring wars, entering treaties, violating national treaty commitments, and levying duties
on imports or exports. Since they could not imagine
how else local governments might influence foreign
affairs, the legal case against municipal foreign
policies has always seemed obvious. But almost all of
the municipal activism now underway does not fall
into any of these forbidden categories. And as attor-
neys and courts have examined specific municipal
foreign policies, they have found that countervailing
constitutional principles render the general legal wisdom practically meaningless (Shuman, n.d.:31).

A generous reading of local powers under the American Constitution is certainly possible:

> Indeed, the Constitution grants to states and localities numerous foreign policy making powers. The First Amendment guarantees the right of all citizens, even mayors and city council members, to speak out on foreign policy. The Fifth Amendment grants them the right to travel abroad. The Compact Clause allows states and cities to negotiate agreements with jurisdictions abroad, providing Congress does not object. Article III, Section 2, gives federal courts jurisdiction over 'controversies between a State . . . and foreign States' precisely because it envisions communications and deal-making between U.S. local governments and foreign nations. Similarly, when the framers gave Congress the power 'to regulate commerce with foreign nations' (Art. I, Sec. 8), they assumed that vigorous economic intercourse between local and foreign jurisdictions would continue. The Tenth Amendment further underscores that 'powers not delegated to the United States, nor prohibited by it to the States, are reserved to the States respectively, or to the people.'[18]

Be that as it may, conservative courts and state officials still take the view that matters of foreign and defence policy are properly within the jurisdiction of the national government alone. In Massachusetts the attorney-general consistently refused, between 1983 and 1987, to register NFZ bylaws adopted by town meetings on the grounds that they involved unconstitutional incursions on the federal powers to provide for the common defence and determine the foreign policies of the United States. Concerns were also raised by the attorney-general and other commentators about possible interferences with interstate commerce, vested property rights, and rights of free inquiry (NFA, n.d.c:15-26).[19] It was on such grounds that the tough NFZ resolution in Oakland, California, was overturned by the courts in 1989 as a result of a private suit by a military researcher supported both by a conservative "public interest" group and by the federal Department of Justice (*New Abolitionist*, 1989b:1,5; *New Abolitionist*, 1989c:1,5).[20] Some of the space left to municipalities is a result of inaction by the senior governments and could be closed off by adverse legislation or even executive decrees.

However, the British experience suggests that even a tightly centralized and strongly led government like Mrs. Thatcher's can run into serious difficulties in trying to impose its policies on determined local authorities. There are striking parallels, for instance, in the fate of civil defence in the two countries in the early 1980s. The U.S. Federal Emergency Management Agency ultimately had to abandon a new civil defence scheme because it could not generate enough support at the state and local level and could not get Congress to force the junior governments into line, something that Congress could in theory have done.[21] Margaret Thatcher's ministers had the support of a tame Parliament and theoretically had the means to impose whatever duties they liked upon "nuclear-free" authorities. Civil defence planning was nonetheless an exercise in frustration for the Conservative government throughout the 1980s.

Problems began for it in 1980, when the British Home Office issued a pamphlet entitled *Protect and Survive* (U.K., 1980a), intended to tell people what to do in case of a nuclear attack. E.P. Thompson's brilliant riposte, *Protest and Survive* (Thompson and Smith, 1980), was a propaganda triumph for the resurgent nuclear disarmament movement, not least because the government's advice about hiding under a table in the parlour was so silly. Two years later the Nuclear Free Zone authorities had their turn, when they responded to the government's civil defence exercise, "Hard Rock," with a peace campaign under the slogan, "Hard Luck" (Manchester, 1987:43-45). So many local authorities refused to participate in the exercise that the government was forced to cancel it. Embarrassed, the Conservatives responded with their own propaganda campaign, emphasizing the need for "all hazards" planning for disasters ranging from major fires to nuclear wars. They stressed the prospect of conventional attack on Britain (NSC, 1986b), evoking memories of the blitz, and they criticized the dissident Labour authorities for politicizing what ought to have been an uncontroversial process of emergency planning. More forcefully, they required the local authorities to prepare plans under the new Civil Defence Emergency Regulations of 1983.

This might have ended the matter, but the NFZ authorities complained that they lacked the information necessary to prepare for nuclear war. They needed to know where and how they could expect to be hit in a nuclear attack, the extent of the likely damage, and so on. When the government responded with planning assumptions that offered only sketchy information, the dissident authorities began their own planning assumptions studies and insisted that they could not comply with the government's requirements until these were complete (NSC, 1986c). The best publicized of these studies, the GLAWARS Report on Greater London (GLAWARS, 1986), was another propaganda success for the NFZs, because it detailed the horrific effects of an attack on London, suggested that civil defence was largely useless, and pointed to the need for action to prevent nuclear war. The government again was embarrassed and it brought in new legislation, the Civil Protection in Peacetime Act of 1986 to bury civil defence in an "all hazards" approach to emergency planning (NSC, 1987a). By separate legislation it abolished the Greater London Council and other metropolitan authorities, which had responsibility for civil defence in the major cities, and replaced them with new special-purpose bodies, including Fire and Civil Defence Authorities. The powers of the latter were carefully circumscribed so that it was clear that they could plan only for the consequences of nuclear war and were not allowed to explore the possibilities for preventing it (NSC, 1986d). That same year, all the local authorities responsible for civil protection were given deadlines for completion of their nuclear plans.

The NFZ authorities, whose representatives dominated many of the new Fire and Civil Defence Authorities as well as most of the key urban local councils, responded with a strategy of "critical compliance" (NSC, 1988a). They proceeded with planning but at every stage made it clear that they were being asked to work with unrealistic assumptions and without the resources to do the job anticipated. They managed to get deadlines extended and meanwhile pressed their case publicly, trying to show that the government was actually sacrificing the opportunity to develop an effective national system for responding to civil disasters by diverting scarce resources into a futile war planning scheme that had more to do with keeping people out of the military's way than with protecting civilian lives. Again, local authority propaganda on this and other matters proved to be quite effective. The government tried to control it by legislating new limits on local authority "publicity" (U.K., 1986:s.2; U.K., 1988:s.27). This was supposed to make it impossible for local councils to engage in "propaganda on the rates." However, as an NFZ legal opinion indicates (NSC, 1988b), the legislation still leaves scope for carefully constructed information campaigns, since the government did not dare go so far as to silence the local authorities altogether. They were entitled, as ever, to advance their own policies with respect to their own activities, which included civil defence.

At each stage in this battle, it became more difficult for the local authorities to pursue their dissident policies; however, it never became impossible for them to act critically. The government's 1988 legislation removed the right of local authorities to impose "contract compliance" conditions extraneous to the business at hand, and thus shut off the possibility of following the American lead in boycotting nuclear weapons contractors. However, this only showed up the fact that the NFZ authorities had been laggard in making use of their powers in this respect. As an NFZ working party reported in 1987 (NSC, 1987b):

> NFZ Authorities have, over the last 5 years, contributed positively to public debate about nuclear issues, and have given significant support to the wider movement for peace. However, when NFZ Authorities are publicly visible it is often because of symbolic initiatives such as NFZ road signs, stickers, or peace gardens. Where those initiatives have been pursued without a complementary development of policy in respect of those responsibilities of the local authority which are affected by the actual activities of the nuclear State, NFZ Authorities have become vulnerable to attack and ridicule. An overemphasis on the symbolic to the detriment of policy development may also have limited the number of authorities who are willing to spend money on NFZ initiatives. If it is accepted that this is the case, then it is recommended that the NSC [National Steering Committee] should give emphasis to substantive policy development on nuclear issues in its work programme. This policy should be developed in respect of those responsibilities of the local authority which are affected by the nuclear State, in particular an authority's responsibilities for its citizens' safety, general education, and future livelihood and well-being.

In response to the Chernobyl disaster a year earlier, the NFZ authorities agreed to campaign against nuclear power as well as nuclear weapons, and this facilitated a "shift to the mainstream" in the development of NFZ policies.[22] For local authorities responsible for public health and safety, there clearly were a range of practical issues related to nuclear accidents and radiation levels with which they ought to deal. These issues arose in relation to nuclear power plants and weapons facilities, disposal sites for nuclear materials, and shipments of nuclear fuels, reactors, weapons, and wastes. Although the national government might claim to have all these matters under control, it was obviously sensible for local authorities to take an interest as well.

Thus, NFZ authorities took it upon themselves to monitor radiation levels (NSC, 1987e), track nuclear convoys (NSC, 1987f), publicize nuclear hazards (NSC, 1988c), educate people about the dangers of nuclear materials, and, of course, nuclear war (NSC, 1987g; NSC, 1988d), develop plans for nuclear accidents (NSC, 1988e; NSC, 1989), and lobby the central government continuously for more information. The complaint that the government was denying the public what they needed to know for their own safety was crucial to the continuing campaign against the nuclear State. Demands for information about the transport of nuclear materials might still seem like posturing if the local authorities had no power to regulate shipments, but it was posturing related to an issue close to the centre of local government responsibilities, and as such had greater legitimacy. Similar was the campaign around the "conversion" of nuclear plants (NSC, 1988f), weapons installations, and armaments factories. Clearly, the closure of such facilities would have serious effects on the local economy, so it was logical enough for a local authority to explore the possibilities for conversion or diversification before the event happened. This implied long-term discussions with local defence contractors and their employees, the logic of which was recognized even by local councils that had little sympathy with the NFZ movement (NSC, 1988g).

The "shift to the mainstream" in British NFZ policy involved a retreat to the redoubts of local authority, where dissident activity could not easily be controlled by the national government. Within these redoubts, practical work could be done which related to a wide range of popular concerns. This helped to legitimize peace action that might otherwise have appeared quixotic. It also made an essential connection between the foreign policy initiatives of the dissident authorities and the traditional concerns of local government.

Healthy Cities

Issues of war and peace are not the only ones that engage municipalities in activities that transcend the limits of national policy. Municipalities are the primary environmental authorities and thus have a legitimate interest in many issues of global concern, including ozone depletion, acid rain, and toxic waste disposal. One response for a local council dissatisfied with national government is to make common cause with its counterparts elsewhere. This is the logic implicit in the activities of the recently formed International Council for Local Environmental Initiatives. As Jeb Brugmann, acting secretary-general, indicated in 1990:

> Right now, there are a handful of municipalities in the position to test new and risky strategies for environmental protection. Without a vehicle for the transfer of successful innovations, many years pass before other municipalities, which cannot assume the political or financial risk, begin to adopt proven policies and techniques. We'll be trying to speed this transfer process by supporting the innovation process, identifying and sharing successes and working directly with communities to implement them (BMFP, 1991:13).

Thus expressed, the role of the Council seems apolitical, but the networks it embodies are the effects of political insurgency. Brugmann, for instance, was the first director of the Peace Commission in Cambridge, Massachusetts, a body established in the wake of the 1981 nuclear freeze initiative in that city. As such, he was involved in campaigns around nuclear disarmament and the conversion of factories to peaceful production, as well as in the development of sister-city relationships and new peace curricula in the local schools (BMFP, 1989f).[23] Later he became field programs director for the Centre for Innovative Diplomacy (CID), which was perhaps the most important agency for promoting radical foreign policy initiatives among American municipalities in the 1980s. It was at a CID-sponsored conference in Irvine, California, that an inter-municipal Stratospheric Protection Accord was first promoted (Bailey, 1989),[24] and the CID was one of the sponsors of the 1990 World Congress of Local Governments for a Sustainable Future, a New York gathering facilitated by both the International Union of Local Authorities and the United Nations Environment Programme. Out of this conference and the activities associated with the Rio Conference on Environment and Development came the new International Council.

This intersection of local and global initiatives had been anticipated within the field of public health. At the 1978 International Conference of Primary Health Care in Alma-Ata, U.S.S.R., the World Health Organization had adopted a new Global Strategy, which "stressed the close and complex links between health and socioeconomic development, and proposed the primary health care approach as the key to attaining health for all" (Law and Larivière, 1988:4). This had two immediate implications: an explicit recognition that poverty and the "inequity" (the World Health Organization's code word for social inequality and economic exploitation) that generated it were at the root of the most serious health problems, and a commitment to "health promotion" as a strategy for dealing with these problems. The latter idea arose largely from the experience of development programmes in Asia, Africa, and Latin America. Efforts at immunization and disease control were often defeated by the desperate poverty that led to poor nutrition and inadequate sanitation. Although economic development was clearly the key to better health, it could not be secured by big projects that bypassed ordinary people and required massive injections of foreign capital and technical assistance. It depended instead on community organization, appropriate technology, social and ecological sensitivity — all of which were also required for health promotion. Outsiders, be they engineers, accountants, or public health nurses, had to support the local people in identifying their priorities, serving as advocates for them to the outside world, and learning to make their expertise, resources, and external connections relevant to the situation at hand. This implied a far more egalitarian relationship than the ones typical of traditional aid programmes.

European municipalities were among the first to reconsider their relationship to third world development in this context. At a 1983 conference in Florence on Towns and Co-operation for Development, delegates from a number of local authorities and nongovernmental organizations (NGOs) agreed to concert their efforts. Two years later they issued the Cologne appeal, "From Justice to Charity," for joint action of NGOs and local communities for North-South development co-operation. The delegates from major NGOs and municipalities in nine European countries looked towards activities that would combine the expertise, experience, and external connections of the NGO development organizations with the organizational resources, legitimacy, and local presence of municipal governments. Thus, they foresaw major educational and informational efforts to raise consciousness about North-South issues, a joint planning process involving all sectors of the community to develop links with the South, and projects for "establishing friendship, solidarity and partnership with towns and rural areas in the South on a community-to-community basis." Linking projects would be guided by the principles developed by the NGOs and their Southern partners, including "equality, reciprocity, absence of paternalism," "focus on the poorest," "recognition of the significance of women," "environmental impact [assessment]" and "[respect for] cultural diversity" (BMFP, 1988d:58-59).

These principles echoed the practices of community development that had been evolving in the rich countries themselves from Saul Alinsky's time onwards. In Toronto these practices fed into the health promotion ideas coming out of the World Health Organization (WHO) and helped to transform the local board of health. In 1978 a radicalized board adopted a new programme that involved "community development and advocacy directed toward the social and political determinants of health" (Hancock et al., 1990:193).[25] Led by a one-time African aid worker and NDP official, the health advocacy unit established an impressive international reputation. In 1984, the board celebrated its centenary with a major international conference under the title of "Healthy Toronto 2000." This proved to be of major significance, because it was here that delegates worked out an agenda for healthy public policies aimed at creating healthy cities by the year 2000. The European region of WHO picked up these concepts and began to promote them under the rubric of its Health For All by the Year 2000 campaign. Thus, a local initiative became much more general.

In Britain, the healthy cities campaign was a godsend to Labour authorities looking to break out of the strictures imposed upon them by the Thatcher government (Lane, 1989:5-12). The Black Report of 1980 (U.K., 1980b), commissioned by the previous Labour government, had documented the connection between ill health and economic and social deprivation in the northern cities. As such, it offered strong evidence that the third world concerns that informed WHO's new Health For All (HFA) global strategy were equally relevant in a first world context. These concerns pointed towards a broader approach to public health, which would emphasize environmental improvements, increased social and economic opportunities for the deprived, and both individual and collective participation in health improvement. Under such an approach, the elected local authorities, which had been pushed to one side by the National Health Service and the district health authorities, would again have a key role to play in public health. Moreover, they would have reason, validated not only by the Black Report but also by the World Health Organization, for pursuing a socialist health strategy, with strong environmentalist, feminist, and collectivist elements.[26]

As Barbara Lane has noted (1989a:7):

> By June 1987, approximately 50 cities in the U.K. were participating [in the Healthy Cities project], some of them communicating with the Regional Co-ordinating Centre at the WHO Europe Office, or with each other informally through the newly formed, loosely-knit U.K. Healthy Cities Network, or a bi-monthly Healthy Cities newsletter published out of Liverpool, or in April 1988, at the first U.K. Health Cities Conference, held in Liverpool. WHO had designated Liverpool and Bloomsbury/Camden as "Project Cities," to be joined in 1988 by Glasgow and Belfast. However, relatively few cities in the U.K. have aligned themselves with WHO, preferring to declare their own projects without waiting for the results from demonstrations projects.

This burst of activity outside the WHO framework reflected the fact that the activist Labour councils already had identified health as an issue that would enable them to re-open the socialist agenda in Britain. As a leading Sheffield activist noted,

> In the years to 1985 claimed for municipal socialism, we used local experience and experiment to create a vision of primary care challenging the dominance of hospitals and medical professionals, democratically accountable to neighbourhood communities, planned to prevent illness and eradicate inequalities in health across the city and building on the skills of grass roots workers like home helps, health visitors, general practitioners and district nurses (Green, 1988).[27]

Similarly, the board of health in Toronto continued to pursue a more radical version of healthy cities after the Conservative federal government gave its blessing to a Canadian Healthy Communities

Project in 1986 (Hancock, 1987:2-4,27; Berlin, 1989:13-15).[28] While other Canadian cities contemplated modest efforts,[29] the Healthy Toronto Subcommittee of the city's board of health advanced a series of bold proposals that would have reoriented local government (Toronto, 1988). These included the creation of a Healthy City Office and a Healthy Public Policy Committee, a food policy council,[30] a "safe city" task force prompted especially by women's concerns, and measures for community empowerment,[31] a healthy housing policy, an environmental bill of rights, and economic sustainability.[32]

Such initiatives illustrate the way that dissident authorities have linked their activities to the broader concerns of progressive social movements. The connective presence of these movements, the stimulative effect of international organizations of all sorts, and the shared experience of social, economic, and environmental problems have all contributed to the development of common fields of action that disrupt the hierarchies of the State system. It is by no means evident that the initiatives of the Toronto board of health, the mayor of Irvine, California, or the Manchester city council are "local" in the sense of "confined to a particular place." Rather, they open up to and are informed by complex international networks that cut across the boundaries between States and create empowering inter-local and global-local relations.

The Scope for Municipal Foreign Policy

The collapse of the Cold War security system, which kept the East "out" and the South "down," has added immeasurably to the uncertainties of international relations. Some of the initiatives of the dissident authorities in the 1980s seem to belong to a world that has passed. Nevertheless, it is clear that borders are less stable and more difficult to police, that individual States have less control of the economy, that disease and decay spread relentlessly over the globe, and that national governments are everywhere struggling to maintain their authority. In this context, both the need and the scope for vigorous municipal action are great. What is apparent from the activities of the 1980s is not that municipalities can easily overcome their own subordination but that determined action at the local level is difficult to crush. In 1987, the Institute for European Defence and Strategic Studies warned of the "potential of the municipal anti-nuclear movement to cause havoc throughout the Western world"

(Regan, 1987), and one of its academic supporters suggested that it might be necessary to suppress democratic local government to protect the State from the "incipient challenge" to its own integrity (Regan, 1987:57).[33] Such alarmist reaction is the sincerest form of flattery and indicates that the most effective limits on municipal action may not be the ones established by States, but rather the ones that exist in the imagination of those who have convinced themselves that local actions cannot have global effects.

Notes

1. This chapter is drawn from a larger study of "radical municipalities" in the U.S.A., Canada, and Britain, financed by a grant from the Social Sciences and Humanities Research Council of Canada. The author is grateful to the Council, to Jerry Wedmedyk and Diane Crossley for their research assistance, and to various local informants, especially Larry Agran, Penny Deleray, Gus Schultz, Nancy Skinner, Ann Fagan Ginger, Geoff Green, Fred Barker, and Jeremy Corbyn.

2. However, see Alger (1990). The best source of information on American municipal initiatives in the latter part of this period is *The Bulletin of Municipal Foreign Policy* (1987-91), published by the Centre for Innovative Diplomacy (then located at 17931 Sky Park Circle, Suite F, Irvine, CA 92714, and subsequently relocated to the Institute for Policy Studies in Washington, DC). See also *The New Abolitionist*, Newsletter of Nuclear Free America, 325 East 25th Street, Baltimore, MD 21218, and *News from MCLI*, Meiklejohn Civil Liberties Institute, Box 673, Berkeley, CA 94701.

3. The first five American congregations to declare sanctuaries for Central American refugees made their announcements on 24 March 1982, the anniversary of Archbishop Romero's assassination. These included the Southside Presbyterian Church in Tucson, Arizona, and the First Lutheran Church in Berkeley, California. My thanks to the Rev. Gus Schultz of First Lutheran for this information.

4. My thanks to Penny Deleray, Administrator of the National Sanctuary Defence Fund, 942 Market Street, Room 708, San Francisco, CA 9412-4008, for supplying this information. Compare the weaker resolution adopted in Takoma Park, MD, reprinted in Shuman (n.d.:52-53).

5. Compare Mayor Tom Bradley's address to the National League of Cities (10 December 1985), reprinted in Shuman (n.d.:4-6). On the ambiguous role of the local diocese of the Roman Catholic Church, see Davis (1990:350-56).

6. On 9 May 1988, the Board of Supervisors declared San Francisco a city of refuge from South Africa and Namibia as well (BMFP, 1988a:42).

7. Compare Solo (1988) and Trinkl (1988:51-62). Attracting less media attention was the Jobs with Peace campaign that began in San Francisco in 1978, and led to ballot initiatives in 85 cities on the redirection of military spending (BMFP, 1989b:18).

8. See Bennett (1987:Appendix D) for a chronological listing. This listing is updated periodically in *The New Abolitionist*.

9. See, for example, NFA (n.d.a). For the most part, penalties for violating such NFZ regulations in the U.S. are minor: Berkeley is exceptional in imposing a

thirty day jail term and a $500 fine for each violation (with each day being considered a separate violation).

10. Takoma Park, Maryland, was in 1983 the first community to adopt a divestment policy with respect to nuclear weaponry, although its initial measure was looser than this. The ordinance is reproduced in Bennett (1987:257-63). A dozen communities had adopted such measures by 1989 (*New Abolitionist*, 1989a:4).

11. Takoma Park also led the way on purchasing and contracting. The Borough of Southwark, England, resolved in December 1982 not to employ any of the firms involved at the Greenham Common Cruise Missile site. Peterborough and Harringay Councils took similar stands with respect to Cruise missile work in 1985. In 1984/85 Hackney and Camden adopted more general resolutions with respect to arms contractors. However, there was little progress in carrying these resolutions into effect before the central government reacted with legislation to curb "contract compliance" policies at the local level (NSC, 1986a). By contrast, American municipalities gradually made their boycotts more effective, by insisting on "nuclear-free" declarations from suppliers and checking them against information supplied by Nuclear Free America and other national research organizations.

12. See the Model Ordinance on Transportation of Hazardous (including radioactive) Materials and Waste, developed by the Environmental Policy Institute, 218 D Street S.E., Washington, DC 20003. "It is based on similar ordinances in large cities, perhaps most closely on Boston's, and is designed primarily for a densely populated city or country" (Dr. Fred Millar, EPI, covering letter.) However, such regulatory activity may be *ultra vires* (Sachnoff et al., 1986:21).

13. The most brilliant examples of this come from Britain, especially Manchester and London. See GLAWARS (1986) and Manchester (1987). However, American cities have not been inactive: "New York and Milwaukee high schools teach 'peace studies' courses. San Francisco, Cambridge, Massachusetts, and Boulder, Colorado, have produced and disseminated pamphlets describing the effects of nuclear war and arguing for a nuclear freeze" (Shuman, 1986:160).

14. Compare BMFP (1988b:3), and BMFP (1988c:28-30). See also BMFP (1989c:40-41). The Chicago Commission received a budget of only $12,000: obviously not enough to do a great deal of work. See Devall (1988:1,9). Compare with BMFP (1989d:30-32).

15. The ordinance itself is reprinted in Shuman (n.d.:53-54).

16. This is part of the "Peace Law Packet" available from the Meiklejohn Institute. Many thanks to Ann Fagan Ginger for these materials. See Bennett (1987:163-84) for similar arguments.

17. See Berkeley Ordinance no. 5784-NS, adopted by initiative in 1986. Available in Meiklejohn (1986).

18. See Shuman (n.d.:31-36) for a fuller analysis.

19. Compare Bennett (1987:164-67).

20. See also BMFP (1989e:35-36) and Swaim (1989:22).

21. "FEMAs problems began in 1982, when it tried implementing 'crisis re-location planning,' which called for the evacuation of two-thirds of the U.S. population from cities to rural areas in the event of mounting international tensions and an imminent nuclear war. The $4.2 billion scheme slid off the drawing boards when more than 120 jurisdictions (representing some 90 million people) officially refused to participate, calling the programme unwork-

able, chaotic, and dangerous" (BMFP, 1987:29). The same article reports that Congress had recently refused funding for a new network of bomb shelters. "Congressional action also forced FEMA to back down from its threats in recent months to cut off funds for all emergency planning (including for fires, floods, and earthquakes) from any state refusing to participate in its so-called 'regional communications exercises,' designed to test civil defense responses after a nuclear strike" (BMFP, 1987:29).

22. "The move to make 'nuclear free' mean exactly that, opposition to the total nuclear fuel cycle, came at the AGM of the NFZ movement at Dundee in September. From now on the terms of reference of the local authorities' National Steering Committee will include a commitment to the phasing out of nuclear power, combined with an equally strong policy to promote alternative energy sources and employment opportunities for displaced nuclear power workers" (CND, 1986:1). Compare NSC (1987c); NSC (1987d).

23. The ordinance establishing Cambridge's Peace Commission is reproduced in Shuman (n.d.:51-52).

24. See also BMFP (1989a:8-12), and Downey, 1989.

25. See also Hancock (1986), Baxter (1986), and MacDougall (1990:283-89).

26. Although coded in other terms, the socialist slant of the WHO Project comes through clearly enough in an early working paper (Hancock and Duhl, 1988:41). Hancock was associate Medical Officer of Health for Toronto, Duhl a Professor at Berkeley.

27. Compare Sheffield (1987).

28. The Canadian Project is jointly sponsored by the Canadian Institute of Planners, the Canadian Public Health Association, and the Federation of Canadian Municipalities, with a grant from the federal government. There is a parallel project in Québec (Lacombe and Poirier, 1989:16-21). The federal government had advanced a new health promotion strategy based on fostering public participation, strengthening community health services, and co-ordinating healthy public policy (Canada, 1986). This fit with WHO's new emphases expressed in the *Ottawa Charter for Health Promotion*, named after a WHO conference in that city (WHO, 1986).

29. See, for instance, Goldblatt (1989), and Kendal (1989). However, see Lane (1989b) for more innovative, participatory strategy. Compare Mathur (1989: 35-44).

30. Sheffield's health plan also contemplates development of a food policy (Sheffield, 1987:20).

31. "City Council [should] develop a Community Development Policy and facilitate community empowerment through its grants, through purchase of service agreements with community groups, where appropriate, and by ensuring that all City departments use community development approaches" (Toronto, 1988:12).

32. The strategy was "to include targets for resources and energy conservation, pollution control, recycling and waste management, and the incorporation of sustainability criteria in the Official Plan" (Toronto, 1988:12).

33. Compare WSJ (1989): "Unless reined in such actions could create a foreign-policy Tower of Babel that would weaken the federal government's ability to further American interests. With members of Congress such as Jim Wright already trying to usurp the role of Secretary of State, the United States has enough trouble developing one foreign policy. It cannot tolerate cities and states developing hundreds of their own."

References

Agran, L., (1989), "There They Go Again," *Bulletin of Municipal Foreign Policy*, 3, 3 (Summer).

Alger, C.F., (1990), "The World Relations of Cities: Closing the Gap Between Social Science Paradigms and Everyday Human Experience," *International Studies Quarterly*, 34, pp.493-518.

Bailey, E., (1989), "Civic Leaders Launch Efforts to Save Ozone: Inability of Nations to Stem Growing Crisis Spurs Action by Delegates at Irvine Conference," *Los Angeles Times* (22 July).

Baxter, D., (1986), "Public Health Planning in the City of Toronto: Part 2. Turning Concepts into Programs," *Canadian Journal of Public Health*, 77 (May/June).

Bennett, G.C., (1987), *The New Abolitionists: The Story of Nuclear Free Zones* (Elgin, Ill.: Brethren Press).

Berlin, S., (1989), "The Canadian Healthy Community Project: Shapes of the Reality," *Plan Canada*, 29, 4 (July).

BMFP, (1987), "FEMA Runs for Shelter," *Bulletin of Municipal Foreign Policy*, 1, 3 (Summer/Autumn).

BMFP, (1988a), *Bulletin of Municipal Foreign Policy*, 2, 3 (Summer).

BMFP, (1988b), "A Sample Ordinance to Study the Local Economic Impacts of Military Spending," *Bulletin of Municipal Foreign Policy*, 2, 4 (Autumn).

BMFP, (1988c), "As It Lay Dying," *Bulletin of Municipal Foreign Policy*, 2, 4 (Autumn).

BMFP, (1988d), "Cologne Appeal: Joint Action of NGOs and Local Communities for North-South Development Co-operation: From Charity to Justice," in *Bulletin of Municipal Foreign Policy*, 2, 4 (Autumn).

BMFP, (1989a), "29 U.S. Cities Declare Themselves Sanctuaries," *Bulletin of Municipal Foreign Policy*, 3, 4 (Autumn).

BMFP, (1989b), "Jobs with Peace: Mayors Should be 'Mad as Hell'," *Bulletin of Municipal Foreign Policy*, 3, 2 (Spring).

BMFP, (1989c), "Chicago: Peace in the Midst of Controversy," *Bulletin of Municipal Foreign Policy*, 3, 2 (Spring).

BMFP, (1989d), "Dealing with Reality: Baltimore Commission Brings the Peace Movement to City Hall," *Bulletin of Municipal Foreign Policy*, 3, 1 (Winter).

BMFP, (1989e), "The Case for Oakland," *Bulletin of Municipal Foreign Policy*, 3, 3 (Summer).

BMFP, (1989f), "Cambridge: Winning the Middle Ground," *Bulletin of Municipal Foreign Policy*, 3, 2 (Spring).

BMFP, (1991), "Local Initiatives: Can They Meet the Environmental Crisis?" *Bulletin of Municipal Foreign Policy*, 5, 1 (Winter).

Canada, (1986), *Achieving Health for All: A Framework for Health Promotion* (Ottawa: Health and Welfare Canada).

Chicago, (1986), "The Nuclear Weapon Free Chicago Ordinance," (City of Chicago: *Municipal Code*).

CND, (1986), *Nuclear Free Zone Bulletin*, (Campaign for Nuclear Disarmament), 12 (December).

Davis, M., (1990), *City of Quartz: Excavating the Future in Los Angeles* (London: Verso, 1990).

Devall, C., (1988), "Seeking a Nuclear-free Economy," *Chicago Tribune* (10 August).

Downey, C., (1989), "Officials Gather in Irvine to Find Local Solutions to Global Problems," *The Orange County Register* (22 July).

Frug, G.E., (1980), "The City as a Legal Concept," *Harvard Law Review*, 93, 6, pp.1059-1154.

Fry, E.H., L.H. Radebaugh, and Panyotis Soldatos, eds., (1989), *The New International Cities Era: The Global Activities of North American Municipal Governments* (Provo, Utah: David M. Kennedy Centre for International Studies, Brigham Young University).

GLAWARS, (1986), *London Under Attack: The Report of the Greater London Area War Risk Study Commission* (Oxford: Basil Blackwell).

Goldblatt, A., (1989), "Edmonton's Healthy Communities Initiative," *Plan Canada*, 29, 4 (July).

Green, G., (1988), "Health and Social Policy in Sheffield," Sheffield District Labour Party Education Paper/Conference of Socialist Economists Discussion Paper (31 October).

Hancock, T., (1986), "Public Health Planning in the City of Toronto: Part 1. Conceptual Planning," *Canadian Journal of Public Health*, 77 (May/June).

Hancock, T., (1987), "Healthy Cities: The Canadian Project," *Health Promotion*, 26, 1 (Summer).

Hancock, T., and L. Duhl, (1988), *Promoting Health in the Urban Context*, WHO Healthy Cities Paper 1 (Copenhagen: FADL).

Hancock, T., B. Pouliot, and P. Duplessis, (1990), "Public Health," in *Urban Policy Issues: Canadian Perspectives*, edited by Richard A. Loreto and Trevor Price (Toronto: McClelland and Stewart).

Isin, E.F., (1992), *Cities without Citizens: The Modernity of the City as a Corporation* (Montreal: Black Rose Books)

Kendal, P.R.W., (1989), "The Healthy Communities Project: Healthy Capital Regional District 2000," *Plan Canada*, 29, 4 (July).

Lacombe, R., and L. Poirier, (1989), "Villes et villages en santé," *Plan Canada*, 29, 4 (July).

Lane, B.J., (1989a), "Healthy Cities in the U.K.: Implications for Canadian Healthy Communities Projects," *Plan Canada*, 29, 4 (July).

Lane, B.J., (1989b), *Canadian Healthy Communities Project: A Conceptual Model for Winnipeg* (Winnipeg: Institute of Urban Studies, University of Winnipeg).

Law, M., and J. Larivière, (1988), "Canada and WHO: Giving and Receiving," *Health Promotion*, 26, 4 (Spring).

Love, J., (1985), *The U.S. Anti-Apartheid Movement: Local Activism in Global Politics* (New York: Praeger).

MacDougall, H., (1990), *Activists and Advocates: Toronto's Health Department, 1883-1993* (Toronto: Dundurn Press).

Magnusson, W., (1986), "Bourgeois Theories of Local Government," *Political Studies*, 34, pp.1-18.

Manchester, (1987), *Manchester: A Nuclear Free City* (Manchester: City Council).

Mathur, B., (1989), "Community Planning and the New Public Health," *Plan Canada*, 29, 4 (July).

Meiklejohn, Civil Liberties Institute, (1986), "Memorandum: Using Peace Law in Local Government Work," *Peace Law Packet* (Berkeley, Cal.: Meiklejohn Civil Liberties Institute).

Merina, V., (1985), "Council Votes 8-6 for LA Sanctuary," *Los Angeles Times* (28 November).

New Abolitionist, (1989a), *The New Abolitionist*, 7, 2 (June/July).

New Abolitionist, (1989b), "Opposition Files Suit Against Oakland NFZ," *The New Abolitionist*, 7, 2 (June/July).

New Abolitionist, (1989c), "Justice Department Files Suit Against Oakland NFZ Law," *The New Abolitionist*, 7, nos. 3 and 4 (November).

NFA, (n.d.a), "Proposed Ordinance Designating Washington County, Indiana, a Nuclear Weapons-Free Zone,", (1984), in "Nuclear Free Zone Legislation," mimeo (Baltimore, Md.: Nuclear Free America).

NFA, (n.d.b), "Sample Legislation on Nuclear Free Investments and Contracts," in "Nuclear Free Zone Legislation," mimeo (Baltimore, Md.: Nuclear Free America).

NFA, (n.d.c), "Nuclear Free Zones and the Law," in "Nuclear Free Zone Legislation," mimeo (Baltimore, Md.: Nuclear Free America).

NSC, (1986a), "Nuclear Free Zones and Contractor Policies," National Steering Committee, Nuclear Free Zone Authorities, NSC Briefing 8 (July).

NSC, (1986b), "Conventional War Planning in a Nuclear Weapon State," National Steering Committee, Nuclear Free Zone Authorities, NSC Briefing 6 (January).

NSC, (1986c), "Planning Assumptions Study: The Basic Guide," National Steering Committee, Nuclear Free Zone Authorities, NSC Briefing 6 (July).

NSC, (1986d), "A Briefing Document for Fire and Civil Defence Authority Members on the NFZ Approach to Civil Defense," National Steering Committee, Nuclear Free Zone Authorities, NSC Briefing 10 (October).

NSC, (1987a), "The Hazards of Promoting Civil Defence: An Examination of the Home Office's 'Civil Protection' Policy," National Steering Committee, Nuclear Free Zone Authorities, NSC Briefing 12(a) (June).

NSC, (1987b), "Report for Resolution," The Secretary, National Conference on Nuclear Free Zone Authorities (27 March).

NSC, (1987c), "Taking NFZ Initiatives into the Mainstream," AGM Report, National Steering Committee, Nuclear Free Zone Authorities, NSC Briefing 15.

NSC, (1987d), "NFZ National Priorities and NSC Work Programme Report," National Steering Committee, Nuclear Free Zone Authorities, NSC Briefing 14 (March).

NSC, (1987e), "Local Authority Radiation Monitoring Conference Documents," National Steering Committee, Nuclear Free Zone Authorities, NSC Briefing 17 (April).

NSC, (1987f), "The Road Transport of Nuclear Warheads," National Steering Committee, Nuclear Free Zone Authorities, NSC Briefing 7 (revised April).

NSC, (1987g), "Peace Education: One Day Local Authority Conference," National Steering Committee, Nuclear Free Zone Authorities, NSC Briefing 16, January

NSC, (1988a), "A Planned Program for Implementation (PPI) for the 1983 Civil Defence Regulations," National Steering Committee, Nuclear Free Zone Authorities, NSC Briefings Nos. 13(a)-(h) (January [1987]-December [1988]).

NSC, (1988b), "Nuclear Issues, Local Authorities, and Publicity: The Legal Framework," National Steering Committee, Nuclear Free Zone Authorities, NSC Briefing 28 (November).

NSC, (1988c), "Radioactive Waste Disposal in the U.K.: Current Position," Humberside County Council for the National Steering Committee, Nuclear Free Zone Authorities, NSC Briefing 27 (November).

NSC, (1988d), "Ministry of Defence Video: 'Keeping the Peace'," National Steering Committee, Nuclear Free Zone Authorities, NSC Briefings Nos. 22(a)-(d) (November [1987]-June [1988]).

NSC, (1988e), "Disaster Planning and Preparedness for Major Nuclear Accidents," National Steering Committee, Nuclear Free Zone Authorities, NSC Briefing 32 (November).

NSC, (1988f), "Alternatives to Nuclear Power: Promoting Energy Efficiency and Energy Conservation," National Steering Committee, Nuclear Free Zone Authorities, NSC Briefing 24 (June).

NSC, (1988g), "The Feasibility of a National Diversification Unit," National Steering Committee, Nuclear Free Zone Authorities, NSC Briefing 31 (September).

NSC, (1989), "Nuclear Facilities and Emergency Planning in the U.K.," National Steering Committee, Nuclear Free Zone Authorities, NSC Briefing 34 (February).

NYT, (1985), "San Francisco Backs Plan to Safeguard Refugees," *New York Times* (25 December).

Regan, D., (1987), *The New City Republics: Municipal Intervention in Defence* (London: Institute for European Defence and Strategic Studies).

Sachnoff, Weaver, and Rubenstein, (1986), *Opinion for Chicago Clergy and Laity Concerned* (25 February).

Sheffield, (1987), *Good Health for All: The Sheffield Plan* (Sheffield: Sheffield City Council).

Shuman, M.H., (n.d.), *Building Municipal Foreign Policies: An Action Handbook for Citizens and Local Elected Officials* (Irvine, Cal.: Centre for Innovative Diplomacy).

Shuman, M.H., (1986), "Dateline Main Street: Local Foreign Policies," *Foreign Policy,* 65 (Winter).

Skinner, N., (1991), "Making Energy Policy, Not War," *Bulletin of Municipal Foreign Policy,* 5 (Spring).

Solo, P., (1988), *From Protest to Policy: Beyond the Freeze to Common Security* (Cambridge, Mass.: Ballinger).

Swaim, W., (1989), "Feds on the Offense?" *Bulletin of Municipal Foreign Policy,* 3, 4 (Autumn).

Thompson, E.P., and D. Smith, eds., (1980), *Protest and Survive* (Harmondsworth: Penguin).

Thompson, E.P., (1980), *Zero Option* (London: Merlin Press).

Toronto, (1988), *Healthy Toronto 2000* (Toronto: Board of Health, City of Toronto).

Trinkl, J., (1988), "Struggles for Disarmament in the U.S.A.," in *Reshaping the U.S. Left: Popular Struggles in the 1980s, The Year Left,* edited by Mike Davis and Michael Sprinker (London: Verso).

U.K., (1980a), *Protect and Survive,* Home Office (London: HMSO).

U.K., (1980b), *Inequalities in Health: Report of a Research Working Group,* Department of Health and Social Security (London: DOHSS).

U.K., (1986), Laws and Statutes, *Local Government Act,* 34 and 35 Eliz. 2.

U.K., (1988), Laws and Statutes, *Local Government Act,* 37 and 38 Eliz. 2.

WSJ, (1989), "Sanity Disarmament," *Wall Street Journal* (8 May).

WHO, (1986), *Ottawa Charter for Health Promotion* (Geneva: World Health Organization).

Also published by

FIELDS, FACTORIES AND WORKSHOPS
Peter Kropotkin

edited, with Afterwords, by George Woodcock

While at one time Kropotkin's view of our future might have been regarded as a utopian dream, today, as a result of the growing realization that the world's resources of energy and raw materials are finite, that food is our most precious commodity and that most people's working lives are futile and stultifying, the lessons of this book, for both the rich world and the poor, are topical and hopeful.

This volume is the 10th in *The Collected Works of Peter Kropotkin*.

255 pages, index
Paperback ISBN: 1-895431-38-7 $19.95
Hardcover ISBN: 1-895413-39-5 $38.95

THE MYTH OF THE MARKET
Promises and Illusions
Jeremy Seabrook

The Myth of the Market *sets out a strong indictment of the market system. The argument is all the more timely with the recent moves in global trade... [Seabrook's] book serves as a good introduction to a complex topic.*
Peace and Environment News

Read Mr. Seabrook's book...There are alternatives to the market, but unless we begin to resist the monetization of all human activity, they will be relegated to museums where, fittingly, you'll pay to see them.
Imprint

200 pages
Paperback ISBN: 1-895431-08-5 $18.99
Hardcover ISBN: 1-895431-09-3 $37.99

HOT MONEY AND THE POLITICS OF DEBT
2nd edition

R.T. NAYLOR

Introduction by Leonard Silk, former financial editor of the New York Times

...a wide angle view of the seamy side of international finance.
New York Times

"As conspiracy theories go, here is one that is truly elegant. It involves everybody."
Washington Post

510 pages, index
Paperback ISBN: 1-895431-94-8 $19.99
Hardcover ISBN: 1-895431-95-6 $38 99

CRITICAL PERSPECTIVES ON HISTORIC ISSUES

This series, from the work of the Karl Polanyi Insitute of Political Economy at Concordia University in Montréal, is intended to present important research by leading international scholars and critics.

The Life and Work of Karl Polanyi, Kari Polanyi-Levitt, ed.
Culture and Social Change, Colin Leys and Marguerite Mendell, eds.
From Political Economy to Anthropology, Colin M. Duncan
    and David W. Tandy, eds.
Europe: Central and East, Marguerite Mendell and Klaus Nielsen, eds.
Artful Practices: The Political Economy of Everyday Life,
    Henri Lustiger-Thaler and Daniel Salée, eds.
The Milano Papers, Michele Cangiani, ed.

BLACK ROSE BOOKS
has also published the following books of related interest

The Political Economy of International Labour Migration, *by Hassan N. Gardezi*
Private Interest, Public Spending, *by William E. Scheurerman and Sidney Plotkin*
Dissidence: Essays Against the Mainstream, *by Dimitrios Rousspoulos*
Shock Waves: Eastern Europe After the Revolutions, *by John Feffer*
Ethics, *by Peter Kropotkin*
Mutual Aid, *by Peter Kropotkin*
Political Arrangements: Power and the City, *edited by Henri Lustiger-Thaler*
Bringing the Economy Home From the Market, *by Ross Dobson*
The Myth of the Market: Promises and Illusions, *by Jeremy Seabrook*
Race, Gender and Work: A Multi-Cultural Economic History of Women in the
    United States, *by Teresa Amott and Julie Matthaei*
Dominion of Debt: Centre, Periphery and the International Economic Order,
    by Jeremy Brecher and Tim Costello
Bankers, Bagmen and Bandits: Business and Politics in the Age of Greed,
    by R.T. Naylor
The Economy of Canada: A Study of Ownership and Control, *by Jorge Niosi*
Essays on Marx's Theory of Value, *by Issak Illich Rubin*

send for a free catalogue of all our titles
BLACK ROSE BOOKS
P.O. Box 1258
Succ. Place du Parc
Montréal, Québec
H3W 2R3 Canada

Printed by the workers of
Les Éditions Marquis
Montmagny, Québec
for Black Rose Books Ltd.